To Al and Ardy for giving me Peggy and
to my grandparents who were great sports
fans.

ACKNOWLEDGMENTS

I would like to thank the coaches and athletes who contributed to my education. Without their cooperation and assistance this book could not have been written.

Special thanks must go to my colleagues for their support, dialogue, interest, and contributions. It is with a deep sense of gratitude that I recognize the significant influences of the following people:

Richard Alderman
Cal Botterill
John Clapp
Peter DuFresne
Deborah Feltz
Dan Gould
Wayne Halliwell
Yuri Hanin
Steve Heyman
Andy Jacobs
Dan Landers
Don McGavern
Frank Macartney
William Morgan
Dave Nesvig
Bruce Ogilvie
Tom O'Hara
Robin Pratt
Candy Reynolds
John Salmela
Dennis Selder
William Straub
Bob Weinberg

Finally, I would like to thank Dr. Jim Harper for his editorial assistance and suggestions.

CONTENTS

Preface VII

Chapter One: Role of the Sport Psychologist 1
    Clinical Sport Psychology 1
    Crisis Intervention 4
    Psychological Assessment 5
    Performance Enhancement 6
    Consultation and Program Development 6
    Prevention and Treatment of Injuries 7

Chapter Two: Ethical Standards for Sport Psychologists 9

Chapter Three: The Need for Psychological Theory 17

Chapter Four: Attentional and Interpersonal Style in Sport 21
    Figure 1: Attention in Athletics 25
    Figure 2: Attention Errors 26
    Figure 3: Attention and Choking 30
    Situational and Interpersonal Factors 32
    Need for Control 33
    Self-Esteem 34
    Obsessiveness 34
    Extroversion-Introversion 35
    Communication Style 36

Chapter Five: Should We Administer Psychological Tests to Athletes? . . . 39

Chapter Six: Uses of Psychological Tests 51
    Knowledge Required of Test Users 51
    Subject's Response Styles 53

Chapter Seven: Focusing the Assessment Process 62
    Operationally Defining the Referral Question 63

Chapter Eight: Introducing Testing and the Feedback Process 67
    Establishing a Contract 68
    Feedback of Test Results 71

Chapter Nine: Assessment Case Histories 78
    Table 1: Test of Attentional and Interpersonal Style-Scales 78
    T-scores, Z-scores, and Percentiles 80
    Skeet Shooting 81
    Figure 4: Profile of a Skeet Shooter 83
    Professional Tennis 84
    Figure 5: Profile of a Tennis Player 90
    Distance Runner 91
    Figure 6: Profile of a Distance Runner 93

Chapter Ten: Team Building 95
    Inter-service Boxers 98
    Gymnastics 106

Chapter Eleven: Consultation and Program Development 111

Chapter Twelve: Crisis Intervention 123
    Recognizing a Crisis 127

Regaining Control 129
Counseling Manual for Coaches 133
Chapter Thirteen: Prevention and Treatment of Injuries 142
Figure 7: Prevention and Treatment of Injury 145
Chapter Fourteen: Treatment Selection 151
Figure 8: Treatment Selection 152
The Placebo Myth 153
Factors in Treatment Selection 160
Chapter Fifteen: Prevention of Chronic Problems 163
Uses of Biofeedback, Progressive Relaxation, & Meditation 167
Biofeedback 167
Meditation 171
Progressive Relaxation 173
Relaxation Procedure 176
Physical Exercise 178
Chapter Sixteen: Hypnosis. 179
Four Stages of Hypnosis 179
Hypnosis and Attention 185
Figure 9: Attentional Processes and Alterations in
Consciousness 187
Applications of Hypnosis to Sport Psychology 188
Setting the Stage 191
Chapter Seventeen: Attention Control Training 193
Centering Procedure 196
Instructions for Centering While Standing 196
Instructions for Centering While Sitting 198
Centering Case Histories 198
Chapter Eighteen: Cognitive Rehearsal Techniques 202
Mental Rehearsal 202
Psycho-Cybernetics 202
Positive Thinking 203
Discriminant Cue Analysis 203
Visuo-motor Behavior Analysis 203
Cognitive Behavior Modification 204
Development of Rehearsal Strategies 205
Case Histories 207
Chapter Nineteen: The Making of a Good Sport Psychologist 212
Self-Awareness 213
Communication Skills 213
Motivation 213
Deductive and Analytical Ability 214
Ability to Empathize 214
Balancing Support with Confrontation 214
Ability to Depersonalize 214
Ability to Self-Disclose 214
Ability to Operationalize 215
Trustworthy. 215
Attentional Flexibility 215
Ability to Function Under Pressure 215
Study Questions 217
Suggested Readings 221
Appendix A: Test of Attentional and Interpersonal
Style (TAIS) 225

PREFACE

Although interest in sport psychology in the United States can be traced to Coleman Griffith's work at the University of Illinois in 1918, the field is much younger than that. It wasn't until the 1950's that we began to see organized research in several locations, and the beginning of communication between researchers. The mid 60's to mid 70's saw the development of both national and international organizations that focused on the psychology of athletics. Included among these were the International Society for Sport Psychology (ISSP), the North American Society for the Psychology of Sport and Physical Activity (NASPSPA), the Canadian Society for Psychomotor Learning and Sport Psychology (CSPLSP), and FEPSAC, the European Sport psychology group.

Even with the development of these major organizations, membership has remained relatively small. As of 1980 there were only about 250 members in NASPSPA, and about 130 in CSPLSP. In addition, a large segment of the membership has had primary research interests, particularly in the areas of motor learning and motor development. It is a small but rapidly growing group of individuals that is interested in the application of psychology to athletics.

Applied interests began developing slowly and in response to some of the theoretical and technical developments occurring within psychology during the 60's and 70's. The work of B. F. Skinner, and the elaboration of operant learning theory had obvious implications for the motivation and training of athletes. The development of a technology that allowed for the immediate feedback of biological information, biofeedback, provided a conceptual bridge between physical and psychological processes. Research in the laboratory and in the field began to clarify the relationship between physiological arousal, anxiety, concentration (attention) and performance. Finally, it was demonstrated experimentally that thought processes or cognitions could be used to modify behavior, attitudes, and physical arousal.

Because of the advances in theory and technique, we began to see a broader interest in applied sport psychology. At this time, professionals in the field were experiencing pressure to become more directly relevant. In Russia, party leader Brezhnev dictated that it was time for science to play a more productive role in society, helping to develop man's capacities and talents. In the United States, athletes who had developed their physical abilities about as far as they could, were experimenting on their own with psychological techniques in an attempt to develop the "winning edge." Individual athletes and a few coaches had made the conceptual leap between their needs for psychological training and some of the newer deveopments in the field of psychology before the psychologist had.

Thus, the demand for service preceded the development of any systematic training or service delivery program. Individuals with limited experience in the field of physical education and/or psychology, quickly became self-proclaimed experts in "sport psychology." Slowly, professional organizations like NASPSPA, and ISSP, became aware of a need to establish some standards for the sport psychologist.

In 1979, an attempt was made to survey those individuals around the world who identified themselves as sport psychologists. This is to be the subject of a book by Dr. John Salmela from the University of Montreal. The goal of the survey was to identify the training received by these people, to list and describe the services that they provided, and to determine the courses they taught and the training they felt should be required of sport psychologists.

At the same time the survey was being conducted, both NASPSPA and CSPLSP established ethics committees. It was to be the responsibility of these committees to determine the need for certification in sport psychology. It was hoped that the committees could make specific recommendations regarding training requirements and certification for those individuals engaged in the provision of services or the application of sport psychology. It was my involvement on both committees that convinced me of the necessity for this book.

At the present time, the title *psychologist,* is a term that is restricted by law in the United States and Canada. Only those individuals who have completed advanced training in the field of psychology, and who have passed a state or national licensing examination can use the title psychologist. This fact is of concern to many of the members of NASPSPA and CSPLSP. Individuals who are actively practicing sport psychology may or may not meet the requirements of various states and provinces.

It can easily be argued that current laws, restricting the use of the title psychologists (and thus the title sport psychologist) are not applicable to the field of sport psychology. Since the term sport is not restricted, there is nothing keeping any psychologist from deciding that he or she is a "sport psychologist." All he or she has to do is apply the label. Psychologists who want to call themselves sport psychologists are not required by law to have any special training. They do not have to have had experience in sport, to understand anything about athletes, competitive pressure, or anything else. Unfortunately, there are psychologists who are calling themselves sport psychologists, without any awareness of their own limitations. They can be insensitive to important issues and actually do more harm than good.

There are other individuals who because they are not licensed, are illegally calling themselves sport psychologists. These people come from education and/or physical education backgrounds. They usually have advanced degrees in P.E. or some related area. More often than not, they have a great deal of experience in sport as a participant and as a coach or trainer. Typically, their experience in the field of psychology is limited to an undergraduate major or minor.

For the protection of both the public and the profession, it is important to define the roles a sport psychologist fills, and to identify the educational experiences that should be prerequisites. It should be obvious that training as it is currently being offered does not prepare an individual to practice sport psychology. At the present time we do not have a defined field of study (at least not within a particular program) that adequately integrates courses in psychology with those in physical education for the practitioner. We need changes in existing laws and in existing programs. In the meantime, how do we function? There are individuals from both types of backgrounds who are qualified to provide psychological services to athletes to function as sport psychologists. In addition, there are a great many other individuals who are competent to function in specialized areas like assessment, stress management, or the use of biofeedback.

I have written this book in the hope that it will provide some direction, or at least a jumping off point for the field of applied sport psychology. In the following chapters I have attempted to identify the roles that I see sport psychologists' filling. I have used my own training, experience, and personal opinions to identify training experiences, skills, and ethical concerns of which I believe the sport psychologist should be aware. Obviously this is only one person's opinion (though an opinion that has been shared with and by many others). The book is not intended to be an end point; rather it is a beginning. It is my hope that the book, in combination with some supervised applied (internship) training in sport psychology, can provide the basis for competent, ethical, professional functioning.

In the material that follows a great deal of case history information is shared. It is important to point out that for the protection of the coaches and athletes involved, important identifying data has been altered.

CHAPTER ROLE OF THE SPORT PSYCHOLOGIST

There are several roles that the applied sport psychologist attempts to fill. As these roles are presented it will become apparent that they require a variety of skills and training experiences. In the future as we attempt to certify sport psychologists it will be important to certify them for certain roles. One of the ways we can protect both the profession and the public prior to the development of integrated training programs, is to identify the competencies required for different roles. In this way both the consumer and the professional can evaluate services that are currently being offered.

CLINICAL SPORT PSYCHOLOGY

Perhaps the role that is most often associated with sport psychologists, is that of psychotherapist. A common misconception is that all a sport psychologist is, is a clinical psychologist or psychiatrist who specializes in working with athletes who have emotional problems like phobias, or neurotic conflicts.

Although there are clinical psychologists who do see athletes with emotional conflicts and underlying psychological problems, this role is probably relatively rare. From the vantage point of the psychotherapist, let me briefly define some of the problems that might be seen by the clinically oriented sport psychologist.

In thinking about severe psychological problems, emphasis is often placed on the athlete experiencing a loss of control. In sport situations we may see athletes who insist that they want to be the best. In observing their performance they have the ability and skill to be great, yet somehow they seem to sabotage their own best efforts. They fall apart in competition, they continually injure themselves at critical times, they develop drug dependencies, and so on. Solutions to their problems seem obvious to the outside observer. If they would only follow instructions things would be so easy. Somehow, they just can't follow through. According to traditional theory there is some underlying conflict that is preventing them from achieving their stated goal. That neurotic conflict must be uncovered and worked through before the sabotage will stop.

Sometimes the underlying conflicts developed very early in the athlete's life. There are individuals who have become involved in sport through their need to be loved by others, rather than by their own desire for competition. Children pushed by parents who want to live through the successes of their sons and daughters can fall into this category. There are many girls and boys who are working and investing themselves in a sport not for the enjoyment of the sport but because they need the love of their coach who has become a parental substitute for them. At times this results in the athlete becoming extremely dependent, making excessive demands on the coach to fill roles other than the simple role of coach. The athlete begins to see and use the coach as a lover, father, mother, etc. When the coach is disapproving, rejecting, or when the athlete must move on, as in going from high school to college, severe emotional problems can become apparent.

Another area in athletics where problems occur involves the transition from being an athlete with a goal to accomplish, and having a focus for one's life, to suddenly finding oneself finished at a very young age. Now, there is no direction because life has been nothing but athletics. Whether one won or lost the gold medal doesn't seem to matter that much. A major clinical depression and loss of self-esteem can occur at this time.

The problems just presented can require fairly traditional long term psychotherapy. Extensive clinical training and an understanding of psychodynamics would appear to be a prerequisite to effective intervention. In effect, the sport psychologist is a clinician. The fact that he or she is interested in athletes and may be familiar with the pressures that an athlete faces makes communication easier. The primary training, however, should be clinical.

A great many practicing sport psychologists do not provide the type of clinical service just outlined. They recognize that their training has not prepared them for that. In addition, their role (if they are involved with an entire team, or hired by management) can prevent them from functioning effectively as a clinician. Let me list some of the problems that can develop when a sport psychologist attempts to function in a clinical role.

First, the number of clinical problems that one encounters when working with groups of athletes (particularly at higher levels) is relatively small. As a group, athletes are fairly well adjusted without the underlying conflicts spoken about earlier.

Next, because the athletic situation emphasizes self-control and confidence, it is typically difficult and often impossible for athletes to ask for psychological help. They simply cannot admit that they are incapable of coping with a problem, nor can they believe that a clinician could help.

When problems are identified, however, and when an athlete does want to work on them, several difficulties occur if the sport psychologist is involved in an ongoing way with the athlete's coach or team.

Traditional therapy requires a very special, confidential relationship. The emotional needs of the athlete take precedence over everything else. The importance of placing the individual's needs first can place

2

sport psychologists in conflict with the responsibility that they have to the team, which may involve getting the athlete to play in spite of emotional pain. Therapy itself is often a stressful, painful process as the individual exposes and begins to work through conflicts. This pain may impair performance, and may even lead to athletes giving up any involvement in sport. The individuals may realize he/she has been working for others, and destroying himself/herself in the process. The sport psychologist who is helping the athlete work through these issues at the same time the coach needs the athlete to win the league championship, may quickly find himself/herself without a job.

As the athletes start to work through some of their underlying conflicts they begin to relate to the therapist in a very primary way. As mentioned with the coach earlier, they begin to see the therapist as a father figure or authority figure. When athletes are insecure they become very dependent on the therapist, relying on them (or attempting to) for things they should get from the coach. The athletes' dependency on the psychologist can become very threatening to the coach.

Finally, therapy is usually an ongoing process, typically involving appointments from one to several times a week. Such a process is all but impossible when the athlete is traveling from city to city, playing one hundred and sixty-two baseball games in a season, or gone for weeks at a time.

Although the role of clinician is one that is often ascribed to sport psychologists, it is probably a role that should be separated and not included as one of the responsibilities of a person who in the future comes to be certified as an applied sport psychologist. This recommendation is made for several reasons: 1) There are too many conflicts of interest that can develop when the psychologist must consider both the team and the coach clients, as well as the individual athlete; 2) Adequate training to function as a clinician, as well as adequate training to function in all of the other roles sport psychologists find themselves in, would require considerably more than four years of graduate training. It would be like combining medicine and psychology and attempting to get both a Ph.D. and M.D. Although such a program could be developed, few people would be willing to delay active involvement in the field long enough to complete it; and 3) By removing the clinical function we may take away the stigma that prevents many athletes from making use of the sport psychologist. They don't have to be "crazy" to see one.

In deference to those individuals who have been or will be trained to function as a clinician, as well as a sport psychologist I would suggest the following. If the role of clinician can be clearly separated from other job responsibilities and confidentiality and trust can be maintained, it may be possible to assume both roles. In this instance, however, it would be best to adopt a policy of never attempting to maintain an ongoing therapeutic relationship with an athlete who is also involved with a team

3

that the psychologist is working with. For trust to be maintained, the contract to work on the emotional conflicts and needs of an individual athlete must be kept separate from the contract to work with a group to improve performance.

Because the clinical role requires clinical training, I will not deal with it in this book. There are many clinical training programs available, and many texts on the subject. These programs teach you to treat clinical problems, independent of the person's occupation or avocation. There is no emphasis on sport.

Although clinical training will not be provided, time will be taken to teach you to recognize when there are underlying issues that need psychotherapeutic intervention. In conjunction with the recognition of severe psychological problems, procedures for making a referral to a clinically trained individual will be discussed.

CRISIS INTERVENTION

Another service that is often associated with applied sport psychology involves crisis intervention. Crises are typically seen as acute situations in which there are very strong emotional responses that interfere with an athlete's ability to perform and/or make important, rational, decisions. Perhaps a few examples will help to illustrate the need for this service.

There are times, within competitive situations, when athletes become so frustrated and angry at their own performance that they lose control, and "choke." On these occasions it is necessary for someone outside, like the sport psychologist or the coach, to help the athlete regain control; the individual simply cannot do it for himself/herself. Another example would involve the situation where an athlete is about to enter his/her first big contest. Before the event even starts, the athlete's anxiety level is so high he/she feels as if he/she is falling apart. He/she wants to run, withdraw, scream, or simply crawl under the stands and hide. Often, it is the sport psychologist who may help this individual calm down.

It is not uncommon to see athletes who become so upset at their early performance, performance in the preliminary round or the first few minutes of a contest, that they begin to lose control, becoming emotionally upset, depressed, crying, talking in self-defeating terms. Once again, some type of crisis intervention is required.

At times, the pressure comes from outside the competition itself, and may involve close personal relationships. Something happens to a friend or family member, there is a fight with a wife, boyfriend, or coach. The importance of the personal relationship and the depth of the emotions involved threaten to damage the athletes' performance and perhaps their entire career. At these times the sport psychologist functions to provide some stability during the crisis and assesses the need for a referral. It may well be that the problem is not only going to interfere with an immediate situation, but it could become chronic as in the case

4

of marital difficulties, and may require more traditional counseling or therapy.

Then too, there are situations that occur in which an athlete or coach appears to have sudden doubts about his/her competence, or whether he/she belongs. The athlete who suddenly disappears from training camp because he/she is homesick. For whatever reason some real doubts have suddenly begun to enter into the athlete's thinking. Enough anxiety is generated that the athlete is in danger of making some hasty, irrational, decision. It may well be the sport psychologist who helps the athlete through.

To be able to provide crisis intervention services, it is necessary to be able to listen, and empathize with an athlete and his/her problems. You must be able to establish a relationship, to get through the athlete's anger, depression, and/or anxiety in order to open up communication. As communication is established, the next step is to assess the situation and to establish some treatment plan. This may involve simply talking out the problem and helping restore the athlete's confidence. It may mean being able to recognize more serious underlying emotional problems and then having the skill to get the athlete to accept a recommendation for counseling or therapy.

In chapter 12 I will provide some of the information needed to function effectively in crisis situations. Details about what to do, and what to avoid will be presented.

PSYCHOLOGICAL ASSESSMENT

Very often, sport psychologists are called upon to use the knowledge they have about testing. Usually, they are given two basic kinds of tasks that can involve the use of tests: 1) They may be asked to make selection and/or screening decisions. Which athlete do you feel will function best in a pressure situation? Who should be selected to be coach? 2) The second type of question involves program development and/or counseling. In these instances test information is used to asses the strengths and weaknesses of an individual or program. The information gained through the testing (assessment) process is used to make decisions regarding what type of training would be helpful to a given individual, team, or organization, under what particular circumstances. A sport psychologist may be asked to assess the need for stress management training, or for the development of communication skills, etc.

There are many different assessment techniques that a sport psychologist might decide to use. These procedures include structured interviews, the making of systematic behavioral observations, the analysis of performance information, the use of paper and pencil tests of personality characteristics, needs, perceptual abilities, habits, etc. It may also include the use of psychophysiological measures like biofeedback.

It would be impossible in this book to review all of the methods and procedures that might be used in assessing athletic situations. Discussion of psychological tests alone could encompass several volumes. Instead, the emphasis here will be on the following: 1) Learning to determine the relevance of a particular test or procedure to the job at hand. How do you select tests? 2) Teaching you to be able to evaluate not only the relevance of a technique from a theoretical and practical perspective, but to be able to evaluate *its* validity and reliability. 3) Learning the ethical concerns and limitations associated with the use of psychological tests. 4) Case history data and test information to aid in the learning of strategies that can help you develop skill in test interpretation and program development. 5) Learning how to establish conditions so that you maximize cooperation when attempting to collect test data. 6) Specific rules to aid in teaching you to provide test feedback to athletes and organizations in a way which will maximize the likelihood they can make effective use of your findings.

PERFORMANCE ENHANCEMENT

There are several ways a sport psychologist can be used to aid in the development and execution of athletic skills. Psychological techniques like biofeedback, progressive relaxation, meditation, hypnosis, and autogenic training can be used to improve the consistency of an athlete's performance by giving him/her greater sensitivity to, and control over, his/her physiological arousal.

Techniques like Attention Control Training, Cognitive Behavior Modification, Mental Rehearsal are often used to aid in the identification of performance problems, and to speed the learning of new skills. It is possible for the sport psychologist to facilitate the learning process, reducing the number of errors an athlete makes during skill acquisition.

Often, skills in psychological assessment are used to facilitate performance by team building. Through testing and behavioral observations the sport psychologist identifies ways in which athletes can communicate more effectively with each other, with coaches, trainers, etc. It may be the sport psychologist's job to identify interpersonal factors affecting performance, and to then work with the individuals involved to develop better communication and coping strategies. This team building process is related to the consultation and supervision services discussed below.

Finally, sport psychologists may be asked to use their knowledge of human behavior to aid in motivating athletes. What can be done to increase enthusiasm, enjoyment, and involvement in sport.

Section three of this book will provide information about the different techniques that are most often used by sport psychologists to improve performance. Strategies will be presented to help you decide which technique to apply to a given individual, in a specified situation.

CONSULTATION AND PROGRAM DEVELOPMENT SERVICES

In many ways the sport psychologist functions as a bridge between

6

two fields, psychology and athletics. Often, particularly when working with elite athletes, or with athletes who have extremely close relationships to their coach, the sport psychologist is not the best person to provide services. It may be that he/she does not know enough about the technical aspects of a sport to provide the interface with psychology. It may be necessary to train the athlete or the coach to provide the service or intervention. Sometimes the level of trust between athlete and psychologist, or coach and psychologist is such that it is much easier to provide training and supervision in the use of a particular technique to the coach than it is to try and do it yourself. Then too, the sport psychologist may not be around when a particular service is required. Few sport psychologists are willing to travel throughout the season with a professional baseball team that must play 160 plus games a year.

When time, your own limited expertise, and/or trust become issues, teaching and supervising others can provide a very effective method for meeting the psychological needs of athletes. Chapter 2 deals with some of the ethical, structural, and organizational issues that are involved in training others to provide services, or to monitor training programs that you develop.

PREVENTION AND TREATMENT OF INJURIES

It is commonly assumed that increasing pressure and anxiety can both increase the likelihood of the development of an injury, and act to exacerbate pre-existing injuries. Because of the role of anxiety, and the interaction with physical processes, the sport psychologist may be called upon to reduce the athlete's perception of pain, to help him/her control muscle tension that is aggravating a problem, and to reduce stress as a preventive measure.

Chapter 13 discusses the inter-relationship between mental and physical processes as they relate to injury. Techniques that the sport psychologist can use and their limitations are also discussed in chapters 15, 16, 17 and 18.

These are some of the major services that sport psychologists find themselves engaging in. It is the intent of this book to provide you with a majority of the theoretical and technical information necessary to provide these services. As was mentioned earlier several professional organizations are attempting to determine the best type of training program to offer to meet the needs of sport psychologists. At this time, we are probably several years away from being able to offer an integrated experience which offers training in all of these areas. In the meantime, services are being provided and that it why it is so important to have some explicit ethical standards which guide us in the provision of those services.

I believe it is possible for individuals to pick up skills in psychological assessment, hypnosis, biofeedback, etc. through psychology courses, reading, experience and self-study. Skills developed in this way may provide the technical background required to function in a given area. I think it is critical, however, that this technical expertise or knowledge be supplemented with some type of supervised internship and/or practicum experiences.

Some internship experiences in sport psychology are being developed. As an example, a cooperative program between San Diego State University and the California School of Professional Psychology, has allowed Master's level students in the SDSU program and Doctoral level students at CSPP to work in a supervised setting with various athletic teams at San Diego State University. Students have provided assessment services, crisis intervention, performance improvement, and consultative (team building) services.

It has been our experience that practicum experiences are critical for several reasons. 1) They help to sensitize the student intern to important ethical issues. Under supervision, interns quickly become aware of the conflict of interests that develop as they attempt to please both the coach and the athlete. 2) The internship experience helps interns identify their own needs. They begin to see why they are working with athletes and become more aware of those situations in which they are likely to project their values, attitudes, and beliefs on the athlete. 3) The internship, particularly as the interns begin to work with several athletes over a period of time and are able to see the effects of interventions, helps point out the vast individual differences that exist between athletes. It is this awareness that sensitizes sport psychologists to the need to have several different ways of approaching a given issue. 4) It provides the interns with the opportunity to take a few chances, to risk making a mistake or two, knowing that the supervisor will help out. This opportunity can be a great confidence booster to the interns and may provide the emotional strength they need to be successful. 5) The training experience requires the interns to learn to think on their feet, to react to the unanticipated. There are a great many times when problems develop that a sport psychologist cannot have prepared for. With supervision and experience, the interns learn that they can handle these situations effectively. 6) Finally, the internship helps the interns develop the empathy, language, and sport specific knowledge that is so critical to effective professional functioning.

ETHICAL STANDARDS FOR SPORT PSYCHOLOGISTS

What is presented in this chapter, has not been accepted as the official position of various sport psychology bodies (ISSP, NASPSPA, CSPLSP). Instead, it is an adaptation of the ethical standards for psychologists. Wording has been changed slightly to focus on the field of sport psychology. The proposal that the International Society of Sport Psychology accept these standards has been made by their ethics committee.

It should be pointed out that if the title "sport psycholgist" is to be limited to those individuals who currently qualify as psychologists under existing state and provincial laws, it is not necessary to recommend the acceptance of these standards. By definition, psychologists are already required to abide by these standards. The only issue to be raised regards the appropriateness of imposing these standards on others (non-psychologists) who may be functioning in applied areas. My own personal feeling is that we should accept these standards as they are, and we should expect anyone providing services in the sport psychology area to abide by them. Others would disagree with this position and we may yet see some modifications.

For a full examination of the standards that have been established for psychology you should write to: American Psychological Association, 1200 Seventeenth St. N.W., Washington, D.C. 20046. Two of their publications would be especially relevant to sport psychologists; 1) *Ethical Standards of Psychologists,* and 2) *Standards for Educational and Psychological Tests.*

In this chapter the intent is to discuss some of the basic reasons for establishing an explicit set of ethical standards. In addition, a summary of the major principles the American Psychological Association addresses, is presented.

Each individual has inside themselves some implicit set of values and ethical standards. Typically, these values or ethical principles guide our behavior, but they do not become explicitly stated. In an ideal world, we would all know what values other people held, what we could expect of them, what their responsibilities were. Fortunately, or unfortunately, the world is more complex than that.

In a jungle where survival of the fittest is the rule, we would not trust anyone. We would all be looking out for number one. Sport psychologists, like clinical psychologists, have defined their role a little differently. They have in effect, called a time out. A public statement is made indicating that they are not in business to serve their own needs first. In describing themselves as a service provider their job is to respond to the needs of the athlete, coach, or team. It is the needs of their clients that must come first. If their own needs are served in the process, and presumably they are, that occurs only through, and secondarily to, the provision of service to others.

Because sport psychologists must have the trust of the individuals they would work with to function effectively, their motives must be clear to the athlete. An explicit ethical code is one way of providing reassurance to people they would serve. It establishes standards by which the profession expects to be judged, and by which it judges itself.

A fear that most professions have is that the public will attempt to legislate their behavior. As psychologists who are highly trained it is difficult to concede that an untrained, unsympathetic group of lay people (no matter how well meaning) would be qualified to tell them how to practice, what to teach, etc. Their development and identity as professionals depend upon their retaining control and assuming responsibility for their own behavior. If they do not want the public to control what they can and cannot do, then they must convince the public that they are capable of responding in a competent and ethical fashion. In effect, the profession must police itself and its members in order to be effective, to have respect, and to survive. Explicit ethical standards that have been adopted by the profession provide the guidance and direction needed to police themselves.

The rules that are established will be critical, for they will be the laws that govern most aspects of our behavior as professionals, and it is important that they be well thought out. Those presented here have been tested in a related profession. They have not provided all of the answers and are not without flaws. However, they do have much to recommend them. I believe the preamble to the Ethical Standards for Psychologists is worth quoting. It is the preamble that describes why we are concerned about the establishment of an explicit ethical code:

> *"Psychologists respect the dignity and worth of the individuals and honor the preservation and protection of fundamental human rights. They are committed to increasing knowledge of human behavior and of people's understanding of themselves and others and to the utilization of such knowledge for the promotion of human welfare. While pursuing these endeavors, they make every effort to protect the welfare of those who seek their services or of any human being or animal that may be the object of study. They use their skills only for purposes consistent with these values and do not knowingly permit their misuse by others. While demanding for themselves freedom of inquiry and communication, psychologists accept the responsibility this freedom requires: competence, objectivity in the application of skills and concern for the best interest of clients, colleagues, and society in general. In the pursuit of these ideals, psychologists subscribe to principles in the following areas:"*

10

RESPONSIBILITY

Sport psychologists value objectivity and integrity. In providing services they maintain the highest standards of their profession. They accept responsibility for their work and attempt to insure that their services are used appropriately.

I am sure that most people would have no trouble subscribing to the principle dealing with responsibility. It makes sense and all of us want to respond in an ethical way. There are times, however, when I feel that no matter how well motivated, our own interests or concerns prevent us from seeing that we are not accepting responsibility for the services we provide. Perhaps a couple of examples will illustrate the point.

Sport psychologists often find themselves using clinical techniques like implosion and systematic desensitization to help athletes control anxiety or fear in competitive situations. Both of these techniques were originally developed for use with neutoric patients — individuals with fairly extreme fears that seemed to be complicated by underlying or unconscious psychological factors. Often the clinician working with the patient had to proceed very cautiously, either to overcome "unconscious resistances" the patient might have to therapy, or to prevent the treatment itself from being so stressful that it resulted in further breakdown and greater problems for the client.

The concern about the possibility of an emotional breakdown, particularly with a vulnerable patient, is raised in the case of implosion. As a therapeutic technique, implosion involves confronting an individual with his/her fear in as dramatic a way as possible. It is like the father who throws his son or daughter into the deep end of the swimming pool because the child is afraid of water.

With a reasonably healthy patient, there are usually few problems encountered in attempting to implode a patient's fear. With a highly anxious patient, however, there can be major problems. It is this fact that necessitates the clinician to have a knowledge of psychodynamics. The clinician who decides to use implosion as a treatment is accepting the risk of possible problems and is willing to take the responsibility for making that decision. Competent acceptance of that responsibility must come from knowing the risks, and from being able to assess the strength of the individual you are working with.

I have heard it argued that sport psychologists are not clinicians (a point I agree with) and that they need not be clinically trained. Instead sport psychologists are described as educators. They are people with certain technical skills or knowledge and they teach others about these skills. The population they work with is athletes and coaches and they automatically define them as normal. They make the assumption that the people they are working with are highly motivated to succeed, have the mental and physical gifts required, and do not have underlying psychological conflicts that are going to prevent them from learning, or that will damage them.

11

Such an assumption is made to justify the use of techniques like implosion by non-clinically trained individuals. In a sense, it is a way of avoiding responsibility for possible negative consequences. Although I believe that it is important to treat athletes as if they are normal and to assume that they are highly motivated, without serious underlying problems, I also believe that it is the sport psychologist's job to be sensitive to the fact that this may not be the case. The sport psychologist must be capable of recognizing when a technique he/she intends to use may be inappropriate. This recognition does not mean that he/she should be capable of providing therapy or of dealing with the underlying dynamic issues. It means he/she should be sensitive to individual differences and recognize when to make a referral and when to move away from a particular treatment approach. It is important that we do not allow our desire to make use of a valuable technique cloud our judgment. Although athletes are not seen as pathological, approximately the same percentage of athletes have relatively severe emotional problems as do people in the general population. In fact, it may well be a large portion of the pathological population (5-10 percent of all athletes) that are drawn to the sport psychologist. Using a technique for anxiety reduction, and teaching it as if you were teaching a skill in math, can be an avoidance of professional responsibility.

There is a second area of concern under the responsibility principle. It is stated that the psychologists try their best to insure that their services are not misused. I have had sport psychologists tell me that coaches have come to them asking them to "brainwash" their athletes. The coaches have had one concern and that has been winning, or getting ready for a particular game. In many instances they are not concerned with the special or personal problems that their athletes may be having. Their priorities are clear, and they may ask the sport psychologist to adopt them, even though they don't fit with that person's ethical standards or principles.

It is very common for management and coaches to ask for psychological information that they are not qualified to interpret. They don't understand the limits to the validity and reliability of test results or a psychologist's conclusions or findings. If the information is simply turned over to them they are quite likely to abuse it. It is for precisely this reason that the American Psychological Association has made very explicit statements about not providing test feedback through the mail. Computerized test interpretations can be provided only to professionals who are capable of interpreting the results and capable of independently assessing their validity and reliability. Most coaches and athletes are not capable of effectively using test information.

COMPETENCE

The maintenance of high standards of competence is a responsibility of all psychologists. Sport psychologists recognize the limits of their techniques and the limits of their own competence. The sport psychologist keeps current in the scientific developments within the areas that they offer service. They limit the techniques they use and the statements they make to those which meet recognized standards.

· Very often the title psychologist carries with it a great deal of meaning for the public at large. This status is especially true in the area of sport psychology. Professionals within the field have not yet agreed upon the functions, services, and expertise that can be considered a part of sport psychology. It is not uncommon for the public to attribute all of the expertise they would grant to a psychiatrist, a clinical psychologist, a hypnotherapist, a stage hypnotist, a parapsychologist, a social psychologist, a psychometrician, and an organizational psychologist, to the sport psychologist. It is the sport psychologist's responsibility to accurately present his/her credentials and training to avoid any possible misunderstanding or misrepresentation.

As it currently stands, any psychologist is entitled to administer any psychological test, or to use any form of psychotherapy he chooses whether that is psychoanalytic therapy, gestalt therapy, rational emotive therapy, or hypnotherapy. Legally, psychologists can use any or all of these techniques, in spite of the fact that their training may not have prepared them to do so. It is the psychologist's ethical code which insures that individuals are competent to provide the services offered.

One of the criticisms that clinicians who have decided to move into the sport psychology area have encountered involves the fact that they know very little about the demands of sport situations. There has been a tendency for clinicians to blindly apply to athletic situations those techniques or theories that they have found useful in clinical practice. In many instances solutions have not fit, and the decisions made without adequate knowledge about athletes or about the athletic environment have occasionally been harmful. To attempt to explain a baseball hitter's slump on the basis of deep underlying neurotic conflict may not only be inaccurate, it can create more problems.

A sport psychologist (or anyone for that matter) who attempts to use psychological techniques like hypnosis to minimize pain, increase endurance, etc. should either know a great deal about human physiology and the demands of a particular sport, or they should be under the direct supervision of someone who does.

A competent professional must be extremely sensitive to individual differences, to the effects age, race, sex, ethnic background, socioeconomic status, coach, etc. can have on different individuals, on test results, interview data, etc.

Competent professionals must be sensitive to their own needs, personality traits, etc., so that they can see when these are getting in the way of the services that they would hope to provide. It is very easy for sport psychologists who have strong competitive needs of their own, to project these on the people they work with. If this happens they may fail to respond to the athletes' needs. They become like the parent who must live through the competitive success of their child. In a similar fashion, I have seen sport psychologists who are very strongly against competition. They believe that competition is bad and this fact influences the way they respond to the needs of athletes. Although these people may be very helpful to those individuals who have low levels of self confidence, and who have been hurt by competition, they have great difficulty relating to the elite athlete or coach who is highly competitive. They cannot rid themselves of their own feelings and biases, and no one would expect them to. What is expected is that sport psychologists be sensitive to those factors that influence their own experience and decisions and take steps to insure that they do not negatively affect the people that they would serve. Often, this difficulty in separating issues means seeking outside supervision and/or a second opinion.

MORAL AND LEGAL STANDARDS

Psychologists' moral, ethical, and legal standards of behavior are a personal matter to the same degree as they are for other individuals, except when these personal standards compromise the fulfillment of professional responsibilities, or reduce the public's trust in psychologists, or psychology. In effect, psychologists like teachers and medical doctors, must place the needs of the public above their own.

A sport psychologist would refuse to participate in practices that are inconsistent with ethical, legal, and moral standards regarding the treatment of athletes. In providing services like testing, the sport psychologist will avoid any action that could violate the legal and civil rights of the athlete or coach.

PUBLIC STATEMENTS

"Public statements, announcements of services, advertising, and promotional activities of psychologists serve the purpose of providing sufficient information to aid the consumer public in making informed judgments and choices. Psychologists represent accurately and objectively their professional qualifications, affiliations, and functions . . . (p. 3)."

CONFIDENTIALITY

It the primary responsibility of the psychologist to safeguard material that is obtained from the client during the provision of psychological services. Material collected during consultive relationships and/or evaluative material concerning athletes, coaches, etc. is discussed only for professional purposes and only with people who are concerned with the case.

"The psychologist is responsible for informing the client of the limits of the confidentiality (p. 4)." For additional information regarding possible

14

violations of the confidentiality standard, and ways to avoid this, see the next standard.

WELFARE OF THE CONSUMER

"Psychologists respect the integrity and protect the welfare of the people and groups with whom they work. When there is a conflict of interest between the client and the psychologist's employing institution, psychologists clarify the nature and direction of their loyalties and responsibilities and keep all parties informed of their commitments. Psychologists fully inform consumers as to the purpose and nature of an evaluative, treatment, educational or training procedure (p. 5). . . ."

Especially in sport psychology there are many areas where potential conflicts of interest can occur. I have already mentioned the conflict that develops when a sport psychologist is hired by a coach or management to prepare a team for competition and then finds himself/herself in the position of providing therapy to an individual on the team. Very often the therapy process or goals are diametrically opposed to the goals of the team.

Throughout the book I will be discussing different kinds of services that sport psychologists can and do offer. As a part of this discussion I will be bringing up examples of violations of various ethical principles, especially this one.

PROFESSIONAL RELATIONSHIPS

"Psychologists act with due regard for the needs, special competencies and obligations of their colleagues in psychology and other professions. Psychologists respect the prerogatives and obligations of the institutions or organizations with which they are associated (p. 5)."

This is a very important principle for the sport psychologist, especially for the sport psychologist who has been clinically trained. The situation within which the sport psychologist works is very different from the traditional clinical situation. There are many others, including trainers, coaches, team physicians, physiologists, etc. who have their own special areas to be concerned about, and who have a clearer mission given the particular situation. The goal for most professional organizations is to win; that is the focus of the situation, and the athletes agree to that when they get involved. The psychologist's own needs and training may cause him/her to attempt to impose his/her values onto the organization. This particular principle emphasizes the importance of respecting the orientations, prerogatives and obligations of the team or organization.

UTILIZATION OF ASSESSMENT TECHNIQUES

"In the development, publication, and utilization of psychological assessment techniques, psychologists observe relevant APA standards.

Persons examined have the right to know the results, the interpretations made, and where appropriate, the original data on which final judgments were based (p. 6)."

Both the ethical standards and the standards the American Psychological Association recommend for the development of psychological tests are discussed in detail in the section of this book dealing with assessment. This particular ethical standard has been repeatedly violated in sport psychology.

PURSUIT OF RESEARCH ACTIVITIES

"The decision to undertake research should rest upon a considered judgment by the individual psychologist about how best to contribute to psychological science and to human welfare. Psychologists carry out their investigations with respect for the people who participate and with concern for their dignity and welfare (p. 7)."

The International Society for Sport Psychology (ISSP) ethics committee has recommended the inclusion of one additional standard or ethical principle. The focus of the tenth principle is on the sport psychologist's responsibility when he/she observes or learns of another colleague conducting research that is not in accordance with the foregoing principles. In this instance it is the observer's responsibility to bring his/her concerns first to the investigator, suggesting that he/she re-examine the research in light of the ethical principles. It is also suggested that the researcher seek out additional consultation from responsible senior colleagues.

3

THE NEED FOR PSYCHOLOGICAL THEORY

It is difficult to imagine a sport psychologist being able to function consistently in an ethical and competent way, without having some theoretical framework that guides his/her practice. Theories are those constructs and rules which help us to understand the people and institutions we find ourselves working with, and provide the basis for our making predictions about an individual or team's behavior. Finally, theories provide the guidance we need in the development of programs that are designed to gain control over, or alter behavior. From a scientist's perspective, a good theory should do all of these things: it should lead to greater *understanding, prediction,* and *control* of human behavior.

As with our ethical standards, each of us has a set of theoretical principles that guide our behavior. Often, especially for the nonscientist, these principles are implicit and can only be made explicit through deduction. Like the "natural athlete," we have never taken the time to sit down and figure out what exactly makes us run. We seem to function on instinct until we look at our own behavior over time. As we begin to do this, we become aware of the fact that we are using certain principles, signals from the environment, from ourselves, etc. to guide our behavior. These principles are the core of our own mini-theory. They provide the framework that allows us to understand, predict, and control behavior.

For the scientist and the sport psychologist, it is important to know what principles are guiding one's own behavior, that is to take the time to figure out what causes you to make a particular decision to "run the way you do." To say it is "intuition" or my "clinical ear" is not sufficient. Especially when the decisions that you make will dramatically affect the lives of others. To be able to recognize the limits to your own competent functioning, to protect the rights of your clients, to be sensitive to cultural, social, economic, and interpersonal differences, to accept responsibility for your decisions, you must make your theoretical constructs public. No matter how good a sport psychologist you are, no one is perfect. By stating your theory explicitly, and by operationalizing your theoretical constructs you create conditions under which the accuracy of

17

your approach can be evaluated.

I used the term operationalize in the preceding sentence and it is important to define what I mean. As mentioned, ideally a theory will act to increase our understanding, prediction, and control of behavior. Unfortunately, this result is not always achieved. One of the major criticisms of psychoanalytic theories is that although they may lead to a greater understanding of behavior (at least as far as the psychologist is concerned), they do not add to our ability to predict and control behavior. The reason for this failure is that the theoretical constructs which underlie a psychoanalytic orientation are not operationally defineable. They have an elastic quality which allows them to explain any behavior an individual engages in. In fact, the theory can be stretched so far that it can explain opposite behaviors by the same person in identical situations.

From an analytical point of view, I might postulate that everyone has a very strong sexual drive. I may further postulate that this drive is unconscious and can be seen when a person is caught off guard. Thus, if I ask you to associate freely to words, or if I examine your doodling on a piece of paper, or if I give you a test that allows you to project your own thoughts and feelings onto the test material, I should see evidence of your sexual drive. To look at these underlying processes, to attempt to validate the theoretical construct of a sexual drive, psychologists have used tests like the Rorschach Ink Blot Test. If expected responses are not forthcoming, then other theoretical constructs such as repression and denial to ward off unacceptable thoughts, have allowed analysts to explain away the failure to elicit the sexual responses subjects were expected to give. In effect, if a subject gives sexual responses on the Rorschach he/she is validating our theoretical construct of a sexual drive. If he/she does not give sexual responses he/she is validating the construct of a sexual drive that is being repressed by the defenses of denial and repression. These two additional constructs are also validated according to the analyst.

To avoid the problem that occurs with many analytical theories, the theorist attempts to operationalize the basic constructs that make up the theory. By operationalize, we mean describe them in a way which makes them testable. If they have value for predicting and controling behavior, there are some lawful operational relationships that exist between the theory and behavior. It is the theorist's job to make these operations explicit. If, as in the case of analytical theories, additional theoretical constructs are added which serve to modulate interpretations, it is the theorist's responsibility to attempt to define the conditions under which this modulation occurs. In this way, predictions can be made in advance rather than waiting until a person responds and then picking the theoretical construct that explains the response.

We have, and occasionally continue to go too far in our attempts to operationalize. We have dramatically simplified our theory in order to improve our ability to predict behavior. As an example, I might say that my theory of behavior consists of the following construct. The best

18

predictor of an athlete's behavior in a very specific situation, is his/her behavior in an identical situation in the past. That is like saying if I want to predict typing speed, I give a person a typing test. Having given that person a test, I then predict that in future situations like the one in which I tested, he/she will perform in a similar way. Such highly operationalized and simplistic theories do indeed improve our predictive abilities in highly specific situations. They do not, however, add much to our understanding of the individual athlete or team. They do not lead to our being able to make other predictions, or to understand one's behavior in other situations.

As sport psychologists, we do not often have the luxury of testing and/or observing an athlete, coach, team, under every possible set of circumstances. We need to be able to anticipate what will happen in the Superbowl, even though the team has never been there before. We need to make some decisions about a rookie's ability to play in the NHL, NFL or NBA. We need to anticipate how a particular coach and athlete will get along and what the effect of success and/or failure will be on an individual's future performance, etc.

A good theory will lead to improvement in the sport psychologist's ability to understand, predict, and control behavior. It is extremely important for us to begin to identify those constructs that might make up such a theory for several reasons:

1) The articulation of theoretical constructs makes it possible for us to test the accuracy, i.e. predictive validity, of the theory;

2) Having operationalized the theory, we can begin to refine it, to make it better when we see where our constructs lead to inaccurate understanding and/or prediction;

3) By making our constructs explicit, we create the conditions under which other people (who may be more objective than we can be with our own theory) can evaluate our work, and place it into some perspective;

4) The articulation of our theory makes it possible for us to communicate (teach) the rules that we use to make decisions, to guide our own behavior. As a sport psychologist, I can train other sport psychologists. It may be true that there are some people (coaches, physicians, athletes) who have tremendous "instincts." Unfortunately, those people are few and far between. If we can begin to articulate what makes those people so special, we can begin to teach others the things they need to do to function more effectively. It is this articulation of ability that a good theory provides.

As a sport psychologist, you will need some kind of theoretical constructs to guide your behavior. You may select some existing theoretical framework, or you may construct your own. You may even decide to use several different theoretical positions, depending upon the particular job you have to perform.

I have attempted to point out some of the advantages to having a theory which guides your behavior. I have emphasized that for ethical reasons, it is imperative that we identify those factors or theoretical rules that are guiding our own behavior. This identification is especially important because the theory that we choose to use has limitations. By definition, one of the things it does is constrict our vision, causing us to look at the world in a certain way or through a certain set of glasses. Since the world is extremely complex, and since we are not likely to develop the perfect theory, it is important that we be open to our blind spots, and that we develop a theory which allows as much flexibility (without being so elastic it explains everything and predicts nothing) as possible.

In the next few pages, I am going to articulate the theoretical constructs that guide my behavior as a sport psychologist. I want to make these constructs as explicit as possible. First, I believe that the constructs that I use to understand, predict, and control behavior, have strong support from both the experimental and clinical literature. That is, they have some empirical and practical validity. Next, although these constructs are rough and by no means a final or polished product, I am convinced that their use by others will improve the quality of services that many of us offer. I think they can improve most people's ability to understand, predict, and control behavior. They represent a "next step" in our theoretical development.

Finally, and perhaps most importantly, it is my theoretical constructs (beliefs, etc.) that guide what I write, as well as how I behave in other ways. It is in both our interests for me to articulate what it is that causes me to see things in a certain way, to have certain opinions. To evaluate what I have to say, to be able to see it the way I do, to be able to compare what guides my behavior with what guides your own, and to be able to put my opinions in perspective, you need to know what underlies them.

4

ATTENTIONAL AND INTERPERSONAL STYLE

Because theories are not perfect and represent attempts to explain, predict, and control the behavior of certain groups of individuals, it is important that these theoretical constructs be responsive to the unique problems and characteristics of the groups whose behavior they attempt to explain. As an example, analytical theories were designed to explain the behavior of neurotic patients. Given that neurotic behavior is often irrational and self-destructive, and given that the patient often fails to see his/her own contributions to problems experienced, constructs such as the unconscious begin to make sense. The population that a sport psychologist deals with, however, is not typically neurotic.

Some of the factors that should be included when developing a theory to explain the behavior of athletes, include the following:

1. There is a dramatic need for the theory to attempt to integrate the relationship between mental and physical processes. Athletic situations typically require an individual to make obvious use of both mental and physical abilities.
2. Neurotic fear is by definition an exaggerated and/or irrational response. In contrast, the athlete's response to pressure or stress is reality-based as athletes must function in situations that are often filled with a great deal of "objective" pressure. They may face very real physical, economic, and social pressure.
3. As a group, athletes are seen as highly motivated, as having reasonably high levels of self-esteem, and as being in control of most situations.
4. In athletic situations, the stimuli that the individual should be responding to as well as the way he/she should respond, can usually be agreed upon. This means that it is easier to define a treatment or training focus, and that the outcome or effectiveness of the training can easily be evaluated. There are certain obvious behavioral changes that should take place when training is effective.

In summary then, a theory of human behavior in sport should attempt to explain the effects of increasing pressure on both mental and physical functioning. The theory should have behavioral relevance, and lead to the development of specific, operational programs designed to increase the athlete's effectiveness. The theory can assume that subjects are highly motivated and relatively free from unconscious conflicts that might cause them to be unresponsive to treatment interventions. Subjects are eager to take control, and to accept responsibility for their own behavior.[1]

As mentioned earlier, in the past, theories have been criticized for either being too all-encompassing and general (explaining everything but predicting nothing), or as being too specific (having good predictive validity in an isolated situation and very little generalizability). Several psychologists have made suggestions about improving on existing, or developing new, theoretical constructs.

First, it was emphasized that existing personality traits (e.g., hostility, extroversion, etc.), at least as measured, lacked the trans-situational generalizability it was hoped they would contain. Thus, although these traits made conceptual sense and gave us a feeling of understanding what was going on, they did not lead to accurate prediction of behavior. Because of the lack of utility of past measures, it was emphasized that we needed to search for new, trans-situational competencies. That is, we had to identify some human characteristics that had behavioral relevance in a wide variety of life situations.

A second factor involves the need to assess the behavioral competency of individuals with reference to specific situations. It was felt that by defining behavior more carefully and be assessing actual behavioral responses of individuals as opposed to their needs, attitudes, or feelings about themselves, we could increase predictive validity.

Next, because of the tremendous influence of situational factors on behavior, it was emphasized that theories should examine the person in relationship to others and to their environment. Thus the theory should be concerned with both inter and intra-personal factors.

Finally, the validation of a theory depends upon the establishment of a lawful relationship, usually evidenced by statistical correlations between the theoretical constructs and actual behavior. Typically, this relationship is established through testing. Instruments, or behavioral situations are constructed which allow an observer to quantify the amount of a particular personality characteristic a person has. Once some value is assigned to individuals, they are then studied to see if there is a correlation between the characteristic that has been measured and actual behavior. As an example, in athletic situations I might theorize that hostility (as a personality characteristic) should be associated with aggressive behavior on the playing field. I develop a measure of hostility (the trait), and I define aggressiveness (the relevant behavior). I then test a group of athletes to determine their levels of hostility, and I observe them in order to quantify their aggressiveness. Finally, I correlate their scores on my measure of hostility with their scores on my measure of aggressiveness. If I get a significant positive correlation (one that is not due to some chance relationship), I conclude that there is some support for my theory.

One of the difficulties that has been encountered in testing, and thus in using tests to establish the validity of theories, is the fact that subjects' attitudes toward the test, and certain response style characteristics (such as the tendency to be defensive in testing situations, or the tendency to exaggerate your own strengths, or the tendency to fake test responses in an attempt to look good or bad) result in inaccurate information about the respondent. To minimize the effects of different response style characteristics and to control subjects' attitudes towards the test, it is suggested that they be informed about what is being measured, and about the relevance the measurement has to their life. This issue will be discussed in great detail later. At a minimum, it is a way of at least being able to anticipate the attitude subjects are most likely to take towards testing. Response bias can at least be anticipated more reliably in this way and thus accounted for when interpreting the test results.

The theory of attentional and interpersonal style was designed with the criticisms just mentioned in mind. It was felt that a focus on attentional factors would respond to the concern that we identify competencies that have relevance to a variety of life situations. In addition, it was felt that the attentional constructs would have behavioral relevance, and should lead directly to the identification of performance weaknesses, and to suggesting steps for remediation.

It was believed that attentional constructs could be used to integrate mental and physical functions. There was a great deal of research data showing a predictable relationship between the ability to direct and control attentional processes and increasing pressure or arousal. Thus a careful examination of an athlete's attentional abilities, and an understanding of the relationship between attention, increasing arousal, and performance, should lead to better prediction and control of behavior.

In constructing a test to examine the theoretical constructs, every attempt was made to develop behaviorally-anchored items. In this way, it was hoped that individuals would be more capable of assessing their own abilities objectively.

Finally, the theory attempted to look at more traditional psychological traits (needs and modes of responding that other theorists have been concerned with), such as the need for control, level of self-esteem, whether or not the athlete is extroverted, introverted, expresses himself/herself emotionally, intellectually, and so on. These factors, however, are always examined within a context. Thus, the concern is not simply how strong a person's need for control is, but further, how his/her score compares with the scores of others with whom he/she must interact.

The theoretical importance of placing more traditional characteristics in a specific situation cannot be over-emphasized. The importance is derived not just because we know that situational factors influence behavior, but because examination within an interpersonal context allows us to anticipate situations which will act to increase and/or decrease an individual's level of arousal. For example, a person with a high need for control is much more likely to have a high level of arousal when interacting with an individual who also has a high need for control, than when interacting with someone with a low need for control. Because of the strong relationship between increasing arousal and attention, and because of the role both attention and arousal play in performance, the addition of personality traits and needs, interpreted within the confines of interpersonal relationships, can act to increase the ability to predict and control behavior. By seeing how people react attentionally, and by knowing the situations likely to affect attentional control, we can develop specific programs to minimize weakness and/or to maximize strength.

ATTENTIONAL PROCESSES

It has been suggested that one of the problems with existing trait theories involves the fact that the characteristics measured do not seem to be behaviorally relevant across a variety of life situations. A review of the research and theoretical literature in psychology seems to suggest that this lack of generalizability would not prove to be the case with attentional processes. In fact, it is difficult to conceive a single situation in which an individual's ability to pay attention and concentrate on certain things while ignoring others is not critical to effective performance. It doesn't matter if the person is involved in a complex sport, walking across the street, reading a book, or making a simple decision. It is disturbances in normal attentional processes that have been used to explain everything from schizophrenia to altered states of consciousness.

In the discussion that follows, several theoretical assumptions are made regarding attentional processes and their role in performance. To aid in understanding the material that is presented it is important to make those assumptions explicit:

1. There are several attentional dimensions that are related to effective performance including width and direction of attentional focus.
2. Attentional processes can be thought of as having both state and trait components.
3. The ability to control attention, and to shift from one attentional focus to another, is related to arousal.
4. Individuals tend to have preferred attentional styles. There are individual differences in attentional abilities and each of us has our own relative attentional strengths and weaknesses.

In talking about the role of attention in performance, it is necessary not only to think about an individual athlete's ability to develop certain types of attention, but about the attentional demands of the specific athletic situation. The sport psychologist in attempting to predict and control an athlete's behavior must be able to assess the athlete's attentional abilities and the attentional demands of the sport environment.

The goal is to be able to train the athlete to control attention so that he/she can match the changing attentional demands in sport situations.

There are at least three aspects of attention that must be considered if we hope to predict performance. These include width of attention, direction of attentional focus, and the ability to shift from one type of attention to another.

Width of attention can be thought of in terms of how much information an individual must attend to, within a given time frame. Some athletic situations, such as lining up a putt in golf, require a very narrow focus. Other situations require a broad focus. A three on two fast break in basketball requires the athlete to attend to a number of different cues in a short period of time. A great many sports require that the athlete shift rapidly from a broad focus of attention to a narrow focus. In fact, it is possible to think of the broad focus of attention as serving primarily an assessment function. It is this type of attentional focus the athlete uses to determine a course of action. As a decision is reached, attention is typically narrowed to allow for the execution of a response like shooting at the basket or passing the ball.

The direction of attention refers to whether the athlete is attending to his/her own thoughts and/or feelings, internal cues, or to things going on around him/her, external cues. It is assumed that attention cannot be directed internally and externally at the same moment. Thus, the athlete must be able to shift rapidly from one focus to another. Figure 1 illustrates the four types of attention that develop when we combine the dimensions of width and direction.

Figure 1. Attention in Athletics

External

Broad-External	Narrow-External
Optimal for reading complex sport situations. For assessing the environment. Used in team sports. Athletes with this ability have great anticipation.	This type of attention is required at the moment a response is given. Attention is narrowed and focused externally in order to hit a ball, react to an individual opponent.
Broad-Internal	Narrow-Internal
Optimal for analyzing sport. Coaches use it to make game plans, to anticipate the future and to recall past information. Quick learners have this ability.	Optimal for learning to become sensitive to your own body. Type of attention required in order to center and calm oneself, to rehearse a particular skill or move mentally.

Broad ← → Narrow

Internal

The second assumption that was made about attentional processes, involved the belief that there are state and trait components associated with each of the attentional abilities (Broad-External; Broad-Internal; Narrow-External; Narrow-Internal). To understand the implications of this for the sport psychologist, it is necessary to bring in another of the theoretical assumptions.

The fourth assumption that was made suggests that there are individual differences in terms of the ability to develop the four types of attention described in Figure 1. As an example, some coaches are seen as being dominated by a Broad-Internal focus of attention. They seem to have great difficulty shifting to the other types of attention even when the coaching situation would require it. As a result, they are always analyzing. The mistake that they make results from a failure to pay attention to what is going on around them, or to the need(s) of an individual athlete. Figure 2 illustrates some of the problems that occur when an athlete or coach tends to be dominated by a particular attentional style.

Figure 2. Attentional Errors

External

Broad-External

These individuals are too busy reading and reacting to the environment to think. They make the same mistakes over, getting suckered by their opponent. Behavior is externally controlled rather than internally controlled.

Narrow-External

These athletes do not adjust to changing situations. They get a plan or response in mind and stick to it no matter what.

Narrow-Internal

These individuals are often seen as "choker's." They become so focused on their own feelings that they can't function. For example, the end in football concentrating so hard on remembering the pattern that he forgets to catch the ball.

Broad-Internal

These athletes overanalyze and out-think themselves. They are inside their heads thinking about what will happen or has happened, rather than attending to the game.

Broad

Narrow

Internal

If we can identify the attentional demands of a sport, and if we can measure the ability of an athlete to meet these demands we are in a position to be able either to select athletes on the basis of attentional

26

abilities, or to train them to meet the needs of the sport. Given that there are pre-existing individual differences, the concept of using these to make selection and screening decisions makes sense, *provided we can accurately measure relevant attentional abilities.* In terms of training athletes to meet the demands of a sport, we must be sensitive to the assumption of state and trait components of attention.

Ideally we would like to think of both mental and physical abilities as permanent traits — as being highly stable across situations. In fact, to have any predictive utility, there must be some portion of the abilities that we are measuring that are trait like, or trans-situational. By the same token, to be able to modify behavior, to improve performance, we would hope that these so called traits would not be too stable. Since we cannot have it both ways, and since we do know that there is considerable flexibility or variability in the performance of most athletes, we talk about state and trait components of most abilities. As the state component of an ability, the ability to shift attention from one focus to another, increases, our ability to predict performance decreases, unless we can identify the specific situational influences that are affecting the state component of attention.

A major goal for the sport psychologist is to be able to measure the base level of an athlete's abilities (the trait component), and then to identify those situational factors that act to improve or increase the abilities. In the example that follows I am making the assumption that an athlete's worst performance (within a given time frame, in this instance a year) can be used to estimate the "base level" or trait portion of a given ability. I am also assuming that the difference between this base level and the athlete's best performance provides an indication of the state component of the ability. Obviously this is an oversimplification since the development of new skills, use of new techniques, development of compensatory behaviors, physical and mental maturation, etc. may significantly alter the athlete's base level. All of these factors are a part of the developmental process for any athlete. As development takes place it is necessary to modify our conceptions of the trait components of a given athlete's ability (this is especially important for younger athletes due to their rapid growth and development). Nevertheless, it is possible to select a time frame (longer with older athletes) and to use it to determine the amount of flexibility an individual has in given abilities. It is this flexibility (state portion) that the sport psychologist manipulates in order to improve performance. Generally speaking, the greater the performance variability (the larger the state component) the greater the likelihood that rapid and dramatic changes can occur.

As an example, let's consider a skeet shooter who has developed a very high degree of physical and technical skill. Over a year we record the number of targets this individual breaks for every one hundred shots taken. In this analysis we include practice rounds and competitive rounds. We are very careful to record who he/she is shooting with, what the weather conditions and field conditions are like, how important the shoot is, where on the field he/she is shooting from (skeet shooters must shoot from eight different stations, some being more difficult than others).

As we look at the number of targets the individual has broken, we see that scores have ranged from a low of 86, to a perfect score of 100. We notice too, that there are enough perfect scores to rule out chance as the entire explanation for performance variability. From these scores, we infer that the skeet shooter has the physical and mental abilities required to function at a very high level. Most importantly for our discussion, the athlete has the capacity to develop a narrow-external focus of attention. Under ideal circumstances he/she can sustain it long enough to get a perfect score. Under the worst of conditions he/she still manages to hit 86 of the 100 targets. The number 86 represents the bottom line in terms of the athlete's ability to develop a narrow-external focus of attention, and maintain it. The state component is identified as the range from 86 to 100.

As mentioned earlier, it is conceivable that the trait component of the shooter's ability could be modified by increasing growth and development (there is evidence to suggest that attentional abilities continue to develop through early adolescence). It is also possible that a new gun or development in another ability such as increased strength could act to raise the base level scores. By the same token, advancing age may lower them.

The sport psychologist, however, must begin someplace. For this reason, he/she attempts to control for as many other factors as he/she can and then very carefully examines performance variability. To determine what it is that is affecting the shooter, lowering his/her scores from 100 to 86, a very thorough analysis of the types of errors made, shooting conditions, etc. is conducted. Obviously, this process could be like looking for a needle in a haystack, so where do you begin? Since attentional control is seen as the most critical variable (given adequate skill and good technique), we must ask what is it that is likely to affect attention. It is here that we become concerned with the concept of arousal and with increasing pressure.

There is a great deal of clinical and research evidence that describes the interaction between attentional processes and increasing arousal. First, from a clinical perspective it is assumed that as pressure increases there is a tendency for individuals to play to their attentional strengths. This means that if one type of attention, say the ability to develop a broad-internal focus seems more developed than the others, the athlete will tend to rely on that particular attentional ability whether or not it is appropriate.

As an example, consider the skeet shooter mentioned earlier. An identification of the athlete's attentional abilities indicates that he/she is capable of developing all four types of attention presented in Figure 1. From what we know about his/her shooting, it is apparent that he/she can develop and sustain a narrow-external focus well enough to break

100 targets in a row. At the same time, testing reveals that he/she is even better at developing a broad-internal focus of attention, that is, at being analytical. What we see, as pressure begins to increase for the skeet shooter, at least initially, is the tendency to become more analytical. When he/she does this while shooting, he/she begins to make mistakes because he/she is not narrowing and focusing attention externally, on the target. Instead, he/she is internally focused, trying to analyze what he/she should be doing, what he/she should be preparing for, or worse, what is going wrong. The necessary shift of attention in response to changing environmental demands does not occur.

The next thing that happens to attention as pressure increases, is a tendency to narrow involuntarily. Thus, an athlete who was capable of attending to and integrating several things at the same time, has this ability interfered with. Whether or not this narrowing of attention will help or hinder performance depends on several factors including: 1) How complex the performance situation is. That is, how great the attentional demands are; 2) The base level ability of the athlete to begin with. As mentioned, some athletes seem more capable than others of developing a broad focus of attention. Those who can attend to more things to begin with have greater capacity to deal with increasing pressure — they have more room to move.

Finally, as pressure becomes even greater, a third thing happens to attention. Narrowing of attention is usually followed by the development of an internal focus. In part because increasing arousal results in physical changes in heart-rate, muscle tension, blood pressure, respiration-rate, the athlete begins to pay more attention to thoughts and feelings and less attention to things going on around him/her. The development of a narrow-internal focus in a performance situation is what usually causes the phenomena we refer to as choking. Arousal has caused attention to narrow and to become internally focused. This attentional shift results in performance errors because the athlete fails to attend to relevant external information. In addition, increasing arousal causes physiological changes such as increased muscle tension and alterations in breathing that affect fine motor coordination and timing. The combination of attentional disturbances and physical changes begin to feed on each other as attention becomes focused on internal processes and performance errors result. This feedback loop leads to further increases in muscle tension, creating further disturbances in attention and so on. The downward spiral that follows can be seen in Figure 3.

Since attention is so directly relevant to effective performance, and since arousal affects the state portion of the athlete's attentional abilities and physiological responses, it is critical that the sport psychologist determine those factors that affect a given athlete's level of arousal. By looking at error patterns in an athlete's performance, it is possible to do two things: 1) we can deduce whether or not arousal is too high or too low; 2) we can identify those situational and interper-

Figure 3. Situational Stressor

First time to compete in the Olympic Trials in gymnastics.

Physical Response to Stress

Increased perspiration, tendency to hyperventilate, feeling slightly unsteady. Increased neck and shoulder muscle tension, bracing of muscles which will interfere with coordination and timing.

Psychological Response

Narrow internal focus of attention resulting in a feeling of being rushed. Things seem to be happening more quickly and there is a greater tendency to be distracted by one's own thoughts and feelings (e.g. increased heart rate, fear of failure).

Performance Consequences

As timing and coordination are interfered with, mistakes are made in the routine. The feeling of being rushed causes the gymnast to initiate moves too quickly killing his/her ability to get maximum extension and height. Increased neck and shoulder tension interferes with rotation on difficult moves and results in not getting all the way around.

sonal factors that are stressful or arousing for a given athlete and that are most likely to affect attention control.

Using the skeet shooter as an example, in looking at shooting scores we noticed that the average score per 100 rounds in practice was 92, compared to an average of 97 for every 100 rounds in competition. From the difference in scores we might infer that arousal levels were too low in practice. It would appear for this athlete, as though the increasing pressure associated with competition was acting to narrow attention and to improve performance. The person might describe himself/herself as more focused, more ready and able to concentrate with fewer distractions. On the other hand, if the average scores were reversed so the person were hitting 97 targets in practice, and 92 in competition, we would infer that increasing arousal was acting to interfere with performance. In

30

this instance we would assume attention was narrowing and becoming internally focused. It would be necessary to teach the athlete to reduce arousal in the competitive situation in order to get him/her to improve his/her scores.

Since a major emphasis in many sport psychology situations involves reducing arousal in order to increase performance and control, another example of the reverse may be helpful. This one comes from a world championship boxing match between Roberto Duran of Panama, and Sugar Ray Leonard of the United States.

Roberto Duran is a fighter who is famous for his intensity in the ring, for his anger and "killer instinct." This man was raised in the streets of Panama and he seems to have a fire burning inside of him. Pictures of his eyes during a fight have been on the cover of national magazines because of the intense focus and anger.

In the fight, Leonard was the champion and the favorite. Duran had just moved up in weight and was not expected to be able to beat a boxer with as much speed and skill as Leonard had displayed. The experts were wrong, and Duran won the fight. Looking back on the match, it seems to me as if Leonard made a mistake in his psychological preparations. In an interview prior to the fight the champion indicated that he wanted to make Leonard so angry that he would make mistakes.

Because of the relationship between arousal, attention, and performance, Leonard's strategy makes some sense. Presumably a frustrated fighter would begin to tie up. In the case of Duran, however, there were several things wrong with the strategy. First, anger was something that the man from Panama had lived with all his life. It was his anger and his intensity that got him up and made a fighter out of him. If he relied more heavily on being smooth, etc., then the anger might have gotten in the way. Next, boxing in general, but especially when the fighting style is the rough-house style that Duran uses, does not require a low level of arousal. Finally, so long as Duran's anger was directed at the champion, attention was directed appropriately. This point about the direction of attention is perhaps the most important of all.

Each insult or punch that Duran received helped him to direct attention externally. He was not frightened by the champion, he did not lack confidence, he believed he could win. Without anxiety to cause an internal focus, increasing arousal just made Duran more determined and helped him stay after the champion.

If Duran had become angry at himself for his inability to hit a boxer (had the champion danced away), his performance would have been interfered with. Had Duran been over confident, or unable to use his anger, his arousal level would have been too low prior to the fight and he might not have trained as hard as he needed to. Unfortunately for the champion, given the sport, the challenger's fighting style, the anger and level of arousal that the challenger was used to, the psychological tactics proved to be a liabjlity rather than an asset. A narrow focus of attention, if it is externally focused, can be a decided asset.

Now, before discussing the identification of situational and interpersonal factors that are likely to affect the arousal levels of athletes, let me summarize the affects of increasing arousal on attention:

1. There is initially a breakdown in the ability to shift from one type of attention to another. This occurs because the athlete starts to rely on his/her most dominant attentional style.

2. Attention begins to involuntarily narrow as arousal levels increase. This reduces the amount of information an athlete can deal with. The person narrowing may attend more effectively to a few cues if he/she maintains an external focus. If the situation is complex, however, requiring attention to many different things, he/she will have problems.

3. Finally, attention begins to become more internally focused. It is narrowed, and the athlete locks in on his/her own thoughts and feelings. This is the type of attention associated with "choking."

SITUATIONAL AND INTERPERSONAL FACTORS

There is probably no end to the list of situational and interpersonal factors that we could identify as arousing, or at least potentially arousing for a group of athletes. Somehow, the sport psychologist must select out some of these as most likely starting places to attempt to identify potential trouble spots.

The example with the skeet shooter pointed out a common assumption regarding arousal. It is generally assumed that increasing the level of competition, or the emotional, social, and physical threat of any situation, will increase arousal in an individual. As a result, error patterns are routinely examined as a function of the level of social, emotional, economic, and physical threat associated with them. Beyond that general assumption, however, there may also be individual personality characteristics or traits that allow the sport psychologist to anticipate some individual differences in how athletes will respond.

Although there are some general assumptions we can make about factors that increase arousal levels, we also know that there are tremendous individual differences. It is important for the sport psychologist to be able to look at individual differences and to then use these to make differential predictions about the types of situations to which particular athletes will and will not respond.

In the past, personality traits or needs such as the need for control or the trait of extroversion, have failed to have as much predictive validity as we might have liked. One of the reasons for this failure has been the assumption that these needs are related to actual performance competency. It should be obvious that the preference for being with other people (extroversion), or the need to be in control of interpersonal situations, does not have to be associated with being socially competent (as we might assume an extrovert is) or with having the skill to actually be in control.

32

By looking at personality traits as needs, desires, and attitudes, and then seeing how these interact with attentional abilities we should be able to be more responsive to situational factors. Let me give an example. Let us say that an athlete is determined to be an extreme introvert. It would be a mistake to assume that because of this he/she would automatically perform poorly in those situations that require him/her to be more outgoing. In fact, he/she might do very well in many social situations. If, on the other hand, we assume that the demand that he/she function in an extroverted way denies him/her some of the personal space he/she needs and thus raises arousal, we can then infer that attention and performance will be affected. Whether or not the effect on attention will be sufficient to assist or impair functioning, will depend on the complexity of the situation, and on the athlete's initial attentional abilities. Thus, rather than postulating a direct relationship between a trait like extroversion and performance, we link it with attention. In effect, we look at the relationship between a need and a situation to see if arousal is going to be increased or decreased. Next, we look at the relationship between attentional abilities and attentional demands to see if an athlete has the capability of performing effectively. Finally, we relate the arousal level that has been inferred from the athlete's needs and the environment's ability to meet them, to the athlete's attentional abilities and to the attentional demands of the performance situation. This relationship allows us to predict success or failure, and to anticipate those situations that are likely to prove difficult. It also tells us very specifically, what we need to do to an individual's level of arousal and/or attention to improve performance.

Personality theorists have identified hundreds of needs or attitudes or abilities that they believed were important determinants of behavior. Obviously, the sport psychologist must select a few that seem most promising or relevant to performance situations that occur in sport. The ones that follow are the ones I have found most helpful in anticipating the types of situations that would act to increase or decrease an athlete's arousal. They are common personality characteristics or needs, and we all have them to one degree or another as they come into play in almost any interpersonal situation. It is these personality characteristics that will help determine: 1) which situations will be stressful for a given athlete and; 2) how the athlete is likely to respond, both physically and mentally, to increasing pressure.

NEED FOR CONTROL

Level of competitiveness, need to achieve and leadership ability, are all athlete characteristics that we have assumed influence behavior and arousal. A concept that overlaps with all of these, is the athlete's need for control. Individuals with a high need to achieve, who are competitive and assume leadership, almost by definition are in control and attempt to control interpersonal situations. Athletes high on these needs experience alterations in their arousal level, and in their ability to control attention when they are not able to assume a dominant role. It is arousing to them to have their beliefs, decisions, or leadership challenged. Too low a level of arousal can typically be raised by even small amounts of criticism. These people can be motivated, and will develop an "I'll show you attitude," through personal criticism, challenges to their leadership ability, etc.

In contrast, individuals with a low need for control, who describe themselves as not assuming leadership, experience stress when they are placed in positions that make them responsible for others. Since the athletic situation can be thought of in terms of the demands it places on the individual athlete to assume control and responsibility for self and others, this is an important interpersonal characteristic to measure. It is a personality trait that must be thought of, however, in the context of the sport situations. That is, how does the athlete's need for control (whether it is high or low) interact with the demands of the sport situation, and with the needs of others who are also involved (e.g., coach, teammates, opponents, etc.)? Does an athlete with a high need for control, have the attentional flexibility to deal with the increases in pressure he/she will feel when interacting with someone who is trying to take control away from him/her during competition?

SELF ESTEEM

Athletes who have low levels of self-esteem are very likely to have a negative response to criticism. Instead of reacting to a coach's criticism as a challenge, their attention begins to narrow and to become internally focused. It is the low level of confidence that results in the internal focus — a focus that interferes with performance. Instead of narrowing and focusing externally in a way which could enhance performance, they begin to attend to their own thoughts. A coach who makes a habit of motivating athletes by calling them names, trying to get them mad, will only make matters worse. Often, even positive feedback doesn't help. During the competition, the positive feedback acts to put pressure on the athlete to live up to the expectancies of others. The best technique to use when an athlete has a very low level of self-esteem may involve distraction. By distracting him/her, getting him/her to pay attention to neutral or positive stimuli, or to stimuli that are not task-related, you may allow his/her arousal level to go down and help attention return to normal. In this way mental and physical disturbances can be kept to a minimum. You avoid the development of the downward performance spiral that is often associated with choking.

OBSESSIVENESS

One of the characteristics associated with individuals whom a psychologist might describe as obsessive, is the apparent inability to make a decision. They seem to ruminate and worry for hours or even days before making up their mind about something. The tendency to ruminate and to have difficulty making decisions, or the opposite tendency to make decisions very quickly, almost impulsively, can have important implications for athletic performance.

Those athletes who make decisions very quickly are stressed by delays; they can be psyched out in competition when others take control away from them and force them to wait. In contrast, the athletes who tends to be more thoughtful has a need to be extremely well prepared. These individuals become stressed when other players, coaches, or the situation forces them to respond before they feel they have been given adequate time to prepare. They tend to describe themselves as very thorough and recognize that others seem to get ready more quickly than they. They tend to attribute this readiness to a lack of concern or sloppiness on the part of others (if their own level of self-esteem is high), or to their own slow learning (if their self-esteem is low).

To imagine the problems that can develop one only needs to think of a coach who scores in a direction indicating that it is very easy for him/her to make decisions. The coach sees a change that needs to be made and tells an athlete to make it. Typically, the coach's decision is not encumbered by a lot of "what if" questions? The athlete, however, does have "what if" questions. There is a strong need to be sure that the change is appropriate and to be sure that he/she has anticipated all of the possible consequences of the adjustment.

I know a female figure skater who was constantly frustrating her coach because the two differed dramatically on the basis of the speed with which they made decisions. The coach kept telling her that she was ready to use a new skating program in competition and she kept having tantrums and refusing. When he finally forced her to use the program she was stressed to the point of being unable to concentrate effectively and she skated very poorly. Her performance proved to her that she was right and that her coach was unreasonable. In fact, the coach was right, at least half right. She was ready physically to do the program. Unfortunately, she was not ready mentally. As a result her attitude and inability to concentrate kept her from responding at the physical level of which she was capable.

EXTROVERSION − INTROVERSION

Another personality trait that seems to differentiate between individual athletes involves their need for people. There are those athletes who would be described as more introverted, needing personal space and distance. This need may increase as pressure increases, for example, just before a competition. A coach who forces team involvement (because he/she happens to be more extroverted) or who requires that an athlete room with someone who won't respect that athlete's privacy, can raise the introverted athlete's arousal level beyond the maximally productive point.

Competitive situations that interfere with personal privacy and preparation, for example, chromosomal checks, or forcing athletes to sit together in a very small space prior to competition as the Russians did to the divers during the games in Moscow, can be very damaging. Introverted athletes need privacy. For these individuals, having to sit in a small room with forty or more competitors while waiting for their next dive can prevent adequate mental preparation.

In a similar way, isolation of more extroverted individuals can result in excessively high levels of arousal. The coach who insists that all athletes sit quietly and prepare for competition may be taking away the technique that the extroverted athlete uses to control his/her arousal level and his/her ability to concentrate. Many of these individuals use their own outgoing nature to distract themselves, and to relieve the internal build-up of pressure.

Because of the individual differences in terms of characteristics like introversion and extroversion, it is important for the sport psychologist to be sensitive to different situational demands and different athlete needs. When things are out of balance, special techniques can be used to help the athlete compensate, and occasionally the situational demands can be changed.

COMMUNICATION STYLE

Athletes and coaches differ dramatically in terms of how they express themselves. Some individuals are seen as relatively unemotional, that is, as expressing themselves almost exclusively in intellectual ways. An example of this type of expression, at least as presented in the popular press, is Tom Landry, coach of the Dallas Cowboys football team. Other coaches, for example, John Wooden, may be seen as much more supportive in his expression of a great deal of positive support and feedback. Still others have the image of being extremely demanding and critical, expressing a great deal of anger. Woody Hayes had a public image of being extremely critical of players.

Each of the styles, whether intellectual or emotional, positive or negative, can be effective in the right circumstances with the right players. Generally speaking, however, the more flexible the coach and the more sensitive he/she is to individual differences, the greater the chance of success.

How individuals choose to express themselves can be of great significance to the sport psychologist. The more an individual is dominated by one type of expression, the easier it is to anticipate trouble spots or stressful situations. For example, athletes who do not express themselves intellectually, often fail to because they lack confidence in their own intellectual abilities. It can be anticipated that these individuals will be stressed by demands to be analytical (especially in front of others), such as in answering a coach's questions when review- ing game films. The more open ended the question and the more analytical, the greater the anxiety. A lot of instruction just prior to com- petition can overload these individuals and interfere with performance.

In a similar way, athletes who seem to express positive feelings almost to the exclusion of negative ones, are often stressed themselves by negative feedback. They find it very hard to hear criticism and they find it hard to have to give it. Coaches who have difficulty expressing negative feelings tend to have problems because they don't set limits. They often allow situations to go too far before they are finally forced to step in.

Finally, the tendency to be dominated by negative affective expres- sion can result in the coach or athlete being isolated. The coach who is extremely critical will stress many athletes to the point of driving them away. Unfortunately, the athletes with lower levels of self-esteem will be likely to see themselves as having the problem. The lower the level of self-esteem, the greater the need for some positive support. When positive feedback is lacking, these individuals begin to feel worthless and withdraw.

SUMMARY

In the preceding pages I have tried to emphasize the importance of theory to the functioning of sport psychologists. It has been suggested that without some underlying theoretical constructs to guide in the assessment of performance related problems, and in the development of treatment or training programs, it is impossible to function in an ethical way.

An overview of the fields of psychology and physical education would indicate that there is no shortage of theoretical constructs. The need is to find some constructs that add significantly to our ability to understand, predict, and control behavior in sport situations. This chapter has emphasized the central role that the ability to control width and focus of attention has for performance across virtually every sport situation imaginable.

It has been pointed out that the ability to attend or concentrate in the most task relevant way is affected by alterations in an athlete's level of arousal. As arousal increases, attention becomes less flexible, then begins to narrow, and finally becomes increasingly internally focused. These changes have obvious implications for performance.

Finally, the sport psychologist should attempt to examine certain per- sonality characteristics, such as the athlete's need for control and level of self-esteem, within various interpersonal and situational contexts. It is this examination that allows us to predict the type of situations that will be arousing to a given athlete. Having access to this information, and having some knowledge of the athlete's attentional abilities and of the attentional demands of the sport, provides the basis for understanding, predicting and controlling behavior. It is this information that will lead to the prediction of success or failure, and to the development of specific training programs.

Throughout the remainder of the book the attentional and interpersonal factors that have been discussed here will be used to analyze athlete behavior. To understand the programs that will be developed for training athletes, and to understand why a particular psychological technique is employed, it will be necessary to understand the theory that has been presented.

In an attempt to examine the validity of the theory presented, a paper and pencil test was developed. The Test of Attentional and Interpersonal Style consists of 144 items designed to provide information about an athlete's ability to develop the attentional styles described in this chapter. In addition, the test attempts to measure those interpersonal characteristics that are seen as interacting with attention and arousal to affect performance. The instrument has been found to have some good validity and reliability. As will be seen later it has been used as the basis for developing performance improvement programs. For those who are interested, information about the *Test of Attentional and Interpersonal Style* (TAIS) is provided in Appendix A.

---

[1]When this proves not to be the case (e.g. the athlete seems incapable of following instructions and modifying behavior), it may be necessary to adopt a more traditional-clinical theoretical framework.

5

SHOULD WE ADMINISTER PSYCHOLOGICAL TESTS TO ATHLETES?

There are many people who would insist that the future of psychology (applied psychology) depends very strongly upon practitioners developing their skills in designing, administering, validating, and interpreting psychological tests (Rotter, 1973). It is through the development of tests which can aid in our understanding, predicting, and controlling behavior, that we can talk about applied psychology as a science.

In spite of the fact that many professionals and scientists see testing as the cornerstone of an applied profession, there is an equally large group that would like to do away with the use of psychological tests altogether. Whether or not we should use psychological tests in the field of sport psychology is an emotional issue that at times clouds our own professional judgments. My own emotions tend to fall on the side that is supportive of the use of psychological tests. I am sure that at times my own presentation of issues becomes somewhat clouded by my feelings. In subsequent pages I have tried to respond to issues in an impartial way, or to label my own bias when it occurs. Since we are not always the best observers of our own behavior, you as reader should retain your own critical judgment and determine for yourself the validity of the issues.

It is important to understand where some of the strong anti-testing feelings come from. First, because psychologists have used a professional language, a language that the general public does not understand, there has been confusion regarding just what the psychologist is saying on the basis of test data. Then too, because psychologists are often asked to explain extremely deviant behavior, behavior that seems crazy and irrational to others, the procedures by which they do this (testing) often appear to be somewhat mystical or magical. Following testing and/or an interview I have rarely heard a psychologist admit that he/she could not understand a person's behavior. Instead, he/she seems to explain extremely deviant behavior, with great confidence, in a language that sounds impressive, but is not understood by the general public.

39

Several things have resulted from past inappropriate use of tests. For one, many people have become defensive, frightened by what they fear may be revealed through testing. Somehow the tests are given a great deal of power. It means a great deal more emotionally if a psychologist makes a pronouncement about personality or behavior that is based on test data, than it does if a friend or coach has said the same thing, but without testing. It is easier to question the judgment of a friend or coach, to defend against their findings, than it is to question the test, although in reality the test is not infallible.

As we have become more sophisticated and aware of the limitations of tests and of testors, the general public has been made aware of the fact that very important decisions are being made on the basis of very imperfect data. Tests have been used to make decisions about hiring and firing athletes and coaches. Tests have been used to make decisions about which athletes to play under what conditions. In recent years we have become sensitized to the fact that the accuracy of these very important decisions can be dramatically affected by educational factors, cultural factors, response style characteristics, personality traits, attitudes and behaviors of the testor, situational factors, and so on. In fact, these extraneous factors can often be more important than the "performance relevant characteristic" we presume to measure.

As a result of our increasing awareness of the limits to the validity or accuracy of predictions based on test results, individuals who have very strong personal feelings about discrimination seriously question the use of tests at all. Unfortunately, although there are real issues that must be addressed to minimize test bias, an overly emotional response is not helpful. Too often our ideal humanistic philosophy becomes confused with practical reality. We relate to the world not as it is, but as we would have it to be. At times this response can force change. On the other hand, extreme emotional responses typically result in discrimination in reverse, or worse. This point will be discussed in more detail in succeeding pages.

It is understandable that within the field of sport psychology there would be some negative reactions to the use of psychological tests. There are several reasons for this negativity, and I would like to discuss them. First, however, I would like to point out that if the current recommendations regarding the administration and use of psychological tests had been followed we would not have the problems that currently exist.

In the past, athletes have often been asked to take psychological tests as a part of research. More often than not, they have not been told why they were being tested, what the results indicate, and how the information gained was to be used. It was only natural that this lack of knowledge would lead to their assumption that the testing process was contributing to any negative decisions that were subsequently made (e.g. a decision to trade an athlete).

Then too, there have been those situations where psychologists have been called in as consultants to management. The coach or general

40

manager may have been interested in using the psychologist's knowledge to help him/her communicate more effectively with an athlete, or to respond to the individual athlete's needs. The psychologist tests the athlete but does not provide the athlete feedback. The test results are used and what conclusions are drawn remain a mystery as far as the athlete is concerned. Too often, whether it is true or not, the athlete feels betrayed. It was this type of situation that led the National Football League Players Association to develop a ruling against the use of psychological tests in the NFL.

Finally, we have seen attempts in the past to mass market tests results that presumably have relevance to understanding and predicting an athlete's performance. Test results have been sent by mail, to coaches and other individuals who have not been qualified to interpret them. The results have been less than satisfactory.

As mentioned, had behavior been more closely guided by the ethical standards established by APA, the problems described above would not have developed. Let me describe some of the explicit ethical principles that apply, and then let me address some of the common misconceptions associated with issues of validity and reliability of psychological tests.

The individual being tested has certain rights, and had these rights been protected, many of the concerns of the National Football League would have been alleviated.

1. The individual being tested has the right to know, why he/she is being tested.
2. The individual being tested has the right to know the conclusions drawn on the basis of test information.
3. The individual tested has the right to know how the information is being used.

There are several other ethical standards that interact with the rights of the person being tested to prevent or minimize the possibility of test bias. Many of these ethical principles are concerned with the communication of test findings.

1. The person tested has a right to know to whom the test results will be commuicated, as well as what will be said.
2. It is the psychologist's responsibility to place the interpretations or conclusions that are reached into a specific situational context. This placement is done to prevent others from over-generalizing and drawing inappropriate conclusions. For example, you don't simply indicate that an athlete is likely to choke; you describe the specific situations within which choking is likely to occur.
3. It is the psychologist's responsibility to communicate results in a clear, concise, unambiguous way. The use of professional jargon and/or terms that do not have clear meanings is inappropriate.
4. Test reports are given only to people who are qualified to interpret them. This principle forbids the provision of testing by mail services to individuals without professional training, or to consumers.

It is the psychologist's responsibility when providing feedback to nonprofessionals to do this in a way (i.e., in person) which will protect against any misinterpretation or misunderstanding.

As you can see, the effective use of test materials requires that the sport psychologist establish a good working relationship, and a clear service contract with the athlete and the organization. In addition, it is critical that the sport psychologist be knowledgeable about testing and that he/she be highly skilled in interpersonal communication. There are some additional ethical principles that become important in determining who can administer and interpret psychological tests.

The American Psychological Association stops short of insisting that only qualified psychologists can administer and interpret psychological tests. What it does insist upon is that the individual has some "formal training," and that he/she is capable of responding to the following ethical standards.

1. The user of tests must be knowledgeable about testing principles. He/she must understand the concept of measurement error, and be able to use that concept in the interpretation of an obtained test score.

2. A test user should know his/her own qualifications. The use of a test requires an understanding of the theory that underlies the test's development. In addition, the user must have the experience and skill to be able to relate the theory to the particular individual and/or situation that he/she must work within. Thus, the sport psychologist must not only have a knowledge of the test and its validity and reliability, but he/she must have a tremendous knowledge of the sport.

3. A test user must know and understand the literature that is relevant to the test.

4. Test users must have enough technical knowledge about test construction, and validation to determine the relevance of the test to decisions that they must make.

5. The choice of a particular test, or battery of tests, should be based on clearly formulated hypotheses and goals. This point is critical for the sport psychologist. Unless some theoretical constructs underlie and guide the behavior of the sport psychologist, it is impossible to validate or invalidate (in any controlled scientific way) any of the tests being used, decisions being made, etc. The use of a theory leads to predictions about performance. These predictions can then be objectively tested. Without a theory, or with poorly defined and elastic theoretical constructs we might be able to explain anything yet accurately predict nothing.

6. A test user should consider more than one variable for assessment and the assessment of any given variable by more than one method. In effect, because there are limits to the validity of any procedure, it is important to validate findings consensually. It would be inappropriate to draw conclusions blindly about an

athlete on the basis of data found in a single test. The sport psychologist should attempt to validate this data consensually by using other measures (e.g. tests, interviews, behavioral observations, etc.).

There are other suggestions and principles. For the most part these principles indicate some of the specific things the psychologist should consider in order to minimize measurement error and test bias. As an example, it is emphasized that the psychologist be aware of the appropriateness of established test norms for the population being tested. It is also emphasized that cultural, attitudinal, social, economic, and interpersonal factors be considered when making test interpetations.

Because of past abuses in the administration and use of psychological tests, the profession has become very concerned with the protection of the individuals we attempt to serve. Emphasis has been placed upon becoming more aware of and sensitive to our own limitations, and the limitations of our techniques. At the same time, there has been a cry for greater objectivity in the assessment process. Unfortunately, I believe that many people are carrying some of these issues too far. There has been a tendency by the general public and by many professionals as well, to misunderstand and misuse testing concepts like objectivity, validity, and reliability. Difficulties occur when the following assumptions (explicit or implicit) guide people's behavior:

1. Objectivity is something to be maximized in psychological assessment; objectivity is "good."
2. Subjectivity in the assessment process should be avoided at all costs; subjectivity is "bad."
3. Bias is something that could and should be entirely eliminated from the assessment process. Unless such a guarantee can be made we should not engage in tesing.
4. We should attempt to develop instruments that are perfectly valid and reliable. It is naively assumed that such a process is possible, and desirable.
5. Whenever possible, specific weights should be assigned to various factors that are considered in a selection process. For example, time in the forty yard dash counts for a specific number of points, leg strength counts for a specific number of points, attitude counts for a specific number of points, etc. Decisions are made on a strict mathematical basis.
6. Behavioral observations and past history are seen as more objective than test data.
7. In the absence of validity data that is specific to the type of athlete and situation you are investigating, testing should not be used.
8. Unless tests provide new information, information that is not found elsewhere, they should not be used.

It is not my intent to argue with the importance of behavioral observations, past history, or with the importance of concepts like validity,

43

reliability, and objectivity. These are very important and relevant to testing, but they must be placed in proper perspective.

Many psychologists tend to confuse or compound the meaning of the word "objective" when they talk about testing. They seem to imply that an objective test is somehow unbiased and valid. In fact, all we can really say about an objective test is that it reduces the number of interpretations the examiner needs to make (either to score the test, or to interpret the results). Instead of being dependent on the subjective opinions of the examiner, who it should be pointed out has the advantage of observing and interacting with the person taking the test, we rely on the perceptions, subjective opinions, and biases of the person(s) who developed the test and the scoring or interpretation system. Obviously the "objective" test is not really objective, not in an absolute sense; and it certainly isn't free of bias. Objective tests do insure that different examiners will come up with similar scores and conclusions. These need not be accurate however. As sport psychologists, we do ourselves and those we would serve, a disservice if we assume that objectivity means anything more than reliable or repeatable.

One of the major concerns over the inappropriate use of tests has developed out of the use of intelligence tests like the Wechsler Adult Intelligence Scale (WAIS) on minority groups for whom norms had not been established. Because the scoring of the WAIS was objective (relatively speaking), many professionals began treating the test as if it were somehow more valid and reliable. A reading of the first few chapters of Matarazzo's definitive text: *Wechsler's Measurement and Appraisal of Adult Intelligence,* indicates that people like Binet and Wechsler were only too aware that intelligence tests were not innately objective, valid, and reliable. The simple assignment of numerical scores and the fact that these could be shown to be normally distributed in the population, did not insure validity. The developers of the tests insisted that trained, clinically sensitive individuals use the tests since the interpretation of scores depended upon the integration of many other factors. These factors included the influence of the testing situation, subject's motivation, level of anxiety, relationships to the examiner, personality, and so on. When the ability of the examiner to consider these other factors subjectively, to use them to modify interpretations was taken away, we began to worship the god of objectivity. It was at this point that we began to see wide scale test abuse, and cultural bias. So long as individuals remain sensitive to the fact that other factors (sources of measurement error) exist which affect test scores, we will be able to make effective, humanitarian use of test information.

The subtle inference that validity and reliability are, or should be, absolute concepts creates as many problems as the idea that certain tests are truly objective and unbiased. To emphasize this point it is worthwhile to review the statistical concepts of validity and reliability.

First, reliability as it is used in testing refers only to the replicability of something. A reliability coefficient can tell us the likelihood that a person when re-tested on a given test will obtain a score that is similar to the first one. An inter-rater reliability coefficient can tell us the likelihood that two different raters of the same test information will reach similar conclusions.

In contrast to reliability, validity refers to the extent to which a test actually measures those concepts, or traits, or needs, or abilities that the instrument was designed to measure. As with reliability, we most often use a correlation coefficient to assess validity.

Both a theoretical and practical discussion of correlations can be found in most statistics' books. For our purposes, it is only important that the sport psychologist have a good conceptual understanding of what a correlation can and cannot do.

A correlation is a number that ranges from 0.0 to ± 1.0. That number expresses the strength of association between two different events or scores. By squaring the correlation coefficient we can estimate how much we can predict about event (test) B if we know how an athlete scored on event (test) A. As an example, A and B represented the scores of an entire physical education class on two different tests with A being a test of speed in the 100 yard dash, and B being a test of ability in the broad-jump. If the correlation between the two sets were + 1.0 we could rank order the student's performance perfectly on either test by knowing their scores on the other one. Thus, if we knew the students' times in the 100 yard dash, we could rank order them in terms of distance they would be able to jump. If the correlation between the two tests were .71 we could only account for about fifty percent of the variability in test scores. This limitation results because we can estimate only the amount of variance being accounted for by squaring the correlation (.71 squared equals about .50). Although our predictive accuracy is considerably reduced, there is still a strong predictive relationship between speed in the 100 yard dash and the distance an individual can jump in the broad jump. If the correlation were 0.0, we could not predict anything. In effect, there is no relationship between the two scores.

There is a point that needs to be emphasized here. The correlation that we obtain provides evidence of a relationship (a predictable one) between two events. It does not, however, allow us to infer a causal relationship.

When we want to establish the validity and/or reliability for a test we attempt to correlate the test with something else (e.g., actual performance). The obvious question that occurs when we do this, is, what constitutes a significant and/or valid correlation? How strong a relationship do we need before assuming that we have evidence of validity and reliability? Does the relationship have to be a perfect 1.0? There are two criteria with which we should be concerned.

First, we need to insist that the correlation be large enough to rule out the possibility that the association we see between two events or tests could be due to chance. Typically we establish some statistical criteria.

For example, we may insist that a correlation as strong as the one that we obtain should occur on the basis of chance, only one time in a hundred (a reasonably conservative criteria). The size of the correlation required will then depend upon the number of subjects we test. With only three subjects we would need a correlation of 1.0 to rule out chance factors. Thus, a correlation this high, with only three subjects, would occur less than one time in a hundred on the basis of chance alone. With a thousand subjects the size or the correlation required for statistical significance drops dramatically. In fact, we only need a correlation of .08 to rule out chance.

A second factor to be considered involves determining when you have a useful correlation (when you have established already that a statistically significant relationship exists). Determination of the usefulness of a correlation involves a more subjective judgment. A correlation of 1.0 or .71 accounts for a good deal of the variability in scores and provides considerable predictive utility. It should be obvious, however, that a correlation of .08 does not meet the requirement of usefulness or utility, or does it? Lets say that there is a correlation of .08 between the amount of money put in a slot machine in a Las Vegas casino, and the profit that the house shows. Is that a significant correlation? You bet it is, no pun intended. If the correlation were much higher, favoring the house more, people would have less of a feeling of "beating the machine." With less reinforcement to them, they might stop playing altogether. As it is, the relatively small correlation keeps them playing, and keeps the house winning. The one half of one percent that the correlation accounts for is highly useful and significant.

In contrast, there are times when a correlation of .95 (accounting for 90 percent of the variance) is not large enough. For example, if that correlation were between a set of test scores, and whether or not people paid their utility bill (e.g. by testing we could predict with 90 percent accuracy who would pay their utility bill), most of us would still not want the test to be used. To apply the test blindly would result in a percentage of the population who would pay their bill, being denied service.

It should be obvious that how large a correlation is required by the sport psychologist will depend upon several factors, including the philosophical, moral, and ethical values of the psychologist, of the organization the psychologist is working for, and of society in general. We are not likely to get a consensus on what should be required and it is here that our own emotions get involved. An athlete being tested to determine his/her selection in the draft would demand a much higher correlation, than management would. Often management is interested in the long run and they can afford a few mistakes if the odds are in their favor over time. The individual is concerned about the immediate decision. Somehow, the sport psychologist must satisfy both people. When this is not possible, he/she must at a minimum, make the criteria used to make his/her decisions public. If the coach or athlete assumes that

46

we should have perfect reliability, the assumption makes the sport psychologist's job almost impossible. It is possible, however, and, in fact, necessary, to justify decisions based on less than perfect criteria. At the same time we can improve the quality of services that we offer, and still respond to athletes in a humanistic way.

It is not uncommon to hear people complaining about the fact that we do not have perfect correlations. These individuals don't seem to understand that with a large number of subjects we should never expect a perfect correlation, no matter what we are attempting to correlate, be it psychological or physiological. We could look at the behavior of computers, humans, plants, etc., and we will still fall short of perfect predictability. It is a fact that most of the physiological measures which we attempt to correlate with performance or behavior, correlate no more highly than psychological measures. Even when we are dealing with "absolutes" and very concrete physical realities, correlations are less than perfect. The instruments that we use to measure (e.g., computers) break down, and in the universe we have not found any "universal truths." The fact that man and his world are not perfect, I find comforting.

Too often it is inferred that the stronger a validity coefficient, the more objective and unbiased a procedure. Unfortunately, this inference need not be true; it could simply be a measurement or sampling artifact — an artifact that leads to erroneous conclusions. A perfect correlation would build in bias and cover up individual differences. First, it would indicate that people don't change, thus we couldn't learn from our mistakes or from experience. More importantly, it would seem to say that factors like racial differences, cultural differences, intellectual differences, moral differences, physical differences, etc. do not affect the way we answer items on a test, or the way we relate to people and situations. In fact, athletes, coaches, and sport psychologists need to be able to modify their approach and behavior in response to different people and conditions. This flexibility, though demanded of the individual, is inconsistent with the concept of perfect validity and reliability.

Once again, I do not want to imply that validity and reliability are not important. We must recognize, however, that it is critical for decision makers to be able to move along a continuum which allows for both subjectivity and objectivity in the decision making process. This freedom is especially necessary when the sport psychologist is involved in selection and screening and must make decisions about people who differ dramatically from each other on the basis of factors such as race and educational background.

The need for flexibility can be seen as we consider the consequences of developing objective, standardized weighting scores (e.g., how much tests, past history, interviews, current behavior, etc. count) to make important selection, screening, and training decisions. Such a formula destroys the flexibility that allows us to make individual decisions. It may be that in some cases a single factor outweighs all others, or that a factor

47

which has not been included in the equation at all should over-ride the entire process. An athlete may have sustained an injury, or he/she may be a drug addict. To collect certain commonly accepted bits of information mechanically, and make decisions based on these would be inappropriate and inhumane. Such a procedure would rule out positive exceptions as well, and we would not make special allowances for educational disadvantages, cultural deprivation, character change, and personal growth.

At some level, and this varies from situation to situation, selection, screening, and training decisions should be a combination of empirical, objective, and subjective factors. It can help a great deal to know (through statistical validation) that nine times out of ten a person with a certain score will have problem A. That is a valuable bit of information that the sport psychologist should have. At the same time, it is critical that the sport psychologist be sensitive to measurement error and to individual differences. In this way, you can determine if the person in front of you is an exception to the statistical rule.

There is another misconception that I would like to deal with before attempting to draw some conclusions regarding where we go from here. It is often assumed that the information gained from a test is redundant, providing little more than might be obtained through observation, history, and/or interview. This assumption is probably accurate and in and of itself, is not bad. When it is also assumed that for this reason testing is a waste of time, problems develop.

It can be pointed out that there are very few validity studies that relate directly to athletes. From those studies that do exist, there are still dramatic differences in racial, educational, cultural, social, and intellectual factors that have been detailed if we wish to compare groups of athletes for whom validity data has been established to those with whom we are involved. This means that to make use of existing testing procedures (and any that are likely to be developed in the future), the sport psychologist must be able to make inferences from populations that differ from their own. As a sport psychologist, I must anticipate how the cultural and educational differences between the athletes I am working with, and those the test was developed on, will affect test scores. By basing my inferences on some sound theoretical base, I can begin to determine their validity, and the utility of a given test for my particular problem. In addition, the search for redundancy in material collected becomes very important.

To counter the disturbing fact that we do not have perfectly valid measures, the American Psychological Association established standards for the users of psychological tests. A major focus of those standards is to sensitize psychologists to sources of measurement error and to emphasize the need for consensual validation of any findings. It is redundancy, seeing the same thing under different conditions or in different measurement and observation techniques that provides consen-

48

sual validation and gives us confidence in our interpretations and conclusions.

Almost any sport psychologist can talk to you about the athlete who looked and sounded terrific in an interview, but couldn't perform on the field. Somehow the interview did not tap into his/her problem areas. The reverse is also true. There are athletes who perform at super levels, they have an instinct for the game, yet they present themselves very poorly in interviews and on tests. Redundancy is not something that can be taken for granted. Its presence is comforting; its absence should raise important questions.

There are other reasons for testing that need not be dealt with in detail. Testing should lead to a shortening of the time required to reach a decision or to develop a training program. Testing should introduce some objectivity into the situation. Testing can provide a framework for providing feedback. Finally, through consensual validation, testing can increase the confidence of the sport psychologist.

Testing is not without problems, so where do we go from here? There is a place for testing in sport psychology. It is imperative, however, that testing be done in an appropriate way, with consideration of the ethical standards established by the American Psychological Association. Appropriate use of tests implies the following:

1. That the constructs being measured have some construct validity. That is, it can be shown conceptually that the constructs have relevance to the decision that is being made.
2. That some concurrent and predictive validity has been established for the test's constructs. Ideally this will be on a population that is highly similar to the group the sport psychologist is working with. Minimally, it will be established with other populations.
3. That the results have been consensually validated: consensual validation is important no matter what the source of the data. Material gained through the interview, history, etc. should also be consensually validated.
4. Sources of measurement error must be minimized as much as possible and/or accounted for in test interpretations.
5. Conclusions drawn on the basis of test information must be operational, concrete, clear, concise, and placed within a specific situational context.

Under the above set of conditions, sport psychologists will be making the best possible decision they can. That is not to say that errors will not still occur. What it does say is that the margin for error has been reduced as much as possible.

A problem that adds to the confusion when we decide whether or not to use psychological tests involves the unreasonable expectancies that we often have for the assessment process. We become upset when we demonstrate empirically the limited validity of tests. Too often there is a tendency to reject tests, feeling if they aren't perfect they shouldn't be used. Somehow we don't stop to think that decisions will be made anyway. If the truth were known, decisions based on interview, history, etc. are no less subject to bias, and are no more valid. We don't have correlation coefficients, however, that remind us of the limitations of other decision-making techniques.

It is amazing to me that people will talk about giving up testing, but they will not talk about giving up a screening process altogether. The reason testing is picked on is because it is more objective, because we can see how useful and reliable it is, and because people have misunderstood concepts like validity and reliability. We can see that tests aren't perfect and we want to throw them out. We recognize a need for something, so we hang on to the interview. We have confidence in our own judgment, and when the basis for the judgment is not articulated, who is to say we are wrong?

At the present time we have laws that require users of tests to demonstrate the relevance of those things being measured, to actual job performance. Testing requires that we make a public statement about our decision criteria. More than that, it forces us to demonstrate the validity of the data we obtain. These facts result in a protection for athletes when tests are used as a part of a decision making process.

Testing should help us to identify performance relevant strengths and weaknesses. It should help us articulate the specific conditions under which an athlete is likely to have problems as well as those conditions that are likely to maximize success. Testing, when properly conducted, can help us maintain an appropriate balance between the delusion that we can be totally objective on the one hand, and the notion that we should be totally subjective on the other.

Both the public and the profession have a right to know the state of our "art." We don't have to be ashamed because we don't have all the answers. The biggest danger comes from trying to convince ourselves and others that we do. If we can be honest with ourselves we will be able to make decisions on the basis of the best information we have. No one can ask for more, and as a profession we shouldn't ask for less.

6

USES OF PSYCHOLOGICAL TESTS

Tests are potentially very powerful tools that can be of immense social, economic, and personal value. When applied correctly, they reduce discrimination, they increase productivity, and cost efficiency, and they reduce personal trauma and injury. Tests can be used to facilitate both personal and interpersonal functioning. At the same time tests can be, and have been abused.

A lack of knowledge on the part of an examiner with respect to the validity of a test, and its relevance to a particular use, or with a particular population, has resulted in test abuse and damage to those taking the tests. When instruments are inappropriately used in the course of selection and screening the result is discrimination against individuals. The discrimination is due to measurement error and can result in bias against cultural, minority, or ethnic groups. Too often this bias is not detected because people making decisions on the basis of test data have hidden behind the test scores. They have suspended their own judgment and placed too much confidence in the tests.

WHAT KNOWLEDGE IS REQUIRED OF TEST USERS?

Although formal education is open to interpretation, at least as recommended by the American Psychological Association, the principles and knowledge that test users should have are fairly explicit and include:

1. An understanding of testing principles and the concept of measurement error.
2. The ability and knowledge to evaluate the validity of a test for the purposes (decisions) for which it is to be employed.
3. Self-awareness — a sensitivity to one's own qualifications and limitations.

What is required in order to have a grasp of testing principles and the concept of measurement error? First, a clear understanding of certain statistical concepts is necessary. Users must understand correlational

51

statistics, measures of central tendency (mean, median, mode), variance, standard deviation, and standard error. Users must know about the different types of validity and reliability, and should be able to evaluate a test's validity and reliability for the decisions and problems they hope to use it with.

Users must recognize that test results are not absolute or irrefutable, and that there are many sources of measurement error. For example, they must be aware of the potential influence of situational factors as well as inter and intrapersonal characteristics that may alter the way test scores are interpreted. They must be aware that cultural, social, educational and racial factors can all invalidate results. They must be aware of as many of the sources of measurement error as possible, and do everything they can to reduce or minimize them.

The factor that goes furthest in reducing measurement error with a particular test is the knowledge that allows an examiner to select valid instruments and validate results consensually. To be able to do both of these, it is necessary to be able to define the specific abilities and/or behaviors that are job related. Once this definition has been articulated, tests can be examined to see how valid and reliable they are. Without such operationalization, however, the validity of an instrument can neither be evaluated, nor established.

Often tests are abused because we are unaware of our own limitations. We may lack the job-related experience to identify actual performance-relevant abilities. This naivete is especially dangerous if we know little about the actual physical demands of the sport with which we intend to work. We rely on what we "intuit" or "feel" is important. Often these feelings are ill-defined, global constructs that have no validity or reliability. "I want to feel good about the person." "I want to control anxiety." "I want to see that they can relate." "I want them to have drive, be hungry, have heart."

Test users may assume that instruments provide this type of general non-specific information. Often the interpretations offered are based first on the person's job title, and then on the test score(s). We assume we know what the coach means by hungry. As an example, we may assume that a measure of "need to achieve" is the same thing as a measure of "hunger." Such an assumption is likely to be inaccurate. It is our professional and ethical responsibility to know what it is we are measuring. Somehow we must help the coach or person making the referral to define his/her questions operationally. It is unfortunate that decisions are often made on invalid, idiosyncratic interpretations of referral questions, and test data. To make matters even worse, we very rarely follow up to see if the decisions we make have any basis in fact. Because of the lack of follow through, we perpetuate our mistakes.

Human beings are unique animals, and can convince themselves of almost anything. When that cognitive ability is combined with a need for structure and security, strange things happen. Statisticians become married to a particular statistical procedure, scientists become attached to particular pieces of equipment, coaches get stuck with certain training methods and myths, and sport psychologists adopt certain tests and techniques. Unless we are very careful, we can become overly dependent, true believers in our tests. When this happens we become dangerous because we lose the ability to ask critical questions; we fit people to tests rather than tests to people and jobs. We "become the tools of our tools."

In the next few pages I am going to write about issues involved in the interpretation and communication of test results. Your understanding of these issues will have important implications for your ability to function ethically.

SUBJECT'S RESPONSE STYLES:

How valid and reliable are the test scores that are obtained in most testing situations? How much are a person's responses influenced by the setting, the test itself, the examiner, or his/her mood at the time? Is the test really reflecting some consistent personality characteristics, or only immediate feelings and situational factors?

Certainly situational factors can influence the subject's responses. How important are the influences? Can they lead to response styles that completely invalidate the test? Is the situation one in which the subject will try to look good, or is he/she trying to look bad? Is the athlete taking the test angry and uncooperative? In answering test questions does he/she tend to exaggerate, or minimize his/her weaknesses? Is he/she guarded, or defensive?

Because response styles are important sources of measurement error, the questions listed above are very important. What can be done to detect and minimize the influence of response styles? When are response styles most likely to develop?

WHEN RESPONSE STYLES ARE OF MOST CONCERN:

It is possible to divide the use of tests into two broad areas. The first involves selection and screening of individuals for jobs, training programs, and other career choices. In these situations test information is used to make yes or no decisions about the suitability of an individual for a job or position. Typically test input is used only once (during the decision making; it is not used to design training), and the emphasis is on discriminating *between* athletes. The goal is to identify that athlete or group of athletes best suited to a particular sport. The type of questions being asked include: "Is this person a team leader?" "Should the person be accepted as a member of the team?" "Will the athlete continue to be a coaching problem?"

When tests are being used for selection and screening purposes, response styles become critical. Since comparisons are made between subjects, subject A may be handicapped (not selected) if he has a conservative response style. He may be every bit as good as athlete B, or even better. Because B is less inhibited about admitting abilities and responding to test items, or because B has an inflated self-image, subject A loses out. The influence and power of response styles can be seen in many testing situations in sport, and these styles do influence conclusions that are drawn.

It is fairly common practice to do some kind of testing when athletes return to training camp to begin another season, or when Olympic athletes enter the Olympic training camp for the first time. Many times conclusions are drawn regarding the predictive validity of tests without taking into account the operation of some fairly general response style characteristics.

Let's take the administration of psychological tests to an NBA basketball team at the start of the season. Players on the team can be divided into two groups: 1) a group composed mainly of veterans who know that they have a spot on the team, and who know that they can play ball in the NBA; and, 2) a group composed mainly of rookies who want to prove themselves, but who aren't very secure.

At the start of the season the sport psychologist is introduced. It is announced that this person will be working with the players to help them live up to their potential, by playing their best. It is emphasized that this person is not there to select and screen, but to make sure everyone has a fair chance. The players are then asked to take some tests which the psychologist and coach feel will be helpful to them in understanding and working with the athletes. The explanation could have been different and it really wouldn't have mattered much. The coach and psychologist might have said that they were going to use the results for research to see how the test might be used in the future. In this case it would be emphasized that results would not influence whether or not the player made the team. The players could, however, by cooperating, help future athletes and perhaps learn something about themselves in the process.

In either case, response style characteristics would be operative. The rookies, and those players who are less secure about their making the team would want to look good. They would be trying to convince themselves as much as the coach and/or psychologist. Inside their own heads they would be reminded of things like "if you don't believe in yourself, who can you believe in." "You can't be a winner unless you think like one."

In contrast to the rookies, the veterans and those players who are confident about making the team approach the test with more openness. They are not as afraid or mistrusting. As a result, they are much less likely to exaggerate their strengths and minimize their weaknesses. They are typically open, hoping to learn something that will make them even better. The rookies on the other hand need the test to confirm their promise.

54

It is easy to see the operation of these response styles by testing athletes across time. At an Olympic training camp, those athletes who already know that they have a spot on the team tied down, behave like the veterans. The other athletes are still trying to believe in themselves. As a result, there are often differences at this stage which indicate that those people who are ultimately selected for the team score lower on measures of self-esteem, and control.

After a few days or weeks in the training camp, however, all of the athletes become only too aware of their relative position. If the sport psychologists do their testing now, they get the results that they might have hoped for. Those individuals who are performing poorly, relative to others, are beginning to get depressed and this process will be reflected in their test scores. On the other hand, with the selection of the team approaching and the Olympics not far off, those people who are out in front will be experiencing a high — they will have some elevations in their test scores. It is at this point that we will begin to see test scores actually reflecting the performance abilities of the athletes. Initial response style differences will have been minimized.

A second general issue raised by response styles is that taking tests in selection and screening situations is often much more stressful than taking them for one's own information (assuming you believe the input of the coach or psychologist). Think of the difference between taking the college entrance exam as opposed to taking a magazine personality test that you self-interpret. The stress in the selection and screening situation can result in an exaggeration of a subject's normal response style. Thus, if I am always a little humble and quiet, under stress I might as well be a corpse.

I just contrasted the situation in which a test is used for selection and screening with the second general area in which tests are used. I am writing here about using tests for counseling, and as a part of ongoing training programs. Here the athlete is not worried about the test resulting in him/her being eliminated from something he/she wants to do. More likely, the test is to help. Although response styles can still be operative in these situations, they become less harmful.

With a subject involved in counseling there is far greater opportunity to evaluate, and validate consensually any interpretations made on the basis of test data. Since the client continues to have contact with the examiner or with the organization, any misinterpretations can be picked up and corrected. In addition, *in counseling situations, using test information to make between subject comparisons becomes far less important.*

In selection and screening the test interpreter must be concerned with the absolute elevation or amplitude of scores. This concern results from the need to compare scores across a group of athletes. When this type of comparison is made, response styles can dramatically affect results. In counseling, the interpreter is concerned more with the client than with comparing the client to other athletes. With the focus on the person, it is the *relative position* of the individual's scores that is emphasized rather than the absolute elevation. As an example, we are more interested in the individual's ability to develop a broad focus of attention, relative to his/her ability to narrow, than we are in comparing his/her ability to broaden attention with that of other athletes.

In counseling, I make *within subject comparisons*. This comparison is done to discover the athlete's relative strengths and weaknesses. The fact that an athlete is more extroverted than introverted becomes useful for talking about preferences the athlete has, independent of its predictive utility when comparing the athlete to others. When making within subject comparisons the sport psychologist can be much less concerned with the influence of response styles. The athlete may still have a conservative style, or he/she may exaggerate, yet such a general style is not likely to affect the relative position of the individual's scores. The highest scores continue to be the highest (even after removal of response style influences) and the lowest continue to be the lowest.

As was implied, there are also other factors that can minimize response styles.

These include increasing the trust and comfort of the athlete, reducing anxiety, and providing them with a response set (e.g. "Answer these questions as they relate to your performances as a tennis player. Attempt to compare yourself and your abilities to those of players you compete against.).

HOW CAN RESPONSE STYLE CHARACTERISTICS BE DETERMINED?

Just as a single attentional or interpersonal characteristic, a response style must be inferred on the basis of a pattern of test scores. The inferences made by the sport psychologist interpreting the test come from the scores themselves, from observations of the subject, from an understanding of the dynamics or demand characteristics of the testing situation, and from a knowledge of what the average responses (for this particular group of athletes, athletes matched on the basis of sport, skill level, sex, education, socio-economic status, intelligence, etc.) are.

A great amount of analytical and deductive ability, that is, a broad-internal focus of attention, is required to use tests effectively. To a good sport psychologist a particular response style can provide very useful information. Faking good on a test may invalidate a particular score (I may not be sure about the subject's actual willingness to express negative feelings.), but it tells a great deal about the subject, his/her needs and behavior. The psychologist may learn that the athlete will be manipulative and cannot be trusted in certain situations. Often, this type of information is more relevant to the selection and screening process than the original question about skill or ability to function under pressure.

In the next few pages I have presented some information regarding the detection of three fairly common response styles: faking good, faking bad, and being overly defensive or guarded.

FAKING GOOD

A prime factor that increases the likelihood that someone will "fake good" is the situation or conditions under which the test is administered. This process can be seen in the following example.

Jerry is a college baseball player who was drafted in the third round by a team that is a pennant contender. The coach of the team is a very confident, authoritarian individual. The coach maintains a personal distance between himself and his players. He is a very private person and the athletes know what he is thinking only when he decides to tell them. He is not outwardly open to input about management of the team or players. When he gets a thought or idea in mind he tries it, whether or not other people like it. Jerry quickly learns that the coach's word is law and that if you don't listen, you are gone.

Suddenly at a team meeting the coach tells the players that he has hired a "team shrink" to do some testing. He feels that the information he gets from the "shrink" will be helpful to the team. In response to a few groans from some of the veterans, he says; "Knock off the crap, I want you to do what the Doc asks. This may be a key to our winning the world series."

Under these circumstances, it is not surprising that Jerry would want to be seen in the best possible light. He would not know how the test information would be used. What he does know is that the coach wants to win at any cost. Jerry's need to make the team, his own insecurity, and his lack of trust in the coach would dramatically increase the likelihood that he would try to look good on the test.

Hopefully, the sport psychologist can be in a position to minimize the conditions that lead to the predicament in which Jerry finds himself. When this is impossible, however, it is important to be able to detect if insecurity and mistrust have been operative.

Think about the way individuals might react to a test if they wanted to look good. Remember that they would not be sure what the test is measuring — they would have to guess at that. The athlete's guess would probably be based on what they personally feel is relevant to their successful performance. They are not likely to be thinking in terms of all of the personality variables that a sport psychologist might measure.

If Jerry wants to look good taking the test, he will try to anticipate how each item will be interpreted. Without knowing all of the subscales or personality variables measured, and without knowing the theory that underlies the test, he can't anticipate how items will be compared with each other (e.g., Should I respond more strongly to item one than to item two?). Instead, he will adopt a general response strategy that will be equally applied to each item. "Is this something I should be able to do?" "Is this something the coach would value?" The consequences of this type of response set on a multi-item, multi-scale test include:

1. An exaggeration (relative to normative data) of positive abilities, and a minimizing of weaknesses. Scores are often in the top and/or bottom three percent of the normative population.

2. The sport psychologist will detect illogical relationships, assuming several personality traits have been measured. For example, individuals will indicate they are in control of interpersonal situations, assuming leadership, and at the same time deny expressing any negative feelings (if they feel this is how the coach would have them respond). In fact, it would be impossible to be a leader without expressing some negative feelings.

3. Bright capable people trying to look good will simply exaggerate their strengths and weaknesses. Thus, the illogical relationships are not likely to occur. Perceptive athletes respect the intelligence of people administering tests and recognize that they will detect obvious faking. In this instance, the test remains valid for the individual so long as within subject comparisons are being made. Thus, the sport psychologist may be able to use the test results for counseling purposes since the relative position of scores remains unaltered. It would be a mistake, however, to make a selection and screening decision based on the test information alone. Amplitude of scores would be affected and to get a true estimate of the athletes ability relative to others, the sport psychologist would have to seek other sources of information.

4. Subjects who lack respect for the examiner, or who lack self-awareness, will show extreme differences. The fact that the test does not reflect their actual ability becomes immediately apparent in an interview and/or in looking at their athletic history.

The sport psychologists should attempt to detect response style influences by using their own analytical ability to detect logical inconsistencies. When a concern over the possible influence of a response style develops, an attempt should be made in an interview to resolve the inconsistency. It should be emphasized that inconsistent reports don't always mean that individuals are consciously manipulating the examiner. They may really believe what they are saying about themselves. When this is the case, their lack of self-awareness is what is causing most of their problems. When they see themselves dramatically differently from the way others see them, it is an indication that they are unable to listen, to hear what others are saying, or to see what the environment is telling them. This problem is extremely frustrating to the coach and is one the sport psychologist deals with frequently.

Places that can be examined in order to resolve what appear to be inconsistencies in patterns of test scores include asking and attempting to answer the following questions: Does the person (being interviewed) try to control the examiner and his/her perceptions? Is that person controlling of others in his or her interactions? (This information is gained through taking a history, and through behavioral observations.) Does that person indicate that he or she is victimized by others or by the environment, thus in effect placing responsibility for past failure on others.

FAKING BAD

Another response style that can be of concern is the tendency to portray things as being worse than they really are. There are times when a sport psychologist looks at psychological test data and marvels at the fact that the athlete was able to walk into the office. If the individual were really as disturbed as was indicated on the test, he or she would not even be able to compete.

When this self-dramatization occurs, it is important to determine the overall effect on the validity of the test. Before discussing this, however, it should be pointed out that the same basic strategy is used by the athlete to fake bad that is used to fake good. The only difference is that responses tend to be in the opposite direction. The unsophisticated athlete simply adopts the general strategy to answer questions in a way which he or she believes will indicate that he/she is performing poorly, is emotionally upset, lacks confidence, etc. Usually, such a general response style is quickly picked up because of the extreme scores, and because of the logical inconsistencies. Fortunately, such a negative response style is relatively infrequent in sports (it is much more frequent in clinical settings), but it does occur and when it does it is usually a cry for help. An example of this situation where pressure is great, will help clarify the main issue I am discussing.

Sherry is a thirteen-year-old figure skater. She had competed at a national level and had won a title as a twelve-year-old. She had been good enough to place in some open competitions. Sherry's father and mother had invested everything, time, emotion, and money, in their daughter's skating. Her accomplishments were tremendously important to them, and they never let her forget how much they were sacrificing to allow her to pursue "her" goal.

As she moved into the open competition, Sherry found that she was no longer the top skater. Both she and her parents began to increase the pressure. Sherry was still skating well from an outside observer's standpoint. From her own perspective, however, she was going down hill. She was judging her skating by how she finished in contests. As a result, Sherry began to question her ability, her dedication, her emotional stability, etc. She began to look for excuses for her problems. In some ways she hoped that she could find anything other than less talent or ability on which to blame her failure. She wanted someone or something else to be responsible. She needed support and help but didn't know how to ask for it. When she finally took the psychologist's tests, she answered almost everything ina negative direction. Her own perceptions were innacurate in terms of how well she actually performed, but they were accurate descriptions of how she was feeling about herself.

In looking at Sherry's test information the sport psychologist could see that it was invalid for making comparisons between Sherry and other skaters; it was not invalid, however, when it came to telling the psychologist how Sherry was feeling about herself. Talks with Sherry then had to be undertaken to determine where the problems really existed. The psychologist had to help her put her own abilities, mental and physical, into perspective before even the relative positions of test scores would provide meaningful information.

Sherry's case is not typical; there are, however, those athletes who develop a response style that exaggerates weaknesses, thus invalidating between subject comparisons, but who still provide very useful within subject information. That is, the relative positions of their various test scores can be interpreted and used for training purposes.

In contrast to a Muhammad Ali type, John was an athlete who tended to minimize his own strengths. He would talk glowingly of the abilities of others and could be very helpful to and supportive of them. When it came to describing himself, however, he believed in being modest.

John's modesty did not mean he was not competitive; in fact, just the opposite was true. As a result, John was especially attentive to his own areas of weakness and was continually attempting to discover ways to impove. It was this combination of characteristics that caused John to respond to testing in a more open, self-disclosing way than most athletes. He really did want to use the test information to help himself and he was not afraid to talk about his weaknesses. At the same time, his modesty and his tendency to compare himself against perfection, rather than againt other athletes, acted to minimize strengths.

John's response style is much more common in athletics than is Sherry's. Instead of saying indiscriminately that nothing is good and everything is bad, John does make discriminations. It is these discriminations that preserve the integrity of the relative positions of test scores to each other. It would be a mistake to compare John's scores to the norms, or to other athletes since he would look worse than he really is. The information from the test could be used, however, to identify weaker areas and to design training programs.

Typically, the difference between John's and Sherry's responses are obvious in several ways.

1. Sherry's scores are much more extreme than John's. The differences between positive and negative scores are much greater.

2. In an interview it becomes obvious that Sherry is in emotional pain. John, on the other hand, comes across as confident and in control. He is interested in what you find and eager to take control of the information and use it. Sherry feels helpless.

3. Although both persons' test scores may appear to have inconsistencies, there are important differences. Sherry's seem inconsistent in that the whole test appears to inaccurately reflect her ability and past success. Everything is bad and nothing is good.

John's test is inconsistent in other ways. He may indicate that he feels fairly good about himself (has a reasonable level of self-esteem, although not as high as might be expected given his obvious success), and at the same time indicate that he is not in control of attentional processes. Past experience tells the sport psychologist that most people who are out of control attentionally, are also out of control in interpersonal situations, and have low levels of self-esteem. For John, this is not the case. What is reflected here is John's modest but accurate perception of his level of control and confidence. In terms of the attentional scores he has been overly concerned with identifying problems since he wants to use the information to improve performance. The attentional scores will still be useful (the relative positions of a broad focus compared to a narrow focus will remain intact), although the absolute elevations will be inaccurate.

CONSERVATIVE RESPONSE STYLE

The final response style that I want to deal with develops when an athlete's level of trust in the person doing the testing, in the coach, or in the situation itself, is relatively low. In this case the individual is not sure how the test information is going to be used. Very often, these athletes are very bright and aware of the fact that extreme responses in either direction will be picked up. As a result, they don't want to look too good, or too bad.

When this mistrust is present the athletes avoid extreme responses (minimizing both strengths and weaknesses) in two ways: 1) If given a choice of several responses to a question (e.g., indicate the frequency with which each item describes your behavior: rarely, sometimes, frequently, or all the time), they tend to stick to the middle of the response continuum. 2) They will look across items to see how frequently similar things are being asked. In doing this, they will attempt to avoid looking one-sided. As a result, they will not answer in the same direction as frequently as they might if trust levels were higher.

The end result of this conservative response style is that scores become constricted around the mean for the test. Once again, this style can have an invalidating effect on selection and screening decisions. The interview, and/or past history is used to attempt to validate consensually the scores and/or to get a better estimate of the true between subject comparisons. At the same time, the relative position of the scores to each other remains an accurate reflection of within subject strengths and weaknesses. The conservative response style does not invalidate the test for purposes of training, counseling, or team building.

7

FOCUSING THE ASSESSMENT PROCESS

Assessment, as a process, can be thought about as having both formal and informal components. The formal part of the assessment process involves the administration and interpretation of standardized psychological tests. The informal part consists of the questions and special directions that the sport psycholgist decides to take that have not been standardized. Usually, the informal aspects of assessment develop spontaneously, in response to the collection of on-going information. In a very real way, counseling, coaching, teaching, etc., all have large informal assessment components. Throughout the training process the coach is assessing the progress of the athlete and making decisions about future directions.

Assessment could be a never-ending process because there is so much to be learned about the people with whom we work. When we realize that we need to understand something about the athlete, the sport situation, the sport itself, and the athlete's interpersonal involvements with others, we can become so overwhelmed with information that we confuse ourselves and those we would help. It is only too easy to create more problems than we solve by digging up a lot of irrelevant, stressful, and/or confusing information. When individuals come to a sport psychologist with a problem, they come because they don't know what is wrong and because they have been unable to solve that problem on their own. Typically they are anxious (just as anyone would be in going to a physician for a check-up) and they are looking for structure, direction, and answers. It is not difficult, especially in the field of psychology, to find new problems for individuals who come to see you. I have seen sport psychologists respond to an athlete's request for assistance in improving performance in a particular sport, by unearthing marital problems, or interpersonal problems with the coach or a boyfriend that are only tangentially related to the athlete's request for help. When individuals are already anxious, it does not take much to convince them that they have more problems than they realized.

Perhaps one of the most difficult tasks the sport psychologist faces involves the development of an assessment and treatment focus and, at the same time, the avoidance of assisting in the growth of new problems. This potential to do harm is one of the reasons that the selection of a theoretical perspective is so important for the sport psychologist. It is the theory that helps determine the assessment focus. The sport psychologist who operates on the basis of a psychodynamic theory is intent upon the discovery of underlying unconscious conflicts that are interfering with the athlete's functioning. This particular focus requires an extensive assessment of past history, especially as it relates to critical people (e.g., mother and father) and developmental stages. This process is long and involved. It is often stressful and painful and from the athlete's perspective, proceeds without a relevant focus. For most individuals such intensive therapy would be distracting and irrelevant and would create more problems than it solved.

All of this discussion is not to say that in the event the theoretical approach taken by the sport psychologist fails to solve the problem, it would be inappropriate to adopt a dynamically oriented approach. In fact, as suggested earlier, failure to solve the athlete's problems with more behaviorally oriented approaches may be the best indicator of underlying dynamic conflicts. The place to start, however, is from a theoretical perspective that is directly task-relevant, since it is performance with which the athlete is concerned.

The theoretical approach taken here involves an examination of the interrelationships among increasing arousal, accompanying physical and attentional changes, and performance. It is assumed that an assessment of the physical and attentional demands of the sport situation and an assessment of the physical and attentional abilities of the athlete, in combination with an assessment of the conditions that raise and lower the athlete's level of arousal, will provide the information needed to develop a training program. This theoretical approach restricts the assessment process in many ways. First, underlying dynamics are not considered, at least not initially. Past history is relevant only insofar as it provides information about conditions which might be used in the present to increase or decrease arousal, or if it illustrates that the athlete does or does not have the physical and mental abilities required by the sport.

OPERATIONALLY DEFINING THE REFERRAL QUESTION

Theory provides a framework for the assessment process and for the treatment process. This framework is sharpened even more by the specific reason for referral. The first step that the sport psychologist takes as he/she begins to work with an athlete, team, or coach, is to define operationally his/her own task. Why has the sport psychologist been called in?

Although it would seem that the question, "Why do you want me to work with you?" should be easy to answer (operationalize), often it is not. There are several reasons for this. First, it is not at all unusual for the coach or athlete to not have any idea regarding what the sport psychologist can do. They view him or her as somewhat mystical or magical. As a result, referral questions are often quite vague. "Improve her performance." "Get his head screwed on right." "Give him better mental control." "Help her concentrate." "Stop his choking." "Increase her motivation." "Hypnotize her and make her win." "Tell me what's wrong."

Often, sport psychologists take these general questions or statements and attempt to respond to them at face value. For example, in response to the request to "stop his choking," the psychologist trained the athlete to learn to use progressive relaxation procedures. Although the technique was an interesting one and the athlete found it enjoyable, it had little effect on his performance. The psychologist never did find out what the coach meant by "choking," or the conditions under which it supposedly occurred.

Without a knowledge of the mental and physical demands of a sport, and without a sensitivity to the abilities of an athlete and to the factors that interfere with performing at her own optimal level, it is impossible to respond ethically to the request to "hypnotize her and make her win." There is nothing to keep the hypnotist from inducing a trance and then making suggestions to increase the athletes' confidence in themselves and to assist them in believing they can be winners. Such suggestions, however, if not based on fact and ability, will either not be responded to, or may lead the athletes to overestimate their own ability and create a very dangerous situation.

A second reason that referral questions are often vague, is that neither coach nor athlete may have the language available to describe what they want the psychologist to do. They have not been sensitized to the psychological variables that sport psychologists see as important and they haven't learned the sport psychologist's language. As a result they may not be sensitive to what is happening to them. Like the sport psychologist, without a theory, they don't know where to look.

The first task of sport psychologists then, is to help the people making the referral operationally define their terms. This is done by asking a series of questions that are directly related to the sport psychologist's theoretical orientation. Taking as an example the request to "Tell me what wrong."

1 . *Circumscribe the problem.* This is accomplished by saying things such as: I need to know what you mean by "wrong." What situations are you talking about? What is it that the athlete is not doing well?

2. *Describe the mistake that is being made.* This is accomplished by asking questions from the theoretical framework, but asking them in ways coaches or athletes can respond to: What is it about their physical performance that is incorrect? Are muscles too tense? Are they too slow in responding? Are they concentrating in the way they should? Do they seem to be distracted? Are they not paying attention because they are inside their own head? Are they distracted by things going on around them, or by their own ideas?

3. *Describe what they should be doing.* This too is accomplished by asking questions that can be related directly to the theoretical framework. If they are reacting too slowly, what should they do to improve that? What could they attend to that would speed up their ability to respond?

Through such a series of questions the sport psychologist should reach a point where the referral question provides a very clear indication of what should be assessed, and what changes should occur for performance to improve. The original request to "Tell me what wrong," might be changed to the following. I am concerned about John's ability to maintain concentration throughout a four minute skating program. He seems to start out fine but after the first minute or so begins to make minor errors. He seems to lose his sharpness, getting sloppy, as if his mind is a thousand miles away and his body is just going through the motions. I want him to be very aware of where he is on the ice at all times. I want him to be sensitive to the audience and to his body. I want him to feel his performance on the ice. He needs more tension.

Given a more complete referral question or request, assessment can be conducted in a way which leads directly to the development of intervention strategies. Now the sport psychologist has direction for the assessment interview, for the selection of tests, and for the interpretation of findings. From this point the psychologist would proceed as follows: 1) a history would be taken; 2) tests would be administered; 3) behavior would be observed; 4) a report would be written and recommendations made; 5) feedback would be offered and the recommendations clarified and/or modified; 6) the program would be implemented; and 7) a follow-up would be conducted.

The goal behind taking a history, making behavioral observations, and testing would be to answer the following questions:

1. Does the capacity for the desired behavior exist? Is the person mature enough, does he/she have the mental and physical skills, etc.?

2. If the behavior has not already been demonstrated in the past, we don't know that it exists, the question becomes can it be learned? Do tests, behavioral observations, and/or history indicate that the person has all of the parts required but just hasn't put them together? If so, what needs to be strengthened, how can they be put together?

3. What is the role of arousal? What negatively and positively influences performance? Here the sport psychologist examines the effects of three areas on physical arousal and concentration. First, what intrapersonal characteristics (personality traits) are affecting performance? Next, what interpersonal characteristics are important? Finally, what situational factors (e.g., composition of the crowd, level of competition, etc.) are affecting performance? This investigation provides information about what specifically needs to be altered to effect the desired changes.

4. History of the problem is important from a prognostic point of view and because it too can provide information about techniques or procedures that might be helpful: Was the onset of the problem acute or chronic? How intense is the disturbance, fear, etc., when it occurs? How frequent is the problem? How long does the problem last once it starts? What attempts have been made in the past to deal with the problem? Which of those attempts have been successful? When attempts failed, did the athlete know why?

In the next few pages I am going to write about the structure of the actual interview and assessment process, that is, how testing can be introduced in order to minimize problems due to response style characteristics. I will also be concerned with describing how feedback can be given to a client in a way which will minimize defensiveness and maximize the likelihood that he or she will be responsive to the recommendations that are made. Following this description some case history information will be presented so you can see the assessment process in action.

8

INTRODUCING TESTING, AND THE FEEDBACK PROCESS

What do you tell an athlete or a team, prior to testing, about the assessment process, and about how test information will be used? Ethically, you are required to tell people why they are being tested, what conclusions are drawn on the basis of the test information, and how the test information will be used. Exactly how this information is provided will change from person to person and from situation-to-situation. What you should be aware of, is the fact, that whatever is said will affect the results of the test and must be considered when making test interpretations.

When an athlete or coach refers himself/herself for psychological assistance and/or testing, his/her attitude towards the process will be much different, than it would have been if he or she had been told to "take some tests." Expect some resistance and defensiveness on the part of athletes who suddenly find themselves being tested without knowing why, or without having their feelings and needs considered.

The actual introduction of testing to individuals who want to be tested is relatively straight forward. They work together with the psychologist to define a problem that they both feel needs to be worked on, or they simply request that the psychologist help them explore some of their own strengths and weaknesses in relation to their involvement with sport. In either case, the reason for testing is clear. All the sport psychologist has to do is to convince them that the particular tests being used have some direct relevance. If that case can be made and the athletes accept it, then they are asked to respond to the tests in as open a way as they can.

To the extent this type of trust and cooperation is established it needs to be taken into account when interpreting the test results. This is especially true if the sport psychologist expects to make some between-athlete comparisons. Because the trust level of the athlete is likely to be higher than the trust level for the group on whom the test was validated, his/her scores on traits that might be seen as negative (e.g., being overloaded attentionally) are likely to be higher.

The situation in which a sport psychologist is called in to test a team, is often much more difficult to deal with. First, it may not be clear how the idea of testing was introduced to the athletes. It may have come as a total surprise; it may seem like a punishment because it follows on the heels of some problem the coach has been unable to work out; or they may have decided as a group that they wanted to be tested. Whatever the reason, the sport psychologist needs to know it in order to anticipate how athletes will approach testing.

Each of the athletes in the group is likely to have a different attitude towards testing. As much as possible, the sport psychologist wants to be aware of the different attitudes, and to do what he/she can to control them by maximizing trust and cooperation. There are some specific steps that can and should be taken to increase cooperation.

ESTABLISH A CONTRACT

When the sport psychologist is called in by management or the coach to provide a service it is critical that a very clear contract be developed. When the services to be provided include testing, the person requesting the service needs to know that the psychologist has a moral and ethical responsibility to inform the athletes with respect to the reason for testing, the conclusions that are drawn, and the recommendations that are made. Responding to this ethical principle prevents the psychologist from accepting a referral or job that is not operationally defined.

In addition, the person requesting testing should understand that it is the responsibility of the psychologist to insure the security of the test data, making sure that it isn't misused. This means that the interpretations that are offered must be validated consensually and that they must be placed within a specific situational context. It would be inappropriate for the psychologist to collect information and then simply turn it over to a coach to use as he/she sees fit, or for the psychologist to go back to old test data (at a later date) with new questions, making the assumption that these questions can be validly answered.

When a coach or manager knows that the sport psychologist's ethics indicate that questions or concerns about the athlete should be shared with the athlete, it forces a sharpening of the coach's questions or concerns. The sport psychologist can often be very helpful in that sharpening process, helping the coach rephrase things in a way which will satisfy the needs of the coach, yet not threaten his/her relationship to the athlete. As an example, a coach might be interested in identifying those athletes that he/she is going to have a problem with because they won't listen. The request may come as "I want to know who the troublemakers are." By talking with the sport psychologist the coach may come to realize that the athletes in and of themselves don't create the problem; the problem occurs as a function of the interaction with the coach. A better way of phrasing the question then might be to say that testing is to help the coach identify those situations where his/her personality characteristics may come into conflict with those of the athletes.

68

In this way the psychologist has helped the coach to see that there are two sides to the problem. In addition, rather than saying "so and so is a troublemaker," the particular circumstances under which trouble is likely to develop will be articulated. The psychologist avoids making gross generalizations that would, in fact, be untrue. No one is always a troublemaker.

Whenever possible, the sport psychologist wants to control the introduction of tests to athletes. Without some knowledge of how the material was introduced, and without an opportunity to establish some trust, it is impossible to anticipate the mental set with which the athlete approaches testing. Accurate interpretations and conclusions require some knowledge of the athletes' mental set. Under ideal situations there would be the opportunity for an individual meeting with each member of a team prior to testing. Unfortunately, this is often not the case. When testing must be conducted in a group, and assuming testing is for purposes of self-improvement, I recommend the following:

1. Take some time to let the athletes find out a little bit about you. You want to attempt to establish a relationship with them. This can be done if you speak their sport specific language, empathize with their task, and with their situation. Elevate them, and make yourself human. They are the experts in what they do. Together you might be able to take some of the things you know about (psychology) and combine it with their help and expertise (in their sport) to make them even more effective than they are already.
2. Share with them the reasons you were called in. What is it that the coach wants you to do? How do you hope to be able to use the test information? How will you provide them with feedback? What information will you provide the coach, and how will you clear that with them first? It may be that you don't need to say anything to the coach. My belief is that it is best if you can get the coach to agree that you will only share what the athlete wants you to. You will then work with the athletes to determine not only what will be shared, but how it will be stated.
3. Talk to them about the test, about what it measures, and describe why that is important to them. To cooperate, the athletes need to believe that the test questions have some relevance.
4. Ask them to be as open and honest as they can. Emphasize that confidentiality will be maintained (you will share things only with their permission).
5. Give them the opportunity to ask any questions that they might have.
6. Let them know that you will meet with them individually to work together to determine how accurate the test results are. In effect, you need this opportunity to consensually validate and/or invalidate findings, and to determine how best to use the information.

7. When possible provide the athlete with a mental set to use when answering the questions. For example, "to the best of your ability I would like you to respond to the questions in terms of how they describe your behavior in athletic situations. If you can compare yourself and your responses to those of other athletes competing at your level. Are you more or less capable than they are." This instructional set will help minimize the response style differences that affect test scores and reduce their predictive utility.

The preceding assumed that testing was for purposes of counseling, developing performance improvement programs, team building, and related tasks. What about selection and screening?

Remember, to provide input that is used in selection and screening, some between-athlete comparisons must be made. This necessity means that response style influences and other sources of measurement error become much more important. Because predictability is limited and because decisions that are made can have profound effects on an individual's life, the sport psychologist should seriously question the legitimacy of engaging in any selection and/or screening process.

First, it should be emphasized that the decision regarding whether or not an athlete is selected, placed in a certain position, or used at a particular point in time is the coach's! The actual decision regarding selection or screening is not the sport psychologist's. Management or the coach may work with the psychologist to determine the type of input that they feel the psychologist is qualified to provide. This task means articulating very clearly those psychological factors that are directly relevant to the athlete's success or failure. The psychologist then attempts to identify those factors, to measure them and to define the conditions under which success is more likely to be probable, or within which failure is more likely to occur. It should be clear that the psychologist is not talking in absolute terms. Instead, he or she is attempting to estimate relative probabilities. Those probabilities should be based on previous research that has established their validity.

The psychologist then tells the person who is responsible for making the decision what he or she sees as well as why and how he/she feels what is seen is important. It is then up to the decision-maker to decide how to use that information along with all of the other input. In this process, it is absolutely imperative that the psychologist let the decision-maker know the limitations of the information that has been provided!

When attempting to use tests to provide input to a selection and screening process, it is still important to have some control over how the tests are introduced:

1. Meet with the athletes and let them know what your function is. "My job is to test you and to then provide feedback to the coach regarding your coachability, intelligence, leadership, ability to play under pressure, etc."

2. "I would like you to take some tests which I believe will help me

answer these questions. You do not have to take the tests but you should know that the coach must make a decision with or without this information. If you refuse all I can say to the coach is that you wouldn't take the tests." If I know how the coach will respond to this lack of cooperation, I will tell them."

3. "After testing I will look at the information that I have gained and then go over it with you. I will need your help to check out the accuracy of it, and I want you to know what I am going to say to the coach."

4. At this point I would empathize with the anxiety and anger that some of the athletes might be feeling. I would try to minimize those feelings as much as possible and I would answer any questions that they had.

FEEDBACK OF TEST RESULTS

Once a sport psychologist has managed to administer and interpret psychological tests, his or her job is just beginning. Now the problem becomes one of finding a way to provide feedback so that it can be maximally useful to the athlete.

Tests and the information provided generate fear in people for several reasons: 1) Anxiety is increased anytime a person loses control, doesn't know what the test will show, or how the test results will be interpreted; 2) In the past psychological tests have been associated with problems and with the identification of pathology — it is frightening to the athletes to think that tests might expose such pathology in them; 3) Tests have been abused in ways which have led to the labeling of some, and to discrimination against others; 4) There is a tendency to attribute special powers to tests. An athlete's spouse can tell him/her that he/she is angry and hostile and the athlete can soften what is said by seeing the anger and hostility as his/her spouse's problem as well. When a test indicates that an athlete is angry and hostile it becomes a different matter. Somehow, it is more difficult to defend against the test.

Coaches and athletes have a curious mixture of feelings. They are often drawn to experience things that are exciting and threatening. Tests are like that. There is something exciting about taking a look inside ourselves so we take tests, but occasionally we have difficulty coping with the feedback. The athlete closes his/her eyes and ears, not listening — hearing only part of the feedback. Some individuals will openly attempt to deny the weaknesses shown, others embrace them too readily beating themselves with their negative points. The trick, and the sport psychologist's responsibility, is to avoid these over-reactions.

The first step in effective communication is to be sensitive to the anxiety generated by the feedback process, and to know the effects this anxiety will have on the ability of athletes to hear what you have to say. It is important to know that increasing pressure will cause them to attend to the feedback in an intermittent way. They will start to listen, hear the

71

first part, and then drift off defending against what they think you are saying. Often they misinterpret because they only hear the first part of the feedback. They fail to hear the qualifier, or to hear you place the comment in perspective. In addition, the anxiety narrows attention, reducing their ability to integrate a large amount of information. They become overloaded and confused more easily than they would under less stressful circumstances.

Sensitivity to the effects of anxiety on attention can allow you to compensate for the athletes if you:

1. Provide written as well as verbal feedback. This dual approach allows the client to re-read material after the initial anxiety has passed.

2. Provide the opportunity a few hours or a few days later for the athletes to ask questions. Again, this provides time for the individuals to calm down. He also has time to observe for himself, and can begin to place the issues you have pointed out into perspective.

3. *Most importantly,* keep your feedback limited to a few things that are directly related to the referral question. Don't try and tell them everything and *don't create new problems.* Stick to the two or three most relevant points.

4. Be very careful to avoid psychological jargon. Be concrete and operationalize any terms you use by providing the athletes with behavioral examples (e.g., of distractability due to an excessively broad-external focus of attention. "You may have noticed at times that your ability to concentrate during a football game gets interfered with because you become aware of the crowd, cheerleaders, etc."). Try to make sure the examples provided come from the athlete's own background, or at least from his/her sport.

It is worth your while to take the time to try and place yourself in the shoes of some of the people to whom you will be providing feedback. Imagine how they must feel receiving feedback from you, and then imagine how those feelings will affect what you have to say. For example, imagine that you have looked at an athlete's test scores and it indicates the following:

1. The individual is extremely confident and has a very high level of self-esteem. At the same time, he has difficulty listening to others' opinions, especially if those are different from, or critical of, his own.

2. The type of attentional error that is most likely to occur with this athlete, is to react too quickly to a situation. He is not analytical enough, especially under pressure.

3. He has a great deal of anger, and this can result in his losing his cool, and being ejected from a game. He has a tendency to get down on others, blaming them in an open angry way for problems that he, or the team may be experiencing.

Somehow you want to communicate the above information to an athlete who you can already tell, that under the best of circumstances, will have difficulty listening. Now let me fill out the description of the feedback situation to make it even more difficult. It is this part of the process that is designed to increase your empathy for the athlete, and to help you defuse some of the defensiveness.

You walk into a room with an athlete who is a world class competitor in the discus. He is six feet five inches, 280 pounds and has been competing in the discus for fifteen years. He has won national and international competitions and he feels that a high arousal level and controlled anger are important aspects of his sport.

As the athlete walks into the room he looks at you and sees a person who is five feet eleven inches, 170 pounds, and out of shape. He sees you as a person who has exercised the mind, not the body. On the one hand he is slightly anxious about what you are thinking, on the other, since he didn't ask to be tested in the first place (selection to a national team resulted in his being asked to take the tests), he is thinking the following: "What can this shrimpy egghead possibly know about track, and about the discus. He has probably never thrown a discus in his life. Who does he think he is trying to tell athletes how to do their job? It pisses me off that I am spending my time in here when I could be out on the field practicing. How the hell do the coaches expect us to win if they keep putting us through this kind of crap."

As you think about it, you realize that from his perspective, the athlete is absolutely right. To communicate with the athlete, you are going to have to employ some of the following rules:

1. Provide for support and a balance between confrontation with what you perceive to be a weakness, and support for the athlete's strengths.
2. Don't "root out evil," control it. Even negative characteristics have their good points.
3. Reduce the athlete's inability to listen by depersonalizing feedback.
4. Avoid psychological jargon and emotionally ladened terms.
5. Be concrete and specific about feedback. Provide examples that are behaviorally relevant and show your knowledge of his/her sport.
6. Be content at times to "cast pearls." Don't feel that the athlete's immediate agreement with your interpretations is necessary.
7. Limit the amount of information you try to communicate.
8. Provide the opportunity for follow-up.

BALANCE THE POSITIVE AND NEGATIVE ASPECTS OF FEEDBACK

Effective teaching, counseling, or test feedback involves the ability to walk a fine line: A line between confronting the athlete with a weakness and providing support for his/her strengths. It is this balance that a coach uses to provide the motivation for an athlete to try harder, and it is the same balance the sport psychologist must develop to get the person to hear test feedback. If the confrontation part of the message is too strong the athlete will either block everything out and fight back, not hearing, or (when self-esteem is low) he/she will withdraw, cover-up and run. Without some confrontation the individual may fail to see important areas on which to work. A distinct advantage that the sport psychologist has over the clinical psychologist, is that athletes usually want to improve and work. Thus, they will listen and respond if they believe that you have something to say, and if you can say it in a way that doesn't draw out instinctive defenses. As a sport psychologist, and as a coach, you learn to provide support even when someone fails. "Yes you failed, but at least you had the courage to try and I know that you will have the strength to pick yourself up again and try harder."

There are many ways to provide a balance between support and confrontation when giving feedback:

1. *Point out both the positive and negative aspects of a score.* In the case of the discus thrower it can be pointed out that the positive aspect of his anger is that he has used it well in competition. He has been able to take the anger and use it to generate arousal, helping him throw the discus farther. Unfortunately, there are occasions when he let the anger get the best of him and he lost control. His feelings may have been legitimate, after all, the official did make a big mistake, but his angry outburst resulted in a loss of control. He got kicked out of the track meet and didn't get the opportunity to show what he was really capable of. This example also relates to the next point.

2. *Recognize and balance emotional and behavioral realities.* The emotional reaction against structure, rules, limitations of freedom and creativity may indeed be legitimate. The necessity to impose constraints over your own reactions to those limitations in order to win in the long run, and protect some of those freedoms, may be a reality. We may not like it, but if we want to be a winner in a game that is controlled by others as most sports are, we may have to live with it.

3. *Place negative feedback into perspective by showing that it is not an indictment.* This can be done by empathizing. "I would have felt the same way you did." "I remember swimming in a race and getting disqualified because the official felt I didn't touch with both hands on the breast stroke. I had, and I was so mad I wanted to kill him. The coach pulled me away because he knew that if I was kicked out entirely, we would lose the relay and the meet. That was the pits."

   This can also be accomplished by letting the athlete know that even those people he places on pedestals have similar weaknesses. "I was talking with __the other day and he told me . . ."

4. *Emphasize that you are concerned with control, not with a label or personality characteristic.* Each of us has come to attach fairly strong negative emotional feelings to certain words or personality traits. Chances are, in the feedback process even with the best of intentions, the sports psychologist will use some of these emotionally charged terms. Some athletes are upset by being seen as hostile, aggressive, etc. Others would enjoy those adjectives and are more upset by being seen as dependent, seductive, distractable, etc. The point for the sport psychologist to make is that any characteristic that dominates a persons style, or that becomes less flexible as pressure increases can under certain circumstances (and these must be specified for the athlete) become a problem. By the same token, there are inevitably times when the characteristic that has caused the athlete difficulty in the past, is the most appropriate way to respond. The trick is for the athlete to control the personality trait, rather than the other way around.

REDUCE THE INABILITY TO LISTEN BY DEPERSONALIZING FEEDBACK

One of the threatening things about test results and the feedback of experts is the authority attributed to both. Clients feel vulnerable and exposed and take the feedback personally. Often, they have a difficult time depersonalizing it, seeing it objectively and putting it in a broader perspective. They need the help of the sport psychologist to do that.

1. *Explain to the athlete about the reliability of test scores and what that means.* Often, a client confronted with what he/she believes to be a negative characteristic will ask. "But couldn't that just have been my feeling at the moment?" My own response to such a question is : "Yes, but let me explain something to you. When we give tests and then readminister them later the test-retest reliability is very high. This means that in *most* instances the test is reflecting more than a momentary feeling. Obviously that is not always the case. If I were you and I were uncomfortable with a score I wouldn't take it as some absolute truth, it could be wrong and you may be one of the exceptions to the general rule. To be sure, however, I would keep my eyes open because if it turned out to be accurate I might want to do something about it."

2. Explain that you (the person administering and interpreting the test) and the test are not attributing things to people; you are simply providing them with feedback about how they have described themselves.

3. Point out the difference between how you interpret a behavior and how they interpret it. *Depersonalize it by talking about it in the context of an interpersonal situation.* For example, an athlete who

75

scored high on a measure of obsessiveness might describe his/her own behavior as "careful, cautious, thoughtful." The sport psychologist can describe the athlete in the same way, and then point out that people the athlete sees as "impulsive, thoughtless, etc., would describe the athlete as "ruminative, obsessive, unable to make decisions." The point made to the athlete is that behavior is only seen as good or bad in the context of interpersonal and performance situations. An individual, need not feel indicted; instead it can be pointed out that his/her style interacts with others to create problems to which they both contribute.

RESPECT THE STRENGTH, INTELLIGENCE, AND INTEGRITY OF THE ATHLETE

Respect is shown in a large number of ways. A good sport psychologist shows it by not hiding behind technical jargon on the one hand, nor talking down to the athlete, on the other. It is shown by recognizing that the athlete could be right, and may have a much better feeling for what is gong on than the sport psychologist does. In the case of the discus thrower some of the defensiveness and anger is defused if the sport psychologist starts out by owning up to the fact that he/she doesn't know nearly as much about throwing the discus, about track, or about what it feels like to compete at an international level as the athlete. "I have a great deal to learn from you. I hope that we can combine some of the things we know, and both benefit." Finally, and most importantly, a good sport psychologist shows respect by listening and receiving feedback as well as by giving it.

1. Before making recommendations, and while making them, consult the athlete. "What do you think?" "How do you see the problem or the situation I've described?" "What have you tried?" Tie your own feedback into the information that comes back from the athlete and be supportive: "Good point I noticed the same thing when . . . " "I hadn't thought about that but it would explain . . ." "I think your solution was the right one; that's what I would recommend.' "Why do you think what you tried before failed, and what could be done to change that?"

2. *Work with the athlete to consensually validate the test.* Often, I will begin a feedback session by emphasizing that tests don't provide absolute truths. They do give me ideas about possible strengths and weaknesses, potential problem areas, but I really need to "check those out with you." "Let me tell you what I see and then you tell me where you agree and/or disagree."

3. This process allows me to create a feedback loop, clarifying and correcting any misperceptions I have, and any misunderstandings the athlete may have. I can place the things I have to say into very concrete performance relevant situations with the athlete's help.

3. You can show respect by presenting information and then asking

rhetorical questions. "I noticed . . .; do you suppose that has any relevance to throwing the discus in the upcoming meet?"

OPERATIONALIZE, BE CONCRETE

This point is a very important point that is much easier to accomplish if you have already operationally defined the referral question. To say to an athlete that he/she is "choking" or that he/she "has a temper problem" is not helpful. Those are labels that generate strong emotional responses. In addition, they are non-specific because they do not provide direction.

Remember athletes, coaches and sport psychologists all need direction and structure when they are under pressure. They need a focus, and answers. Vague, ambiguous terms only increase anxiety, giving them more to worry about and creating additional poblems.

BE CONTENT TO "CAST PEARLS"

This point is especially true when you are trying to provide feedback to individuals who cannot or will not listen to the interpretation. It is either too threatening, or they need to be in control, and/or to hear it on their own terms.

As resistance to an interpretation mounts, I'll begin to back off. However, especially with a person who is fighting for control, or who has authority conflicts, I'll throw out a parting challenge: "You may be right. It is possible that my interpretation of your situation is wrong. In fact, I hope that is the case, that would make both of us very happy. If I am not wrong though, it would be wise for you to keep your eyes open."

LIMIT THE AMOUNT OF INFORMATION YOU FEEDBACK

This point is important for two distinct reasons. First, those of us who get into sport psychology often tend to be very analytically oriented. We are dominated by a broad-internal focus of attention. Our ability helps us analyze; we are able to pull things together from many different areas. It is this ability that makes us good at assessment and at program development. However, not everyone is an analytical as we are and in our enthusiam it is only too easy to overload others.

A second factor makes the tendency to overload others even worse. As anxiety goes up for the athlete, the ability to deal with a lot of information decreases. Don't try to do too much! Organize the feedback and the report around a couple of very specific points.

9

CASE HISTORIES

The test reports presented here were written to be used as a basis for feedback to the individual athletes being tested. Some modifications have been made in the section of the report that deals with the reason for referral. In addition, minor modifications have been made to conceal the identities of the athletes.

There are a wide variety of tests in fairly common use with athletes. Included in the list would be the California Psychological Inventory, State-Trait Anxiety Inventory, Minnesota Multiphasic Personality Inventory, Edwards Personal Preference Test, Cattel 16 PF, Eysenck Personality Inventory, Somatic Perception Questionnaire, Depression Adjective Checklist, Profile of Mood States, AMI, and many others. The choice of a particular test would depend upon the theoretical orientation of the sport psychologist, and upon the referral question.

In the present material, the Test of Attentional and Interpersonal Style (TAIS) was used. This particular instrument was selected because it was designed to measure those attentional and interpersonal characteristics associated with the theory presented in chapter 4. In addition, the test has some obvious relevance to the development of individualized training programs. Items on the test are relatively non-threatening and test scores lend themselves to direct feedback. This operational quality is in marked contrast to tests like the Minnesota Multiphasic Personality Inventory. Table 1 provides a description of the seventeen attentional and interpersonal factors measured by the TAIS.

TABLE 1
Test of Attentional and Interpersonal (TAIS) Scales

Scale	Abbreviation	Description
Broad external attentional focus	BET	High scores on this scale are obtained by individuals who describe themselves as being able to effectively integrate many external stimuli at one time.
Overloaded by external stimuli	OET	The higher the score, the more athletes make mistakes because they become confused and overloaded with external stimuli.
Broad internal attentional focus	BIT	High scores indicate that athletes see themselves as able to effectively integrate ideas and information from several different areas. They are analytical.

Table 1 — Continued
Test of Attentional and Interpersonal (TAIS) Scales

Scale	Abbreviation	Description
Overloaded by internal Stimuli	OET	The higher the score, the more mistakes athletes make because they confuse themselves by thinking about too many things at once.
Narrow attentional focus	NAR	The higher the score, the more effective athletes see themselves with respect to being able to narrow their attention when they need to.
Reduced attentional focus	RED	A high score on this scale indicates the athletes make mistakes because they narrow attention too much.
Information processing	INFP	High scores tend to process a great deal of stimulus information. They have high energy levels. Their perceptual-cognitive worlds are busy.
Behavior control	BCON	A high score indicates that athletes tend to be somewhat impulsive. In addition, they engage in behavior that could be considered antisocial, though not necessarily harmful.
Control scale	CON	A high score indicates the athlete is in control of most situations. Leaders score high. Extremely high scores are associated with authority conflicts.
Self-esteem	SES	The higher the score, the more highly the athletes think of themselves and the more highly they feel others would see them.
Physical orientation	P/O	High scorers enjoy, and participate in, competitive athletics.
Obsessive	OBS	High scores are associated with rumination and worry. The scale indicates speed of decision making. Low scorers make decisions very quickly.
Extroversion	EXT	A high score indicates the athlete is warm, outgoing and needs to be with other people.
Introversion	INT	High scorers enjoy being alone, need personal space and privacy.
Intellectual expression	IEX	High scorers express their thoughts and ideas to other people.
Negative affect expression	NAE	A high score indicates that the athletes express their anger and negative feelings to others.
Positive affect expression	PAE	A high score indicates that the individuals express their feelings of affection to others in both physical and verbal ways.

The first case presented involves a competitor in international skeet. This particular case is presented to illustrate the information that can be gained from a careful analysis of performance errors. By looking at the

79

errors in relationship to situational factors it is possible to see the role of arousal in the disturbance of attention and performance. This information then provides the key for the development of performance improvement programs. As will be seen, error information provides confirmation for the test data and vice-versa. Unfortunately, limitations in the athlete's resources, practice time, and other demands resulted in his discontinuing competitive shooting shortly after the report was written.

The second case involves a professional tennis player. This case is presented because follow-up information is available and because it illustrates how specific recommendations can flow directly from test material.

The third case involves a world class distance runner. Testing material in this instance illustrates the importance of making interpretations based on within subject data. Response style characteristics and situational factors played a very large role in determining the absolute elevation of scores on the test. In spite of this fact, the relative position of test scores to each other continues to provide useful information. The sport psychologist who makes a blind interpretation of this data, however, attempting to compare this athlete to others, would draw incorrect conclusions.

Prior to presentation of the actual case material it would be useful to provide a brief description of the Test of Attentional and Interpersonal Style (TAIS) profile sheet. Figures 4, 5, and 6 present the test results for the three cases being discussed.

A subject's responses to the 144 TAIS items are scored and then his/her total raw score on each of the seventeen subscales is computed. These raw scores are then plotted on the profile sheets presented in Figures 4, 5, and 6. In these three cases, the athletes' attentional and interpersonal abilities are being compared with those of a typical college population (athlete and nonathlete). Thus, if we were interested in making between subject comparisons the following rules would apply:

Percentage of the population scoring *below* the corresponding T and Z scores.

T	Z	Percentile
20	-3.0	1%
30	-2.0	3%
40	-1.0	16%
50	0.0	50%
60	1.0	84%
70	2.0	97%
80	3.0	99%

To illustrate the use of the information provided above, consider the following example: The skeet shooter in case number one had a raw score of seventeen on the TAIS scale measuring the tendency to become overloaded and distracted by external stimuli (OET). This score is equivalent to a Z score of 0.0 and a T score of 50. If we were to com-

80

pare this athlete's tendency to become overloaded and distracted to the normative population's, we would say that he is about average, since 50 percent of the college population scores higher than he does on this scale and 50 percent scores lower.

Name: Mike
Age: 32
Date: 8-12-76

SOURCE AND REASON FOR REFERRAL:

Mike shoots international skeet and is interested in developing a program to help him get better control over psychological (mental) processes during competition. During practice he feels that he has better control over both his emotions and his ability to concentrate. He tends to let his temper get the better of him during competition and does not shoot to his capability.

To evaluate his performance and to design a program, Mike was asked to: 1) Take the Test of Attentional and Interpersonal Style; 2) To provide a description of the mental check list he uses to prepare for each shot; and 3) to provide a list of misses for his last 1000 rounds in competition and his last 1000 practice rounds.

ERROR ANALYSIS

Consistent with his self-description, Mike's performance in practice exceeded that during competition. His average per 100 rounds fired was 96.9 in competition and 97.9 in practice. An analysis of the error pattern was interesting in that it illustrated the mental breakdown (particularly during competition) which is responsible for Mike's poorer rounds. First, there is a tendency for Mike to become upset at a particular station. When this occurs he begins to defeat himself before he gets started by worrying about how to correct. For example, he missed High 2 earlier, so he begins reminding himself of things to do and things not to do the next time he gets to that station. The tension this causes in muscles and the mental distraction that results increases the likelihood of another error. This can be seen both in competition and in practice by the string of errors at High 2 in competition, High 4 in practice, Low 5 in competition, and Low 6 in both competition and practice. Mike was able to correct problems at High 2 and Low 5, but has not yet corrected Low 6.

	H_1	L_1	H_2	L_2	H_3	L_3	H_4	L_4	H_5	L_5	H_6	L_6	H_7	L_7	H_8	L_8
Competition	—	—	10	—	2	—	1	2	2	6	—	5	—	—	—	3
Practice	—	—	3	1	1	—	4	2	—	2	—	6	—	—	—	2
Total	—	—	13	1	3	—	5	4	2	8	—	11	—	—	—	5

The second pattern in errors occurs predominantely during competition and not during practice. For Mike, any round in which more than 1 target is missed can be considered a poor round. There were five practice rounds with more than one miss and eight competitive rounds. These are listed below.

Practice	Competitive
$H_2 L_6$	$H_2 L_6$
$H_4 L_6$	$*L_5 L_5$
$H_4 L_6$	$H_2 L_8$

Practice	Competition
$L_2 L_5$	$*L_5 L_5$
$*L_4 L_4$	$*H_2 H_3 L_6$
	$*H_2 L_5 L_6$
	$*H_5 L_5 L_8$
	$*H_2 H_3 H_4 L_4$

The asterix indicates rounds in which Mike had successive misses on targets. As may be seen, he is much more likely to miss shots that come close together during competition (6 out of 8) than during practice (1 out of 5). This, asterix suggests that on a given station, and with a given target, a miss is upsetting enough (during competition) that he cannot clear it from his mind. As with the example presented earlier, he reacts to the miss by giving himself a set of do's and don'ts which continue to upset his muscle tension level and results in a narrow-internal focus of attention. The result is that instead of having one miss and then recovering, he becomes too mechanical and analytical. With the narrowed attention it is easy to get overloaded by his own thoughts and instructions.

PROCEDURES

Mike's rehearsal procedures and check list sounded reasonable except for the tendency to watch the flight path of the target when the shooter in front of him was shooting. In Mike's case, looking for "deviations" can, particularly under pressure and competitive conditions, result in his becoming too analytical and mechanical, overloading himself with instructions and increasing muscle tension.

TEST RESULTS

Mike's test data is important insofar as it provides information about the source of his difficulty and suggests ways for improving. In looking at both his attentional and interpersonal characteristics, he differs from many other individuals in several important ways. These differences mean that some of the remedial procedures others use will not be suitable for Mike.

Attentionally, Mike indicates that he has a tendency to become overloaded by trying to think about too many things at one time. It is precisely this tendency to get overloaded which accounts for his failure to concentrate adequately during a round. The likelihood of becoming overloaded will increase as tension increases, and as Mike tries (during

Name	Mike		Age	32		Date	8-12-76
Norm Group		Psychology Students				Sex	Male

Skeet Shooter

Profile chart — raw scores grouped by domain (circled values = Mike's profile, shown as (n)).

T	Attentional (BET OET BIT OIT NAR RED)	Control (INFP BCON CON)	Interpersonal (SES P/O OBS EXT INT IEX NAE PAE)	T
4•0	36 41 43	68 37 65	43 50 28 35	90
	24 35 32 27 40 42	66 36 64	42 23 48 39 27	
	34 31 26 39 41	65 35 62	41 47 38 32 34	
	23 33 25 38 40	64 34 61	40 22 46 37 26 33	
	32 30 37 39	63 33 60	30 45 36 31 25 32	
3•0	22 31 29 24 36 38	61 59	38 21 44 35 30 24	80
	21 30 28 23 35	60 32 58	37 43 34 29 23 31	
	29 34 37	59 31 57	35 20 42 28 22 30	
	20 28 27 22 33 36	58 30 56	28 41 33 29	
	27 26 21 35	56 29 54	33 27 40 32 27 21 28	
2•0	19 26 32 34	55 28 53	32 26 19 38 31 26 20	70
	25 25 20 31 33	54 52	31 25 37 30 25 19 27	
	18 24 24 19 30 32	53 27 51	30 24 18 36 29 24 18 26	
	18 29 31	51 26 50	29 23 35 28 25	
	17 23 23 28 30	50 25 49	28 22 17 34 23 17	
1•0	22 22 17 27 29	49 24 47	27 (21) 33 27 22 16 24	60
	16 21 21 16 26	48 23 46	26 (20) (16) 32 26 21 15 23	
	20 25 28	46 22 (45)	25 19 31 25 20 14 (22)	
	15 19 20 15 24 (27)	45 (44)	24 18 1(5) 29 24 13 21	
	18 19 14 23 26	44 21 43	22 17 28 23 19	
0•0	14 (17) (22) 25	43 20 42	(21) 16 14 27 22 18 (11) 20	50
	(16) 18 13 21 24	41 19 40	(20) 15 26 21 17 (11) 19	
	13 (15) 17 (12) 20 23	40 (18) 39	19 (25) 16 (10) 18	
	14 (11) 19 22	39 (17) 38	18 14 13 (24) 20 9 17	
	12 13 16 18 21	3(8) 37	17 13 (23) 19 1(5)	
1•0	12 1(5) 10 17 20	(37) 16 36	16 12 12 (22) 18 1(4) 8 16	40
	11 11 (14) 9	35 15 35	15 11 20 (17) (13) 7 15	
	10 16 19	34 14 33	14 10 11 19 16 12 6 14	
	1(0) 9 13 8 15 18	33 13 32	13 9 18 15 5	
	(9) 8 12 7 14 17	32 12 31	12 8 10 17 11 4 13	
2•0	6 13 16	30 30	11 7 16 14 10 12	30
	8 7 11 12 15	29 11 29	10 6 9 15 13 9 3 11	
	6 10 5 11 14	28 10 28	8 5 14 12 8 2 10	
	7 5 4 10 13	27 9 27	7 4 8 13 11 1	
	4 9 9 12	25 8 25	6 3 12 10 7 9	
3•0	6 3 8 3 8 11	24 7 24	5 2 10 9 6 8	20
	2 7 2 7	23 23	4 1 7 9 5 7	
	5 1 6 10	22 6 22	3 8 8 4	
	6 1 5 9	20 5 21	2 6 7 7 6	
	4 5 4 8	19 4 20	1 6 6 3 5	
4•0	3 7	18 3 19	5 5 5 2 4	10

	BET	OET	BIT	OIT	NAR	RED	INFP	BCON	CON	SES	P/O	OBS	EXT	INT	IEX	NAE	PAE
	9	17	14	12	22	27	36	18	45	20	21	16	23	17	13	11	22

Figure 4

competition) to analyze his mistakes, gather additional information about the fields, targets, flight paths, etc. His anxiety, and one or two misses, will cause him to attempt to over prepare for the next shot and this will destroy his natural rhythm and ability.

Interpersonally, Mike is a quiet individual, who tends to be less extroverted and less outwardly expressive both intellectually and emotionally than many of his fellow shooters. He has a slightly lower level of self-esteem and is the type of person who (because of his own quiet, attentive posture) ends up listening to a lot of stories and advice from others. Their inputs can overload him even more.

Under competitive conditions the tendency to listen to advice can become a larger problem because pressure will cause many others to talk and to give advice to anyone who will listen. They reduce their own anxiety by focusing attention on others. Mike can be a good target for the attention because he is quiet, polite, he listens, and he is too nice to tell other competitors to leave him alone.

RECOMMENDATIONS

1. Make a tape to help Mike relax and to rehearse becoming more instinctive and less critical under competitive conditions.
2. Attempt to effect an attitude change. At the present time Mike is shooting to avoid errors, especially during competition. This means that any miss, and some are inevitable, is a sign of total failure. When that happens during competition, anxiety, frustration and anger rise. Mike should attempt to shoot each target as if it were the only shot to be taken in the round.
3. Mike should stop watching the flight of targets when the man in front of him is shooting, especially during competition, and especially when the individual is a poorer shooter and likely to miss.
4. Mike should develop some ways to get away by himself and/or to coach others rather than letting attention focus on him, and his performance. If problems develop he should learn to file them away to be worked on in practice, not during competition. At a shoot he can talk about others' techniques and offer suggestions so long as they distract him from his own worries and pressure.

Name: C
Age: 22
Date: 6-10-79
Occupation: Professional Tennis

REASON FOR TESTING

C has been playing on the professional tour. Although she is perhaps the most physically fit of the younger players on the tour, she has been having trouble with the mental aspects of her game. An injury to her shoulder interfered with her serve (her game is primarily a serve and volley game.). This injury led to a loss of confidence and to her playing far below her capability. The goal of testing is to provide information that will be useful in identifying the types of distractions that disturb concentration and to assist in the development of a performance improvement program.

ATTENTIONAL STRENGTHS AND WEAKNESSES

C has described her greatest attentional strength as her ability to deal with a large amount of external information; to read the environment around her and to be able to react to it. She scores higher than ninety percent of the population on the scale measuring this ability (BET). Although this would indicate that she has the ability to be aware of, and to integrate all of the things going on around her, this asset becomes a liability under pressure. One of C's problems in a match is becoming too aware of things that are external to the play (e.g., a spectator moving, the ball boy, etc.). These distractions tend to grab and hold her attention when she is frustrated with herself or her play. The result is that she fails to narrow and attend to the most relevant cue, the ball.

In terms of her other attentional abilities, C scores at about the 50th percentile. This indicates that she is capable of developing both the narrow focus of attention and the internal analytical focus under less stressful conditions.

CONTROL SCALES

C's information processing score is at about the 80th percentile. This score would indicate that she has a high energy level, and that she has very strong attentional skills (given that she is as effective as she indicates in an environment that is busier than most people's).

C's score on the behavior control scale is below that of 99 percent of the college population. This indicates that she is conservative, and very controlled behaviorally. Her conservativism may be seen as rigidity (being "too good") by some of the other members of the women's tour. Her self-discipline, adherence to the rules, bible study, etc. may threaten others and result in some social isolation.

INTERPERSONAL STYLE

C scores at the 97th and 95th percentiles respectively, on the interpersonal control (CON) and self-esteem (SES) scales. These scores are the kind that would be expected of a leader and winner. They indicate that C has the drive and "killer instinct" necessary to be a winner. The high self-esteem score, though a positive attribute under most conditions, suggests that she is resistant to criticism and may have difficulty listening to a coach, especially under pressure.

During game situations, C can become caught in authority conflicts and battles for control with a coach who scores as high as she does on the need for control and self-esteem scales. The same self-esteem scores that helps C rebound from criticism and keep fighting, keeps her from listening to or accepting help from others.

The need to control, to come out on top, works against her when it keeps her from letting up on herself. There are times when C will not be able to win a point or an argument. As an example, consider a close line call. At the present time, C is unable to relax after a call goes against her. She continues to be preoccupied and this disturbs performance on successive points.

The score on the obsessiveness subscale is at the 70th percentile. This scale indicates a slight tendency to ruminate and worry. This worry can be a major component to increasing neck and shoulder muscle tension during matches. As C begins to get concerned or frustrated over her play she not only becomes less aware of the ball, but there are associated muscle tension increases. These changes in muscle tension result in an inappropriate toss on the serve and in her timing and coordination being impaired. Her problems begin to spiral and feed upon themselves.

C has described herself as intellectually expressive. High scores on this scale are associated with effective academic performance (C had close to a 4.0 in college). This score would indicate that C will take an intellectual approach to her game. High scores here in combination with the high score on control points out the fact that C will need an explanation for (and to understand) all of the psychological techniques she is asked to employ. In addition, she will want to be sure that her ideas and thoughts are listened to, and considered. A coach or psychologist will have to be a good listener as well as a good teacher.

Although C can express both positive and negative feelings, there is a large discrepancy between the two (see NAE and PAE). Scores on the test indicate that she is expressing many more negative feelings than positive ones. Observations of C during a match would support this interpretation. She is especially critical of herself, very sensitive to mistakes and not at all prone to giving positive self-reinforcement. This tendency too is a contributing factor to her increased tension and disturbed concentration and play.

RECOMMENDATIONS

1. *Sensitivity to external cues:* It is unlikely that C will be able to totally avoid distractions. Objects, movements, etc. will come into sight. The goal is not to reduce perception, but to avoid becoming focused on the distractions. C attempts to do this for herself by putting her head under a towel between games (mechanically removing external distractors). During the game it can be accomplished by a thought stopping technique and by getting C to ease up on herself when she is distracted. She must practice

"passively" attending to those distractions (letting them come in and go out without focusing on them). This is where the next step comes in.

2. *Tension control:* Just prior to each of her own serves and after points where she has become frustrated (e.g., at a lines call, missed volley, etc.), C should be taught to quickly implement the Attention Control Training procedure for centering. This will allow her to relax neck and shoulder muscle tension and to maintain a more optimal level of arousal. She should practice this on and off the court developing a 10 point arousal scale, with 5-6 being the optimal level for performance in tennis. 1 on her scale indicates a great deal of tension and 10 indicates that she is so relaxed she is almost asleep. She should learn to use the attention control training procedure to move up and down the scale, depending upon the need for a given situation.*

3. *Need for control and self-criticism:* C should be an active participant in the development and design of a training program. Things cannot come too easy for her (she won't believe them if they do). She needs to become more aware of her strengths and to provide positive self-support as a means of breaking the negative attentional focus. The sport psychologist and her coach should help point out her positive attributes and help her focus on them.

It will be important for the coach to determine in advance where C will let him assert himself when she is under pressure. Since C has a tendency to become angry with herself and others when she is playing below her own expectancy, she can be very difficult to talk with. At these times she is her own worst enemy and needs the help of someone else to break through her negative thoughts and feelings so that she can relax muscle tension and attend more effectively.

During these periods of intense frustration, the coach should simply distract C, talking about something irrelevant, helping her focus on one simple task relevant cue (e.g., the ball), getting her to use the ACT (attention control training) procedure, etc. To be able to do this, however, the coach will have to have C's permission since her initial response to his intervention will be anger because it is reminding her that she is performing poorly.

C is going to have to accept the fact that at times she is out of control. She can become stronger and regain control over herself by first giving up control to the coach. A set of signals can be worked out so that the coach catches C's attention during a crisis period by making a peace sign, tugging at his ear, etc. Once this is done, C attempts to use it to calm herself down and redirect attention. Prior to competition C has practiced laughing at herself and at her loss of control when it occurs. The coach's sign reminds her of what she has been practicing.

87

4. *Increase learning speed:* Relaxation and rehearsal procedures*
   can be used by C to help her in the following ways:
   a. Identify problem areas and practice correcting past mis-
       takes.
   b. To help C build in the ACT procedures before each serve
       and during difficult times so that these procedures become
       a natural reflexive part of her game.
   c. To practice various parts of her game to increase the learn-
       ing speed.
   d. To teach her to anticipate (and desensitize herself to)
       various distractions and frustrations during a match. For
       example, she might mentally rehearse becoming upset at a
       line call, feeling herself beginning to lose control over mus-
       cle tension and concentration. She would then rehearse
       using the ACT procedures to halt the loss of control.

*Thought stopping techniques are discussed in chapter 18, Attention Control Training
(ACT) is the subject of chapter 17, and relaxation and rehearsal procedures in chapters
15 and 18.

Following feedback of the test information C spent two hours per
week for six weeks, working with a sport psychologist to develop the
visualization skills, and control over physical and mental processes suggested in the report. Although plans had been made to integrate this
mental training with work on the court, C could not do this due to a
shoulder and back injury. Thus, for the first four weeks of training C was
unable to see how her practice was going to actually affect her serve and
concentration in a match.

Surprisingly, without much court time (only the last two weeks), C
was playing at a higher level by the end of training. She was serving with
more consistency and enjoying tennis for the first time in a long time.
Prior to the training she had been seriously considering quiting the pro-
tour. She had not been playing as well as she knew she was capable of
playing. She had been frustrated and unable to enjoy the game. Training represented a "last chance" to get it together and to see if she could
achieve her potential.

In the initial tournament after training, C played reasonably well in
her first match. She was more consistent in her play and rarely double
faulted. She had difficulty in that she was overly critical of herself. In the
second match of the tournament she convinced herself prior to walking
on to the court that she would lose to a player who had been on a hot
streak. C allowed her thoughts to affect her own attitude. As a result,
she was out of the match after she lost her serve on the first game. C
began looking for distractions to use as excuses for her own level of
play. As a result of observing the match, the following rather confrontive comments were presented to her by the psychologist (who by this
time had an excellent working relationship with her and could get away
with being confrontive).

Immediately after the match the psychologist spoke only briefly to C. The substance of the comments was that he was too mad at this point to talk with her about her performance. He wanted to have time to think, to put his own thoughts and feelings into perspective before talking. It was agreed that they would meet the following day after they had both had a chance to think about what happened.

In the next few hours the psychologist put down his thoughts and feelings on paper. He believed that C had the self-confidence to be able to deal with some strong confrontation (evidenced by the high self-esteem score on the TAIS). In addition, he knew that he had a good relationship with the athlete and that she would not just get angry and write him off as "not caring" or "dumb."

"I found myself very angry after your second round match, a feeling I don't usually have. In fact, I usually find myself upset and feeling down, as if I have failed when someone I am working with doesn't do well. I think it is important that you understand the difference between these two sets of feelings.

"First, you don't have to win for me. Sure, winning is important and if you lose, I hurt for you and with you. I don't want you to lose, and when you have really tried, put your heart into it, I hurt for you and feel guilty. I didn't do enough to prepare you; it's as much my failure as yours. When you lose under those conditions I don't think any less of you. In fact, just the opposite occurs. Anyone can win when they outclass the opponent. It takes a special person to fight to the last breath, to continue fighting even after they know they have lost. It is that kind of person that is an inspiration. It is that kind of person I admire, wish I could be like, and hurt for. I expect you to be that kind of a person.

"Anger came in your last match because I felt let down. I felt I had invested my time and most importantly my feelings and my caring in you and our work together. You let us both down by your behavior on the court. If I felt you were weak and incapable I could blame that let down on pressure. I could assume you were unable to help yourself, incapable of being anything else. If that were the case I would not be angry, I would be hurting for you. My anger told me that I didn't see you as helpless. Instead, I saw you avoiding responsibility, searching for excuses for your failure instead of playing tennis. I thought you were stubborn and behaved in a childish way, reflecting a lack of respect for yourself and for your opponent.

"Let me put my feelings in perspective by telling you to what I was reacting. First, we have talked about your distractability and the fact that you pay attention to a large number of things going on around you. Although this is true, watching a couple of matches and seeing you play has convinced me that the distractions you experience are very rarely a real problem. Those distractions come and go as the quality of your game comes and goes. It is not that an increase in distractions result in a decrease in performance. In fact, it is just the opposite! As your game deteriorates (and/or, as the other person hits some great shots — like the first game of your second match), you start looking for distractions. These provide you with the excuse you seem to need for your poor play. It's your way of saying to everyone that you are not that bad a player. Well, those excuses are a disservice to you and to your opponent. This was most clear when you felt it necessary to quiet the audience during your service on the first set. As soon as you did that, I knew you were in trouble.

"How good are you? Are you good enough to beat the woman you played? I really don't know. I do know that unless you can find the guts to put it on the line, to learn what it is to be beaten without having excuses, you'll never find out how good you are. You will just continue to roll over and die.

"You walked off the court in your first match complaining 'If I make an approach shot like that, Martina will make me eat it.' If you don't stop making excuses and being so self-critical, you won't have to worry about it, you'll never have to play Martina."

Name C   Age 22   Date 6-10-79

Norm Group   Psychology Students   Sex Female

Professional Tennis

Figure 5

	Attentional	Control	Interpersonal

BET OET BIT OIT NAR RED INFP BCON CON SES P/O OBS EXT INT IEX NAE PAE
18 9 18 11 21 27 47 10 53 31 21 15 28 18 21 13 17

90

C responded very well to the feedback and criticism. Her need for control and high level of self-esteem helped her fight back rather than fold. She began following through on procedures she had learned and gained control over her distractions. Play in singles matches improved a great deal, (moving up more than 70 positions on the ATP ranking) and her play in doubles improved even more.

Given C's broad-external focus of attention, and a serve and volley game, she is a superb doubles player. In addition, her feelings of responsibility toward her partner (reflected in her score on the behavior control scale — BCON) help keep her from wallowing in self-pity when she makes a mistake. It is easier for her to use the psychological procedures to get out of her head in doubles matches.

Name: J
Age: 32   Date: 5-10-79
Sex: Male   Sport: Distance Running

REASON FOR TESTING

J agreed to take the TAIS as part of a research project being conducted on the use of cognitive strategies for coping with pain during running. J is a world class marathon runner and has enough potential to be a contender for an Olympic gold medal in the event. At the point in time J took the test he had just finished competing in, and winning a major marathon. He was also involved in a large number of business obligations and was experiencing some of the "post competition let down" highly trained athletes often go through.

TEST ADMINISTERED AND RESULTS

At first glance, the test scores on the TAIS are dramatically inconsistent with those that might be expected of a world class runner, and a highly successful one at that. J has indicated that he is feeling out of control. He is highly anxious and ruminating about various concerns. He is overloaded by all of the demands being placed on him. He is having difficulty effectively organizing information and his attentional processes have narrowed to the point that he is making mistakes because he is not dealing with all of the task relevant information.

The profile of J's test results is similar to the profile often found with athletes who have a tendency to choke under pressure, with one notable exception. J's score on the self-esteem scale is higher than scores obtained from athletes who choke. His scores on the attentional scales, however, are highly similar. If we were to make a decision based on the test profile alone, we would not predict much success for J.

When interpreting this test profile there are two response style characteristics that need to be considered. The absolute elevation of the overload scores on the test can be attributed to the following: First, J in responding to the test adopted an attitude that tended to maximize his weaknesses, and minimize his strengths. He knew he could use the test for self improvement and so he tried very hard to focus on those items that were indicative of problems. In addition, in answering the test items, J tended to compare himself to perfection, rather than to other runners. The result of this particular response style is to dramatically elevate the overload scores. Relatively speaking, J does not make many mistakes, thus the test scores would not be particularly valid for making between runner comparisons. Other, less talented runners who when answering the questions compared themselves to their peers, would look better on the test than J did.

In spite of the fact that between subject comparisons of J's scores can be questioned, the test information is still valuable for counseling purposes. The relative position of the effective attentional scales to each other, and of the ineffective scales (OET, OIT, RED) to each other provides the information needed for counseling. J is better at narrowing attention for example, than he is at developing a broad-external focus.

An examination of this athlete's history supports much of the information found in the test results. He does indeed have a fairly high level of anxiety and has had times when he has performed very poorly, much below his expected level. By looking at the relative position of J's test scores, it is possible to begin to integrate his test results with his behavior. It might be pointed out here that this material was communicated to J and that he is in agreement with most of it.

J's greatest attentional strength is his ability to narrow attention. He is better than 97 percent of the population when it comes to being able to lock in on one thing, to discipline himself, and to concentrate in the way an athlete must (with a single minded sense of purpose) to reach the very top. This particular attentional ability is almost a prerequisite to achieving an optimal level of performance in a sport like distance running.

Although J's dominant attentional style (narrowing) may be optimal for distance running and discipline, there are negative consequences to this sense of purpose. These can be seen in J's scores on the overload scales. J finds that performance problems, difficulties making decisions, and trouble responding to interpersonal demands develop because of the extreme narrowing of attention. In effect, attention gets narrowed too much and then J feels pressure and becomes overloaded by trying to deal with all of the information. Pressure is increased by business demands, preparation for competition, etc.

On those occasions when multiple demands are being placed on J, his attentional strength (need to be focused and very thorough and dedicated) becomes a weakness. He finds himself distracted by all of his commitments and anxiety mounts as he begins to feel that he can't give things the attention they deserve. Just as the narrow attention can be positively focused on the attainment of a goal, avoiding distractions, so too it can become focused on J's worry and concern. When this occurs, J experiences increasing tension and performance deteriorates. A

92

Name J   Age 32   Date 5-10-79

Norm Group   Psychology Students   Sex Male

Marathon

Figure 6

	Attentional	Control	Interpersonal	%ile
4•0	36 41 43	68 37	65 43 50	28 35	**90**
	24 35 32 27 40 42	66 36	64 42	23 48 39 27	
	34 31 26 39 41	65 35	62 41	47 38 32 34	
	23 33 25 38 (40)	64 34	61 40	22 46 37 26 33	
	32 30 37 39	63 33	60 30	45 36 31 25 32	
3•0	22 31 29 24 36 38	61	59 38	(21) 44 35 30 24	**80**
	21 30 28 23 35	60 32	58 37	43 34 29 23 31	
	29 34 37	59 31	57 35	(20) 42 28 22 30	
	20 (28) 27 22 33 36	58 30	56 34 28	41 33 29	
	27 26 21 35	56 29	54 33 27	40 32 27 21 28	
2•0	19 26 (32) 34	55 28	53 32 26 19	38 31 26 20	**70**
	25 25 20 31 33	54	52 31 25	37 30 25 19 27	
	18 24 24 19 30 32	53 27	51 30 24 18	36 29 24 18 26	
	18 29 31	51 26	50 29 23	35 28 25	
	17 23 23 28 30	50 (25)	49 28 (22) 17	34 23 17	
1•0	22 22 (17) 27 29	49 24	47 27 21	33 27 22 16 24	**60**
	16 21 21 16 26	48 23	46 26 20 16	32 26 21 15 23	
	20 25 28	46 22	45 25 19	31 25 20 14 22	
	15 19 20 15 24 27	45	44 24 18 15	29 (24) 13 21	
	18 19 14 23 26	44 21	43 (22) 17	28 23 19	
0•0	14 17 22 25	43 20	42 21 16 14	27 22 18 (12) 20	**50**
	16 18 13 21 24	41 19	(40) 20 15	26 21 17 11 19	
	13 15 17 12 20 23	40 18	39 19	25 16 10 18	
	14 11 19 22	39 17	38 18 14 13	(24) 20 9 17	
	12 13 16 18 21	38	37 17 13	23 19 15	
1•0	12 15 10 17 20	(37) 16	36 16 12 12	22 18 14 8 (16)	**40**
	(11) 11 14 9	35 15	35 15 11	20 17 13 7 15	
	10 16 19	34 14	33 14 10 11	19 16 (12) 6 14	
	10 9 (13) 8 15 18	33 13	32 13 9	18 15 5	
	9 8 12 7 14 17	32 12	31 12 8 10	17 11 4 13	
2•0	6 13 16	30	30 11 7	16 14 10 12	**30**
	8 7 11 12 15	29 11	29 10 6 9	15 13 9 3 11	
	6 10 5 11 14	28 10	28 8 5	14 12 8 2 10	
	7 5 4 10 13	27 9	27 7 4 8	13 11 1	
	4 9 9 12	25 8	25 6 3	12 10 7 9	
3•0	6 3 8 3 8 11	24 7	24 5 2	10 9 6 8	**20**
	2 7 2 7	23	23 4 1 7	9 5 7	
	5 1 6 10	22 6	22 3	8 8 4	
	6 1 5 9	20 5	21 2	6 7 7 6	
	4 5 4 8	19 4	20 1	6 6 3 5	
4•0	3 7	18 3	19	5 5 5 2 4	**10**

BET	OET	BIT	OIT	NAR	RED	INFP	BCON	CON	SES	P/O	OBS	EXT	INT	IEX	NAE	PAE
11	28	13	17	32	40	37	25	40	22	22	21	24	24	12	12	16

downward spiral begins and performance goes from bad to worse. It is this downward spiral that has led to J dropping out in the middle of races.

RECOMMENDATIONS

Since demands are increasing as a result of J's success, it would seem imperative that he find someone he can trust to manage his business interests, freeing up his time and concentration for training. It would also be helpful for him to work with a trainer or coach who can run interference for him, handling details about travel, meals, accommodations, etc. This help would prevent or minimize the feelings of being overloaded. In addition, the coach or trainer could help J get out of his head when he begins to become overly concerned about irrelevant issues.

In addition to having someone outside of himself to help, there are psychological techniques that J can learn to use to reduce the effects of the downward spiral that results from being caught in his head. Thought stopping techniques, cognitive behavior modification, attention control training, and meditation: could be tailored to J's special needs.

10

TEAM BUILDING

In contrast to the more subjective goals often associated with traditional psychotherapy, the bottom line for the sport psychologist involves
some objective improvement in performance. The coach or team owner
who places the subjective happiness of the athlete above winning is
rare. It is even rarer to find an owner who will invest dollars in helping
athletes "feel better about themselves and/or the team," unless that in-
vestment also results in greater likelihood of winning. That is not to say
that these individuals don't care about feelings; it only emphasizes that
those concerns come secondary to concerns for success.

Many of the psychological techniques that have been used in
organizational psychology in the past have not been directly focused on
improving performance. Sensitivity training (T groups) and encounter
groups have been used to improve self-awareness, increase empathy
for others, and to develop communication skills. Typically, there has
not been a specific treatment focus. That is, training has not been
designed to improve communication within a particular situation or between certain people. Somehow it is assumed that more generalized
training will magically result in the development of skills that will be used
automatically to improve communication and reduce problems within
the organization. Unfortunately, this is often not the case and in fact,
sensitivity groups and encounter groups often increase pressure, bringing problems into focus. Without follow-up by professionals, participants may have difficulty dealing with their newly discovered
knowledge. Pandora's box has been opened; it can't be closed and
there doesn't seem to be any easy solutions.

Team building, as it is discussed in this chapter is time-limited and has
as a primary focus the improvement of performance. Most often, either
explicitly or implicitly, the consulting sport psychologist is hired for a
short period of time to help athletes, coaches, and teams function at
higher levels. Positive changes in feelings and attitudes are seen as
secondary to improvement in performance. It is assumed that as performance improves, positive feelings towards self and team will also increase. This attitude represents a reversal of the philosophy behind
many sensitivity groups, where positive performance changes are expected to follow from changes in attitudes and beliefs. What this expec-
tation means practically, is that a sport psychologist who decides to use
techniques such as encounter groups, sensitivity training, EST

workshops, Rational Emotive Therapy, etc. would do so only if he/she has a specific behavioral focus and emphasizes the improvement of performance in *specific* situations. Thus, athletes aren't just made more aware of feelings; they are made more aware of their feelings in a situation that is affecting their ability to perform. Following this, they are helped to assume responsibility for changing the situation in ways that will facilitate positive behavioral outcomes for them and for the team.

It is important to identify the similarities and differences between what is being described as team building, and the development of individualized performance improvement programs. First, in both instances the primary concern is the improvement of performance. This concern means that the same theoretical constructs that are important for the development of individual programs, will be important in team building.

Team building involves an assessment of the interactions between the members of a team, identifying their attentional and interpersonal strengths and weaknesses as they relate to each other and to the desired outcome. How can different individual's attentional abilities be used to complement each other? What personality characteristics are complementary, and which ones come into conflict with each other?

When working with individuals, and when working with teams, the sport psychologist is always looking at the relationship between individuals and their environments. The total system needs to be assessed in both cases to determine the most efficient method of treatment. The primary difference between the two, is that in the team building situation, there may be a need to place a group goal or outcome ahead of an individual's goal. In addition, there may be an emphasis placed on teaching members of the team to facilitate the performance of others, independent of their own performance. For example, as a member of a track team it may be in his/her best interests to facilitate the performance of the other members, even when he/she is competing in a highly individualized event (e.g., high jump), or when a teammate may be competing against him/her. By helping someone else the athlete may lose the opportunity to compete in the 100 meter dash, but he/she may improve the performance of the relay team of which they are a member.

The sport psychologist who is in the fortunate position of having an individual athlete come to him/her for help, especially when the athlete is paying for the service, has the luxury of responding in many different ways. A contract may initially be based upon the development of a program for improving the individual's performance. As the program evolves it may become obvious that other factors should take precedence over the development of the individual's skill. For example, the athlete may determine that questions he/she has about continued involvement in sport are more important than increasing performance skill. Or, he/she may decide that team goals are more important than individual goals. When this is the case, it is a simple matter for the sport

96

psychologist and the athlete to renegotiate their contract.

In team building situations the potential for conflict is dramatically increased by the fact that individual goals and team goals do not always go together. The sport psychologist is often caught between the needs and desires of the individual athlete, the needs and desires of the coach or manager, and his/her own moral and philosophical values. Almost before you realize it, problems develop. The types of difficulties that occur can be seen in the two examples that follow. Prior to giving these examples, however, it is important to discuss procedures that can be used to minimize the conflicts of interest that develop.

OPERATIONALIZE THE REFERRAL

As coaches, managers, and owners of teams become increasingly aware of the role of sport psychologists, there will be a corresponding increase in requests for team building services. Often these requests are based on very little real knowledge about the role a sport psychologist can play. Misconceptions regarding the services that sport psychologists have to offer are rampant. For this reason it is critical that the sport psychologist: 1) operationally define the goals that a coach or organization have in mind; 2) inform the person requesting services of the ethical responsibilities associated with the provision of psychological services; 3) determine whether or not he/she is capable of ethically responding to the request; and 4)establish a very explicit service contract.

A few examples of the kinds of requests that come in from coaches might be instructive. Speaking to an Australian sports psychologist, I was both amused and upset by the request he had received from a team in the Victoria Football League to "brainwash the athletes."

It was the opinion of the coaches that not all of the players on the team had the best attitude. It was their hope that the sport psychologist could somehow brainwash them into believing in themselves. More than that, the brainwashing was supposed to increase their mental and physical toughness. Somehow, the sport psychologist was to accomplish what the coach had been unable to. The owners and coaches believed that the sport psychologist had some special magic that would make believers out of the athletes in a very short period of time. The psychologist was not to become a coach, however, and the psychologist could not take time away from practice. In this particular instance the sport psychologist felt that the goals the team wanted to obtain could not be accomplished given the time constraints, economic constraints, and insecurity of the coaches. As a result he refused the contract.

On one occasion a coach approached me and requested that I teach all of his athletes relaxation techniques. This particular coach had read a story about a team employing progressive relaxation as a regular part of their practice. The story was very positive indicating that the performance of the entire team had been upgraded as a function of the training. In talking with the coach it quickly became clear that he didn't have any idea as to how the training would help. He thought that I could come in and, in a session or two, dramatically improve the performance of the athletes. It took some education on my part to make him realize that the employment of the procedures should be based on the needs of individual athletes in specific situations, and with specific goals in mind. He was made aware of the fact that involvement, at least if he wanted to accomplish his goals of improved performance, would require considerably more than an hour-and-a-half's talk to the team.

These next two examples illustrate very graphically some of the difficulties that can arise when attempting to provide services to an entire team. The first involved a request to do some testing of a group of inter-service boxers.

One day I received a call from a captain in the armed forces who was in charge of selecting and training the individuals who would be competing in an inter-service and an international competition. I was informed that they had a group of sixteen individuals that would eventually be reduced to eight. He would like me to come and "test them."

Upon asking why he wanted them tested, he indicated that in talking to a mutual acquaintance, he had learned about a test I had developed. It was his understanding that the test might be useful in improving the performance of his team, and in selecting the final eight athletes.

The captain seemed very enthusiastic over the telephone. He had met my friend at a marathon and they had started talking. He didn't know much about the test, but he remembered the enthusiasm of my friend. As we talked, it became apparent that the captain had never boxed himself. He had been placed in charge of the men in spite of his lack of experience. He had appointed a coach for the team, but not the man he really wanted. The coach had been a competitor but had not been outstanding. There was another individual who the captain felt would have been better, but when this man was told he could not compete and coach at the same time, he elected to compete.

Over the phone I got the captain to provide me with a description of the rules and competitive demands the boxers would face. As a function of the discussion, I felt that I might be able to use the test to provide some feedback to individual team members that they might find helpful in terms of improving their own performance. I also informed him that I might be able to gather information that would help him help them. I told him I did not feel the test could be used for selection, although it would certainly be interesting to see how accurate it might prove to be in predicting actual performance.

It was agreed that I would come out and talk to the team. They were described as a group of eager athletes who would be anxious to learn. I informed the captain that it was my ethical responsibility to inform each of the individuals with respect to how the test information would be used. It was agreed that I would test only those members of the team who volunteered following my talk. In addition, individual appointments

98

would be made with those athletes tested to provide them with feedback about their test results. At this time I would ask them what information they would be willing to have shared with the coach, other team members, or the captain. Finally, I convinced the captain that to be maximally effective it would be necessary for him to take the test too, since his personality undoubtedly had an impact on the team.

As a result of our phone conversation I went to the first meeting with some naive expectations. I was anticipating an eager audience. I had been led to believe that these individuals had very high levels of morale and trust, that they really knew what "team work" was. Most of them had been selected from special warfare units. They were the cream of the crop. They were "one big happy family."

When I arrived for the meeting the captain informed me that he would take a few minutes at the start to deal with a couple of "minor" issues. It turned out that the minor issues consisted of the fact that the training facilities the athletes were to work out in had been torn down before a replacement had been built. If that weren't bad enough, the military had not even prepared the barracks. The athletes had to become cleaners and carpenters, fixing themselves a place where they could train and live.

The captain did his best to respond to the anger and frustration of his men. Unfortunately, his success was limited. Several of the competitors asked about some special equipment (these were individuals who had competed in the past). The captain's response was to give them a lecture on how altering equipment could interfere with their technique. As I looked at the audience, I could see the athletes tuning the captain out and I knew that they were quietly thinking "who the hell does he think he is? He's never competed, doesn't he think we know anything?"

Slowly it began to dawn on me that one of the main reasons I had been called in was to entertain the troops. If I could keep them busy with testing maybe they wouldn't be so upset with the fact that they couldn't practice. My eager audience wasn't so eager.

When I got up in front of the group I was very careful to tell them that I was there to learn. I didn't know very much about boxing. I had studied the martial arts in Japan and had earned a black belt in Aikido so I knew something about some of the skills involved. In addition, I had competed athletically in college and had worked with athletes who competed at national and international levels so I did have a feeling for some of the pressures they faced. Finally, and perhaps most important-ly, I had been in the service as an enlisted man and I could empathize with the crap they were running into. It was so typical of the service to tell you to hurry up and then you would find yourself forced to wait. To make matters worse they lecture you on the importance of your winning for God and country and then they can't even provide you with training facilities.

I told them I had been asked by the captain to come in and administer a test which should provide information about their ability to concentrate. If they were willing, I would come back and talk to them as a group about the test results (not talking about any individual, but talking about the scores of the "average" competitor). Following this, for those who were interested I would meet with them privately and help them deal with any questions, or problems that they might have related to psychological preparation. It was emphasized that results of the tests would be treated confidentially and that nothing could be shared with anyone without their expressed permission.

I responded to questions that they had and was surprised to find that the most hostile responses came from the man that had been pointed out as the coach. He agreed to take the test, but had some serious questions about its usefulness and seemed to be very defensive.

I left tests with the athletes and they all took them. While they were taking the tests I went back and continued talking with the captain. I asked him about the problems that the men were having and told him that I would really be upset if I were in their position. I also asked him if he had discussed my being brought in with the coach. He told me no, and then indicated that the coach had some problems. He really didn't want Jim to be coach; he preferred Al. When Al decided that he wanted to compete more than coach, the captain felt he had no choice but to give the job to Jim. Jim's past dedication to training and to the outfit deserved recognition even though the captain saw him as technically, intellectually, and interpersonally ineffective. He was hoping that I would be able to help the coach decide the best way to break the sixteen competitors up into two groups or teams.

It was obvious that he didn't feel the coach was capable, so he was making decisions for him. If that weren't enough, he wanted to involve me in that process and he had brought in a retired inter-service boxer as a consultant to the coach. This individual was to provide technical expertise, something the coach should be doing. All of these plans were made without considering the coach's needs, concerns, feelings, or knowledge. Already I was beginning to feel caught between the coach and the captain.

Test results were very interesting and provided some insight into the problems that seemed to exist, as well as providing some consensual validation for some of the observations I had made. First, the captain described himself as a very effective individual. He was the kind of person who has a great deal of confidence in himself, and for whom it is difficult to admit that he might possibly make mistakes, or be limited in terms of knowledge. He was a leader, good at giving orders, but not so good at following them, or at allowing others to lead.

The captain's self-confidence was high enough, and his need for control was high enough that it would not occur to him that the fact he had never competed in boxing should have any relevance. Apart from having little empathy with the fact that his men might not feel he was qualified to coach them, there were some specific mistakes he was likely to make.

Attentionally, the captain's greatest asset was his ability to think in analytical terms — to deal with a large amount of information. In addition, he was intellectually expressive and as already mentioned, controlling. This style meant that he was very likely to overload others with information, that he would expect them to deal with too much, and that he would overcoach. His tendency to get involved in testing, to bring in consultants, etc. were all well intended, but in combination with other things they made the situation unnecessarily complicated.

The second type of mistake the captain was likely to make involved delegating responsibility to others, and then taking it back. Being a take-charge person, and describing himself as an individual who makes decisions quickly, he would become impatient and take over. These personality characteristics interacted in a very negative way with the attentional and interpersonal characteristics of the coach. In addition, they were further complicated by the fact that the coach was an enlisted man and the captain firmly believed that officers were innately superior to enlisted men. His first question to me when I returned to discuss the test results was to ask me if the test could pick out the officers in the group.

Results of the coach's test indicated that he was experiencing some anxiety, and that unlike the captain, he had difficulty making decisions. Attentionally, he described himself as overloaded by all of the demands that were being placed on him. In addition, his level of self-esteem was much lower than I would have expected. It was obvious from the test that he was not feeling very effective.

Results of the sixteen athletes' tests were also interesting and tended to fall into one of two general categories. There was a group of individuals who described themselves as being confident and in control. Although this group had areas that could be identified as places to work on in order to improve performance, the general picture was of very effective individuals.

Those effective individuals could be contrasted with a group of athletes who were feeling very much like the coach, overloaded and confused. Their self-esteem was down, and they were very pessimistic about the likelihood of making the team.

As I thought about giving feedback to the individual members of the team I became concerned about several issues. First, I anticipated that the captain would push for information about various members of the team, and given his test scores, I felt that it would be difficult to get him to hear about some of the ways in which he might be contributing to the problems.

I was equally concerned about talking with the coach. I could easily emphathize with him and with the frustration he must feel. At the same time, I knew there was some legitimacy to the concerns that the captain had, and to the frustration that I was sure I would hear from some of the athletes.

I went into the individual feedback sessions reminding myself that I would limit my comments in the following ways:

101

1. I would talk to the individuals about their own test reports. I felt that I could share with them how I felt I would react to some of the problems that we were both aware of. That is, I felt I could use as examples situations and interpersonal experiences that we had both shared (e.g., having the gym torn down).
2. I could encourage them to talk about their concerns and frustrations in relation to training and in relation to the team, coach, and captain. Again, I felt that I could take their expressions at face value and maintain that "if that is an accurate picture, and if I responded to the test in the way you did, here are some of the problems I would see." The emphasis here would be on identifying those things that the athlete could do to improve the situation, rather than placing the blame or responsibility on someone else.
3. When I could see that a problem that they were presenting interacted directly with some of the concerns that I had about others (e.g., they indicated that the captain overloaded them with information), I would ask them if I could share that information. If they agreed we would work out the best way for me to do this, and even come up with the specific language.

There were obviously many things that I could see which I thought might be helpful. Unfortunately, I did not have the power to control other people's responses, or to make decisions about who should coach, etc. (perhaps I should say fortunately). Although the temptation was very strong to jump in and empathize with various people, to take sides on issues, to assume more responsibility than the military was willing to give, I knew that I couldn't. I could not give more than they wanted to receive. I could not assume the administrative responsibility of the captain, nor could I assume the functions of the coach. Neither could I betray the individual's confidences. Such control is not easy when you, the sport psychologist, have as high a need for control and as high a level of self-esteem as the captain of the unit.

Individual meetings went fairly well and provided a great deal of information about the problems that the team was experiencing. Generally speaking, the captain was seen as a typical officer by most of the enlisted men. They felt that he was an okay guy, but that he undercut the coach. They felt that he could be more supportive and would have liked to see him take a more aggressive stance with the "Brass." They wanted him to run administrative interference for them. They felt that he was overloading the coach with administrative responsibilities (e.g., to argue with the military about getting the training facility built; to argue with officers who kept trying to grab the athletes for various work details; and to purchase all of the equipment for training like shoes, etc.).

The coach was seen as ineffective by the men. They felt that he lacked confidence, and that he would not stand up for himself. Many of the team members who scored low on self-esteem complained because the coach was never around to help — he was always off doing ad-

102

ministrative chores and he would turn the coaching over to two of the athletes who were officers.

Those athletes who indicated that they had fairly high levels of self-esteem had responded to the situation by writing off the captain and the coach. "They listened very nicely then went out and did precisely what they wanted." The position was perhaps best described by the individual who had wanted to be both coach and competitor.

Al's test indicated that he was exceptionally effective when it came to controlling attention. He was extremely energetic and scored in the 99th percentile on those scales measuring the need to be in control of interpersonal situations, and self-esteem. In contrast to the coach, he was much more expressive of positive feelings, and more capable of providing support to the other athletes.

He walked into the individual feedback session and said "By now you must be aware of the fact that we really need some help. There are some really good athletes on this team who aren't going to make it unless something is done." I told him that I would really like to hear what he had to say about the situation, but first I would like to provide him with some feedback from his test. He listened very carefully as I told him what his scores indicated. I pointed out that it was my experience that individuals with scores like his were extremely frustrated by what they saw as ineffectiveness or incompetence of others. I told him that I had observed the look on his face in the meeting when he had asked the captain to get some special equipment and had then received a lecture on how it might interfere with his technique.

By the time I had spoken to Al, I had already met with several of the athletes. Two of them had specifically mentioned that Al was the choice for coach, but that he had elected to compete. They emphasized that they had seen him withdraw from the team over the past few days. I asked if I could share this with Al when he came in and they said "yes."

Al's response was understandable, and one that I could respect. He said that he knew the coach was insecure and that he was having a very difficult time. At first Al had tried to help out, but quickly began to feel that his efforts were making the coach's job more difficult. He didn't want to do that so he had withdrawn. At the same time, he expressed a lot of anger because he felt he had a great deal to offer.

We had both been in a lecture that morning given by the consultant. The subject had to do with some of the technical aspects of boxing. During the lecture the consultant pointed out that one of the competitors from another branch of the service would be likely to employ certain tactics. Al said that, in fact, the consultant was basing his feelings on inaccurate information. I asked him how he knew and he said he had boxed the man twice and he had reviewed several fight films of previous bouts. I asked why he didn't share the information with his team and he said for the same reasons discussed earlier, he didn't want to create problems. I pointed out that his withdrawl was creating problems too. I asked him if the opportunity presented itself, could I share some of his concerns with the coach. He indicated that if I thought it would do any good, I could.

When the coach came in he was much less defensive than I thought he would be. He started out by telling me that he felt insecure in his job. He told me that he had been a competitor on the team the year before, but if he had to rank himself now, relative to the sixteen athletes, he would put himself in the fifteenth or sixteenth position. Jim presented this as a reason for feeling insecure. I tried to point out that he could begin to establish a very positive relationship with the men if he would tell them what he just told me. That, at least, would show them that he respected them. I told him that there were several athletes on the team who had not been competitors before who really needed some support and reinforcement from him.

At that point he told me that he was the second choice for coach. He didn't feel that he had the confidence of the captain or of the team. As a result, he avoided assuming very many coaching responsibilities.

I asked him what he felt about my being asked to do some testing and what he thought about the technical consultant. He seemed uncomfortable by my question. That was something the captain wanted so that's the way it is. He seemed to have bought the notion that officers were somehow superior to enlisted men.

I mentioned to him that he had indicated on the test that he was feeling overloaded by all of the demands that were being placed upon him. I asked him if he felt that the captain contributed to this by giving him a lot of administrative responsibility, and by putting time pressures on him. He admitted that this was the case, but seemed only too eager to accept total responsibility for the problem. He should be able to handle all of those things; the captain's expectancies were okay. I shared with him the fact that some of the team members did not share his feelings. They felt that he was being handed too many administrative responsibilities and they would like to see him more available for coaching.

Jim seemed as if he wanted to believe the things I was saying, but somehow just couldn't buy it. He appreciated what I had to say, but he did not want me to share the things he had said with the captain.

As I had anticipated, the first thing the captain wanted to know when I walked into his office was how "his men scored." I told him that first I would like to go over his test information and then I would have somethings I could share with him and perhaps we would come up with some specific questions.

I took considerable time to point out to the captain all of the strengths that his test indicated. He has scored the way "most effective leaders do." "He was obviously a take charge guy, with a lot of confidence and a lot of ideas." "He had to be very effective at what he did or he wouldn't have gotten as far as he had." Then I indicated that people like him make very few mistakes but when they do, they are usually of two types. First, because they are so good at thinking and analyzing situations, and because they deal so effectively with very complex situations

104

and make very difficult decisions, they expect others to behave the same way. The result is that they can overload less capable individuals by expecting too much. At the same time, they may delegate authority and then in their own haste to get things accomplished take it away. For example, he might not see it this way but in some sense my involvement and the involvement of the technical consultant represented this type of behavior.

I shared with the captain the feedback that some of the athletes had indicated I could. I told him that they felt he could run more administrative interference. I also mentioned that many of them wanted to see the coach freed from some of his administrative responsibilities so that he could spend more time coaching. At this the captain indicated that he had tried to do that but that the coach seemed to prefer the administration. In my own head I knew that was the coach's way of avoiding an uncomfortable situation. He was simply too threatened by the officers in the group and by the skill level of many of the athletes to believe he had something to contribute.

I had told the coach and the team in advance that one of the things the captain had asked me to do was to offer some suggestions about how the team might be broken up into two groups to speed up practice. In discussing this issue with the coach and with the various team members I was able to get their feelings about each other, and about who they would like to work with. These conversations allowed me to encourage individuals to seek help from each other, and to not be afraid to ask questions or to offer assistance.

As it turned out, the athletes agreed with the coach — they did not want to be broken up into two groups. They preferred to work together as a team, hoping to develop more of a sense of identity. This agreement provided a boost for the coach because it allowed him to take a stand on an issue and to hold out against the captain. At the same time it gave the individual team members the excuse they needed to begin working with each other independent of the captain and the coach. They went on to field the best team in the service that year in spite of the problems.

In a situation such as this where there are so many obvious problems it is extremely difficult for a sport psychologist to remember ones own limitations. The desire to help and the feeling that one could certainly improve communications is hardly sufficient for believing you can become coach, manager, owner, and athlete all rolled into one. The temptation to overstep your responsibilities can be almost overpowering. Likewise, the temptation to betray a confidence, like the coach's, can be difficult to avoid. Concern for members of the team, the desire to help, the need to feel important, the need to have something concrete to offer, and the need to please the captain can make it very easy to rationalize away an ethical principle for "this little situation." Unfortunately, these "little situations" pop up all the time.

Often, team building begins by first attempting to assess the needs of a particular organization for psychological assistance. There are many ways in which this assessment can be carried out. Group sessions have been used to try to get those athletes and individuals involved to identify problems or needs that they feel exist. Unfortunately, the effectiveness of such sessions are limited by the amount of trust that exists within the group. Very often athletes will not discuss, at least not initially, things that are bothering them in front of a group.

A second way is to identify smaller subgroups and to work first with these. A subgroup might consist of a coach and an athlete, two athletes or several athletes who occupy similar positions (e.g., ends, interior linemen, backs, in football). Starting small and then expanding allows you to develop trust and to avoid opening up a major problem unexpectedly (e.g., the fact that the team hates a particular member or coach). This procedure is not without problems, however, since it requires constant revisions in the contract between psychologist and the ever expanding group, and because it creates a situation in which the psychologist, if not careful, can be used against others. The following example illustrates some of the complications that can develop:

Working with a gymnastics team I was asked to identify some ways in which the coach could improve his ability to deal with each of the athletes on the team. It was agreed that I would provide some general training in the use of relaxation and rehearsal procedures to the entire team, but there was a subset of elite gymnasts ranging in age from 11 to 22 with whom the coach was especially concerned. These were the individuals that he determined to have the most talent, and he wanted to make sure that he was doing the right things.

We decided that the best way to proceed was for the coach to give me his greatest concern with each of the gymnasts. Following his discussion with me, the coach agreed to go to each gymnast and to tell her what he had shared with me. This disclosure allowed me to go to each individual and openly address an issue. I informed the coach that as a part of this process I would begin by first asking the gymnast if she had been told what the coach and I had spoken about. I would then listen to her interpretation of the problem as heard from the coach. I would tell her how I heard the problem, and then I would ask her what her own feelings were. "Do you see it as a real problem?" "What do you think the coach could do to help?" "What do you see as the biggest problem?"

Problems that were identified by the coach ranged from wanting to improve a certain gymnast's ability to concentrate in practice (she concentrated well in competition), to wanting to help an athlete lose weight, to being concerned about how best to relate to a gymnast. In this last instance the coach emphasized that the coaching relationship was particularly frustrating. The gymnast could not take criticism at all, seemed moody and angry no matter what the coach tried to do.

Working with most of the individual problems was not difficult. More often than not, the gymnasts agreed with the coach's assessment and were eager to work out some type of solution. My role in the process was to identify different psychological techniques that would prove useful in improving concentration, losing weight, etc. As these were identified I would work with the coach and athlete to provide the necessary training or to point out where it could be obtained.

The conflict came in that almost every gymnast that came in had a second agenda. The team seemed to be divided into two groups. One was very small consisting of only three people. It was the contention of this contingent that the reason the coach could not communicate with the gymnast whom he saw as a problem was because the coach was unreasonable, he was unpredictable, and he let his own moods affect how he related to the gymnast's.

The other group described the gymnast that the coach was having difficulty with as moody and hard to get along with. They felt that she made no attempt to be a member of the team. Her involvement was damaging to the relationship that the coach had with the other gymnasts because she would upset him and then his frustration would get carried over to practice. It was obvious that many of the gymnasts would be much happier if they could get this one girl off the team.

Suddenly, I found myself in the middle of a problem that it had not been agreed upon that I would work with. The members of the team were doing what they could to get me to take sides. None of them wanted to hurt anyone; but their concern for the team outweighed their concern for the individual.

I felt stuck. I was concerned about going back to the coach with the feelings that had been expressed by many of the team members since I wasn't sure how he would deal with that information. At the time the issue came up with the individual athletes I had felt that I should listen. I was trying to establish a working relationship and I had been afraid that if I told them I didn't want to listen or deal with the problem they would write me off. I don't think that would have happened; but that was what I told myself at the time.

I had been very careful not to take sides in talking with the individual athletes. I had emphathized with the frustration what each of them was expressing but had followed that with a "There must be another side too. I wonder what it seems like from her position?" Most often the response from the athlete would be something like "I'm sure she is upset, the coach can be hard to get along with, but doesn't she care about the team?"

The problem that had begun to surface was a very serious one. It was one that I could not deal with in an ongoing way. I had been called in as a consultant to provide services within a short period of time. I was not going to be around to see this one through. I felt that I had two choices. The first was to ignore the issue, pretending it had never happened. The second was to explore it in more detail and to try and come up with some recommendations for dealing with it. Since I would be leaving, this meant that I would have to trust the integrity and concern of the coach and the athletes. I had to believe that they were capable of following through in a responsible way. I chose the second option.

Susan's side of the story helped me understand a great deal. It also made me want to cry since it seemed as if the situation was pretty hopeless. When she came in to talk I asked if the coach had shared his concerns with her. She said that he had and she began to cry. Her tears were angry tears as she stated that she didn't feel she could work for the coach. She felt that things had been okay for a period of time and then another gymnast had joined the team. This gymnast, though not as good as Susan, had a very bubbly outgoing personality. She always did what the coach asked and she was a real cheerleader for the team. The coach thought she was a super kid and that became obvious to Susan. Susan's jealousy made matters go from bad to worse.

Susan's problems had actually begun long before the arrival of the other gymnast. She had been working in another city with a coach with whom she had a very close relationship. This particular coach had a very different coaching style than the one she was currently involved with. To make matters worse, the coaches didn't like each other. When Susan's parent's moved, she suddenly found herself having to work with an individual that she believed disliked her former coach, and disliked her.

In fact, her perception of the situation was not totally wrong. Her current coach did not get along with Susan's previous coach. In fact, he had refused to accept Susan into the club initially because he felt that her previous coach was trying to tell him how he should deal with Susan before she ever arrived. Susan, aware of this early rejection and very sensitive to rejection to begin with, got off on the wrong foot.

By the time I talked with her it was too late. I asked her what the coach could do to improve their communication and she quite honestly said that she wasn't sure there was anything he could do. She felt it had reached the point where nothing could be done. We discussed what her options were and she decided that at the moment she really didn't have any if she wanted to continue in gymnastics.

I asked Susan if I could share her feelings with the coach. I especially wanted to be able to tell him how she perceived the early involvement and I wanted to sensitize him to the conflict she was experiencing in relationship to her previous coach. From my perception, Susan was a girl who needed a very close relationship with her coach and with the team. She had a close relationship in the past. Unfortunately, for her to get involved and to allow a relationship to develop with her current coach meant an emotional betrayal of her previous relationship. The two coaches didn't get along and so, inside, Susan would feel like a turn coat if she became emotionally involved with the current team.

Her coach was very empathetic and was genuinely concerned with doing whatever was best for Susan. At the same time, he had responsibilities to the team and his own feelings. It was my belief that for the relationship to work out it would involve a lot of work in an ongoing kind of way with a more clinically oriented sport psychologist. I could not fill that role and neither of the participants (Susan or the Coach) seemed interested in going to that extreme to solve the problem.

As it was left, the coach would try to work with Susan and be as sensitive as he could to the underlying issues. Should that fail, however, he would do what he could to help her find another coach with whom she could work. In addition, he agreed to accept part of the responsibility for the problems they were having and to let Susan know this. In this way he could help prevent her self-esteem from going any lower. They managed to stay together for about a month before Susan decided to find another coach.

Team building is a systems approach to the solution of specific performance related problems in sport. The focus of training may be on the development of skills, the establishment of better communication (communication that facilitates performance), making alterations in attitudes or levels of motivation, or changing the situation or environment. The system can be relatively small involving coach-athlete or it can expand dramatically to include members of a team, coaching staff, management and administrative personnel, and in the case of age group sports, parents.

The larger and more extensive the group the more challenging and the more difficult it is to respond in a professional and ethical manner. Let me summarize here the steps I believe should be taken in order to minimize the likelihood of serious problems:

1. Operationalize the referral question and determine whether or not you can respond to it in an ethical fashion.
2. Inform the individuals involved of your ethical responsibilities. These include the following:
    a. To maintain a clear contract with each person knowing what your responsibilities are, to whom you report, what you are looking for, and what you will say.
    b. To maintain the confidentiality of the people with whom you are involved.
    c. To communicate information only within the context of particular situations.
3. Develop a format for how you will proceed once specific behavioral and/or emotional goals have been identified. This format should include your input regarding how best to introduce the program. Provisions should be made for you to:
    a. Get acquainted with the athletes, coaches, etc. involved.
    b. Very clearly establish the rules and goals surrounding your working relationship. These should be made public to the group.
    c. Provide the opportunity for individual contact as well as group contact as a means of validating consensually your observations, checking out the best way to provide feedback, discussing what will and will not be shared with the group as a whole or with various group members.

4. Build into the program places where the goals and contract can be periodically reviewed to make sure that they are being followed, and, should it be desirable, to provide the opportunity to make public changes in the contract.

5. Build in an opportunity for follow-up to assess what the response has been to the various suggestions and changes. This follow-up allows you to deal with any unanticipated problems.

6. Give yourself time to discuss issues in a professional way with a peer (e.g., another sport psychologist who will maintain the confidentiality) who can help you see when you are letting your own needs get involved. Make sure that you are not overstepping your bounds and assuming too much responsibility. *You are not a coach,* and, as a function of your consulting role, *you are not a psychotherapist.*

11

CONSULTATION AND PROGRAM DEVELOPMENT

As is often the case with team building, there are many situations in which it is economically unfeasible to hire a full-time sport psychologist. As a result, skills in developing psychological programs relating to the assessment and enhancement of performance, and the skill to train and supervise others to follow through on those programs are important to the sport psychologist.

Apart from the economics of the situation there are also times when psychological services can be more effectively integrated into an ongoing training program when they are provided by a coach, trainer or members of a team. Sensitivity to the total training program, a sense of timing and the emotional needs of the athletes, and an already established trusting relationship can facilitate learning. Finally, the ability to speak in a language and to use examples that are directly related to the athletes' personal experience is a decided advantage. Often, the sport psychologist is handicapped and does not have the time or sport specific knowledge to be able to do this as effectively as the coach or a team member might.

What are some of the skills that sport psychologists are called upon to teach? What are some of the prerequisites to learning those skills? What are the ethical responsibilities of the sport psychologist?

It is very common for sport psychologists to go into athletic situations and set up behavioral programs (contingency management) designed to alter specific athlete or team behaviors, motivation levels or attitudes. Coaches may be taught the principles behind the use of positive and negative reinforcement in controlling behavior. Often, the psychologist assesses the athletic situation to determine those behaviors and attitudes that need to be changed in order to improve performance and/or attitude. This assessment may be done with formal psychological tests, behavioral observations or through interviews with the athletes and coaches. Following the assessment of target behaviors, the psychologist uses his/her knowledge of human behavior, drives, and motivations to identify positive and negative reinforcers that can be used to develop the desired behavior, or to eliminate an undesirable one.

Once target behaviors have been identified, and reinforcement contingencies have been established, the coach or athlete is taught to implement the program. As an example, I might observe that two or three athletes are engaging in a lot of "horse play" during practice. Their fooling around is dramatically reducing the amount that gets accomplished during a practice session because it distracts and delays everyone. The target behavior that I want to change is the "horse play."

As a sport psychologist I need to be sensitive to what motivates the behavior to begin with, and what keeps it going (what are the positive reinforcers for this negative behavior). Observations indicate that for one of the athletes, it is a way of reducing the anxiety that is associated with practice. For this individual, the fooling around increases as practice requires him to attempt new or difficult tasks. For another individual, the fooling around seems relatively non-contingent. This particular athlete is hyperactive, easily distractable and thus becomes quickly involved whenever anyone else is fooling around.

For both athletes, there is a tension release that is associated with the negative behavior. The individuals are driven by the tension and the initial reinforcement for the behavior comes from the reduction of the tension. The fooling around continues, or is maintained because of the delay it creates (keeping one of the athletes from having to engage in the threatening behavior) and because it gets a lot of attention from the team. Others begin to laugh and occasionally get involved making the two athletes the center of attention, something that is rewarding to them. Finally, it gives the athletes involved a sense of control over the coach. The coach is authoritarian and dominates practice, not giving the athletes much latitude in determining what should be practiced, how it should be practiced, for how long, etc. In part, the fooling around is a way of getting back some of the control that they have given up.

It is the psychologist's training and sensitivity to the dynamics that underlie human behavior that helps him/her understand and identify the reinforcement contingencies. It is unlikely that this sensitivity could be taught to a coach or athlete in a short period of time. A great deal of experience, observation, and training is required to be sensitive to all of the important issues. As a result, it is rare that the sport psychologist attempts to train others to make the assessment of reinforcement contingencies themselves. Without adequate knowledge and experience, they would be in danger of developing a program that would not take into account some of the important underlying factors that are influencing behavior.

In the case just presented it may be easy to see that the fooling around is reinforced by the team getting involved, smiling, etc. It is more difficult, especially for a coach who needs control, for the coach to see that his own controlling behavior is also a contributing factor. Likewise, the fact that anxiety is a contributor for one of the athletes may go unnoticed and denied by the athlete. His need not to feel frightened because that might (in his own mind) signal that he is not strong enough, can result in his denying anxiety, even to himself.

112

Without seeing all of the issues, the coach might establish a program that creates more problems than the fooling around. First, he might order the athletes to avoid any response to the horse play. This order would be an attempt to take away the social reinforcement. Although it could have some effect, this move would increase pressure because it would simply add to the dominance and control against which the athletes are already rebelling. In addition, the coach may decide to remove the individuals who are fooling around from practice. First, this decision would probably not be necessary for the individual who is hyperactive. To a large extent his behavior is triggered by others, and by his own activity level. Control that the coach will get with this person is more likely to develop by altering the environment and distractions and by giving him an appropriate way to release some of the excess energy.

Kicking the individual out of practice whose behavior is motivated by anxiety, would be a stress reducer for him. He would get what he wanted by avoiding practice. In effect, the coach who was behaving as if he believed he was punishing the athlete, was actually rewarding him.

Given that the majority of contingencies are identified, it becomes easier to develop a procedure for controlling practice that responds to the underlying needs. In the example presented, the team might be asked to work together (in a non-punitive way) to come up with some ideas about how they might be able to reduce the horseplay. This process would allow them to have some responsibility and control and would begin to respond to that need.

The coach or psychologist could also take the special needs of the athletes into account without making a public display of it. They may be able to find ways to allow the hyperactive athlete to be productively active during lulls in practice. They are also likely to find that the fooling around for this athete will be dramatically reduced as the team stops reinforcing it (inciting to riot and adding to the attentional overload) because the team decides that they want to make more effective use of practice. In addition, as the anxious athlete finds other ways of dealing with his tension, he will no longer serve as the instigator, starting something that the other athletes own activity level keeps going.

The anxious athlete's behavior could be modified in a number of ways. A direct way (this assumes his is aware that he is anxious) would be to get him to employ some relaxation technique instead of horseplay. Another way would be to allow for some fooling around after a difficult part of practice has been negotiated. This fooling around period would be time limited, and would be engaged in by all of the athletes and the coach.

In the behavioral management situation, the sport psychologist establishes the best way to handle the behavior and then leaves the follow-through to the team and coach. Unfortunately, there are dangers associated with the use of these techniques and some of them have been identified above. When inappropriately applied, it is usually because reinforcement contingencies have been too concretely focused

113

on surface behaviors and on modifying these. Contingencies have not been looked at closely enough to see what the underlying motivations are (something that has to be deduced from behavioral observations). Because the techniques seem fairly simple it is not uncommon to see individuals who become behavioral engineers, oblivious to (at times openly against) the importance of underlying factors. It is on these occasions that we hear athletes cry out about "fascist" techniques.

One more example may help to illustrate the problems. It can be shown by research that getting athletes to make public statements about personal goals in training will increase work output and performance. One technique then of a behavioral management sort might be to use this bit of information in an attempt to increase productivity.

Although it is quite likely that an examination of the entire team's productivity following such a process would result in an overall increase, there would be some individuals for whom this would not be the case. A very important underlying factor that needs to be considered in this situation is the level of self-esteem of the athlete, as well as his/her ability to establish realistic goals. If the coach is not sensitive to these issues, there will be individuals who will place unreasonable expectancies upon themselves and who will increase pressure to the point (having to live up to the expectancies that the team now has for them) of insuring failure. *The global application of any technique or principle or rule is inappropriate and dangerous!* The danger in teaching a few principles to a coach which might allow him/her to develop his/her own behavioral programs is that he/she may have a tendency (due to a lack of experience and knowledge about individual differences) to over generalize.

Before getting into some of the other areas in which sport psychologists might train others to provide psychological services, it would be useful to discuss a couple of the ethical principles which should be used to guide behavior. These principles have direct application to the situations described above.

1. It is the psychologist's responsibility to make sure that the information provided will not be misused.
2. The psychologist must communicate in a clear, concise, unambiguous way, and he/she must place any interpretations that are drawn within specific situational parameters. To prevent misuse of programs or information, the psychologist must specify the explicit circumstances under which those programs apply.
3. The psychologist has a responsibility to protect the public from the abuse or misuse of psychological techniques.

It is possible to teach individuals to apply psychological techniques in an effective, safe way within specific situations. I believe that techniques such as progressive relaxation, behavior modification, hypnosis, self-hypnosis, some types of psychological assessment, and crisis intervention, can be taught to coaches and athletes in a way which protects the public. *If* the applications have been clearly identified, *if* the situations

114

within which the techniques are to be used are highly circumscribed, *if* the individual can be trusted to follow the outlined procedures, and *if* supervision is available from a qualified sport psychologist, it is to our advantage to teach others to apply some of our knowledge.

At this point, I should state that my feelings about teaching individuals to use hypnosis and self-hypnosis are at odds with many of the members of the International Society of Clinical and Experiment Hypnosis. It is the feeling of a large number of the members of this group that individuals without professional training cannot have the background necessary to deal with the special nature of the trance, and the unexpected things that may develop as a function of being hypnotized.

As the example that follows illustrates, I am only too aware of some of the problems that can develop through the use of hypnosis. Nevertheless, I do not believe the ethical standards of the American Psychological Association preclude teaching others to use these techniques, though they do require that if we do, we take every step possible to insure the protection of the public.

Several years ago I wrote a book titled *The Inner Athlete*. One of the chapters in the book dealt with the application of hypnosis to athletics. Included in the chapter was an example of a hypnotic induction technique. The book received fairly wide circulation among coaches and athletes (as well as professionals) and I did my best to present some of the dangers and limitations of the various techniques that were discussed.

Approximately four years after the book was published, I received a call from a diving coach who worked with elite divers. This individual indicated that he had been applying the hypnotic techniques I discussed for purposes of helping divers relax, to develop good imagery of their dives, and to increase motivation and feelings of well being. All of these things had gone very well but recently some things started happening which the coach indicated he didn't understand. He asked if I would be willing to provide some direction for him because he wasn't sure where he should go with the hypnosis.

When I arrived on the scene, the coach relayed the following story. The team had been using hypnosis on a regular basis for several months and by this time, there were a number of members on the team who were excellent subjects. The coach had divided the team up into two groups: those who went under very quickly (in the time it took him to count backwards from 10 to 1 very rapidly), and those who had more difficulty, taking longer and not becoming as deeply hypnotized.

One day during practice, a member of the easily hypnotized group was standing on the 10 meter tower when she suddenly had what appeared to be an epileptic seizure. The coach had no idea what had happened, since the diver had no history of seizures. The coach ran up the ladder to the top of the tower and not knowing what else to do told the diver he was going to "take her down," the coach's language for putting her in a trance. He then counted quickly from 10 to 1 and the diver's seizure disappeared. She responded to questions as she would in a trance, she was relaxed, felt fine, and when he woke her up she continued practice without further incident (and without incident to this day, more than a year later).

It was not too long after this experience, which started the coach's wheels turning, that one of his divers had an accident on the trampoline. He landed on the frame, hitting one of his legs very hard. He was in considerable pain and the coach decided to use the hypnosis to attempt to reduce the pain. As before, he hypnotized the athlete and told him that the pain would lessen and that his leg would begin feeling better. The suggestions seemed to work and both the athlete and coach were amazed at the speed with which the redness went away, at the fact that very little swelling occurred, and at the fact that bruises didn't develop. This was an athlete with a high tolerance for pain under normal circumstances, so the fact that he was feeling the pain to begin with indicated that he had indeed hit very hard.

Finally, the divers were at a national competition when one of them landed flat on her back after attempting a reverse two-and-one-half somersault off the ten meter tower. The damage that can be done hitting the water from so high up with the speed and rotation involved in the dive is considerable. Individuals have separated shoulders, detached retinas, broken most of the peripheral blood vessels in the contact areas, split open scrotums, etc. This particular diver was in considerable pain when she was taken out of the water. Again the coach hypnotized her and dramatically reduced the pain. In fact, the diver was able to continue and executed the best back two-and-one-half of her life on the very next diver off the tower. The following day there was some soreness and stiffness, but nothing like what would have been expected given the landing on the dive.

All of these things were related to hypnosis, and both the coach and the divers were beginning to wonder what magic and what promise hypnosis might hold. They began to experiment with suggestions and the coach found himself in a counseling role with one of his divers. She began to talk with him about personal experiences that were troublesome to her. It was at this point that I was called.

Clearly the coach began to apply hypnosis in areas where his expertise was limited. He was not a psychotherapist and was not qualified to use hypnosis as a counseling or therapy technique. Likewise, although he knew a great deal about human physiology, he was not a physician. His attempts to use hypnosis to deal with pain and with a seizure, though successful up to this point, could lead to problems if suggestions covered up serious medical problems. The coach needed the supervision and involvement of medical experts to use hypnosis in this way.

Finally, and perhaps even more importantly than the above, the coach was becoming a true believer in a technique. He was almost becoming convinced that somehow hypnosis could alter human poten-

116

tial and make his divers capable of things that they couldn't normally do.

As I observed one of the coach's practices, I had the opportunity to see one of his thirteen-year-old divers ready to execute for the first time, a three-and-one-half somersault in the pike position, off the ten meter tower. The dive is one of the most difficult any diver can do and here was a thirteen-year-old about to do it.

To assist the diver the coach employed two techniques that are fairly commonly used. First, when the diver got on top of the tower and signaled to the coach that he was ready, the coach "counted him off." This involved counting fairly quickly from one to five with the diver knowing that on five he is to go. What the counting does is help the diver redirect attention away from his anxiety and fear. Without this redirection, rational thought might tell him he was crazy to launch his body off the tower. The counting provides a new focus, keeping him out of his head. In many ways it accomplishes the same type of attention shift that hypnosis does. The final count of five is a command to go and the diver has agreed to give that control to the coach. As a result, on five he goes.

The thirteen-year-old heard five and without blinking and without hesitation ran to the edge of the tower and threw himself into the dive. The second technique came into play just before the diver hit the water.

The coach, watching the dive, yells at the diver to tell him when to open. In effect the diver has placed total trust in the coach. He believes that the coach will yell at the appropriate time (not to soon and not to late) and that he will open on cue.

Watching the diver I could see that for all practical purposes he was in a hypnotic like state during this experience, in spite of the fact that no formal induction procedure had been used, and in spite of the fact that neither the diver nor the coach identified this set of conditions as hypnosis. Because the two of them hadn't seen what was going on as a special state of consciousness, however, they were not likely to abuse it.

With the techniques of counting and calling the diver out, both coach and athlete were very familiar. Because they didn't attribute special powers to these techniques, they openly used them when the athlete was really ready for a dive. This meant that all of the lead ups for the dive had been accomplished. Both coach and athlete knew that the physical and mental skills were there and that the dive could be safely executed.

Unfortunately, with hypnosis, because neither coach nor diver knew the limitations of the techniques, there was a danger of assuming it could be used to help the diver do something for which he wasn't physically and/or mentally ready. Unreasonable goals and expectancies were likely to be set that could result in permanent injury if a diver attempted something before he was ready.

It is all of these concerns which lead many professionals to insist that hypnosis is not a technique that can be safely used by the general public. Fortunately, in the case cited above the coach called and asked for some supervision. He was thoughtful, concerned himself, and very responsive to suggestions. He was able to listen to my concerns and he was very responsive to limiting his use of hypnosis to highly specified situations — situations that made use of his expertise and skill and that involved the mechanics and execution of dives. Hypnosis was used to help the athletes maintain arousal levels that would facilitate their performance. Hypnosis was used to help them relax and feel good about an upcoming contest. Finally, following the consultation hypnosis was used to help them image various dives, and to detect and correct problem areas. The coach avoided counseling and the treatment of injury.

With behavioral procedures, I emphasized the possibility of making mistakes because of oversimplifying, assuming that less was involved than is likely to be the case. In some ways the types of mistakes that occur with hypnosis are similar even though the hypnotist may assume that more is involved (e.g., the supernatural) than is the case.

Hypnosis is often described as a heightened state of suggestibility. Because of preconceived attitudes and attentional changes (which will be discussed in Chapter 16), the subjects are more likely to respond to suggestions than they would under more "normal" conditions. Many times the hypnotist is not aware of some of the important predetermining factors. Like the behavioral engineer who fails to see the underlying insecurity in the athlete, or the control battle going on between athlete and coach, the hypnotist concretely assumes that the material that will influence hypnosis is all going to occur in the trance.

I remember standing in front of a class of about 400 students one time and doing a group induction. Prior to hypnotizing the class I asked if people had any questions. I wanted to able to reassure them with respect to any misapprehensions that they might have had. Someone asked about the possibility of not waking up on command. I told them that "that is highly unlikely but should it occur, or should you still feel hypnotized, tell me and I will go through the wake up procedure one more time and you will be wide awake."

During the hypnosis I noticed that a woman in the front row seemed to be an exceptional subject. She had responded very rapidly and completely to all of the suggestions that I made. Following the demonstration, I awoke the class and they were all excitedly talking about what it had felt like and so on. As I looked at the woman she seemed dazed. After a few minutes she said "something is not right, I feel funny." I had forgotten what I had said prior to the induction so I responded by saying "Sometimes people get very relaxed and it takes a few minutes for the blood to get circulating again. Why don't you stretch and move around a bit and if you are still not awake at the end of class I'll walk you back to my office and wake you up."

At the end of class she told me that she was still feeling funny. When I asked her to stand up she seemed disoriented and had to hold on to me. She was dizzy and had difficulty walking to my office.

118

This type of experience had never happened to me before and inside I was shaken. I didn't know what was going on. When we got back to the office I had her sit down and went through the procedure of waking her up again. I did this primarily because I didn't know what else to do, but I did not have much faith that it would work. To my surprise and hers, she smiled, seemed totally alert, felt great and walked out happy as could be. As I thought back on the experience I realized that this woman had been influenced by the question that had been asked earlier by someone else, as well as by my response. In effect, she had responded to a "prehypnotic" suggestion not to wake up. She needed me to count twice. Had I not remained outwardly calm, I could have upset the woman a great deal.

In spite of the dangers that do exist, steps can be taken to insure the safety of athletes when coaches or other athletes are taught to use psychological tools. It is a mistake and an injustice to assume that a specific type of education (e.g., training as a psychologist) automatically qualifies a person to apply psychological techniques safely and ethically. Likewise, it is a mistake to assume that an absence of professional training insures that a person is incapable of responding in a safe, ethical fashion.

I doubt that many people would argue that extensive professional training will not increase the ability of an individual to make sounder judgments about the application of psychological techniques. In fact, it is our conviction that this is the case which has caused us to develop training programs and certification standards for psychologists, physicians, coaches, and trainers. High quality performance, however, depends upon natural talent, sensitivity, flexibility, intelligence, as well as formal training and experience. Ideally, whether or not a person is qualified to employ or use a particular technique should be evaluated on the basis of the individual situation.

What are the abilities and characteristics that we assume professionals have which give them license to determine whether or not to use a particular psychological tool?

1. We assume that they have a broad theoretical background that provides them with a sound conceptual base for identifying crucial factors that are affecting behavior. They understand something about human behavior, learning, motivation, cognition, psychopathology.

2. We assume that they are sensitive to "general laws of learning" but that they are equally sensitive to individual differences. They recognize that there are no "universal truths" and they know the importance of being aware of the exceptions to the general rules.

3. Professionals are sensitive to their own limits. They recognize the constraints that are placed on their ability to function effectively and ethically by economics, their own limited knowledge relative to certain techniques, subject populations, situations, and their

own personal abilities. They are aware of the restraints and limitations that are placed on them by the people they must work with and for.

4. Professionals are sensitive to the fact that the conclusions and inferences they draw about human behavior are subject to a variety of sources of measurement error. Cultural, social, interpersonal, personal and situational factors can all influence the conclusions that are drawn. For this reason the professional is careful to consensually validate findings and to place any conclusions drawn into carefully circumscribed situations.

5. Professionals should have the ability and temperment that allows them to function well under pressure, to think on their feet, to deal with the unexpected in a logical way.

6. Above all else, the professionals set their own needs below those of the individual they serve. The health and happiness of the athlete comes first. The professional will not abuse an athlete in order to win.

Each of the points listed above should be considered in determining what skills can be taught to, and turned over to a coach or athlete. They are all important, but especially the last one. I remember a coach telling me that the reason he was coaching diving was for the recognition it brought him. What he wanted was to get a diver to do something that no other diver in the world had ever done. His priorities were to respond to his own needs before the diver's. There was a real danger that he would abuse a diver in order to accomplish his personal goal. With this kind of individual I would be very cautious about turning over any psychological techniques.

As a professional providing training, you can be seen as certifying the competence of an individual to perform certain functions or services. This perception is created by the very fact that you provided the training. You don't have to provide a diploma or anything else. When the public hears that Dr. X trained me in the use of hypnosis that amounts to being certified in their eyes.

As a profession, we have recognized the need to train others to deliver services. Cities throughout the world employ volunteers, non-professionals, to provide crisis intervention services to suicidal patients. Hospitals make use of patients, volunteers, and non-professional staff to deliver a wide variety of medical and psychological services. Community psychology focuses on the use of para-professionals in the prevention and treatment of a wide variety of personal, social, and organizational problems.

In the vast majority of instances, the training of para-professionals to provide psychological services has more than justified itself. This justification is true in the field of sport psychology as well as in the field of clinical psychology. The sport psychologist can provide a tremendous service by training and supervising others in the delivery of services.

This training must be done responsibly, however, and with the protection of the athlete who is to be the recipient of the service in mind.

There are no hard and fast rules about the type of training that should be offered, to whom it should be offered or under what conditions. Each situation must be judged on its own merits, and the sport psychologist can make that judgment by considering the following recommendations, and most importantly by checking his/her own judgments with those of professional colleagues.

1. Operationalize the referral question. What is it that the individual wants to be trained in? As a part of this process, what are the specific goals of training? These must be operationalized (e.g., to keep anxiety under control just prior to competition) and delimited. By delimited, I mean the sport psychologist should attempt to anticipate some of the ways procedures might be inappropriately applied (e.g., hypnosis for counseling) and then sensitize the person being trained to this danger.

2. The individual being trained needs to be assessed along the dimensions presented earlier. The sport psychologist should attempt to see the extent of their theoretical understanding (what they already know, what they need to learn). Are they sensitive to individual differences, are they adequately concerned about the well being of the athlete, do they recognize their own limits, will they stick to the limits you suggest, do they have the ability to deal with the unexpected in a cool, rational, way? Will they ask for help when it is needed?

3. What are the consequences of providing training, and of refusing? What impact will the sport psychologist's involvement, or lack of it, have on the well being of the athletes?

4. What opportunity is there for the sport psychologist to teach? How much time can be given to develop the skills, theoretical understanding, sensitivity to individual differences, etc. that will allow the trainee to function safely?

5. Be as specific and concrete as you can in defining the conditions under which a given technique is to be used. Tell the trainee very explicitly: a) what the procedure is to be used for; b) when the procedure is to be used; c) why the procedure is being used; d) on whom the procedure should be used.

6. Make sure that training includes supervised practicum experience as well as teaching the theory that underlies the procedure and the technique itself. For example, give the trainee the opportunity to apply the technique themselves under supervised conditions, gradually giving them more responsibility and freedom.

7. Make sure that there is opportunity for follow-up and periodic supervision. Make sure that procedures have been established for dealing with the unexpected. Who do you call, where do you go?

8. Provide the individuals with training materials. These may be books, workbooks, audio tapes, etc. The point is he should have material available which reminds him of the critical points and keeps him focused on the original goals of training. The material should help him be more sensitive to his own limitations.

12

CRISIS INTERVENTION

For purposes of this chapter, a crisis within sport psychology involves any situation in which an athlete, or coach, is out of control of their own behavior. It is a situation that requires some type of outside intervention in order for the individual to regain control over feelings and the ability to perform.

Using this definition, there is not an individual in the world who at one time or another isn't "in crisis." In this chapter I intend to look at crisis situations in sport from the theoretical perspective presented in chapter 4. Using this framework it is easy to understand what happens to athletes under extreme pressure. It also becomes relatively simple to identify those characteristics that differentiate athletes who "choke" frequently, from those who function very well under rather extreme pressure. Finally, the inter-relationship between attentional processes, stress, and physical performance, provides the information necessary to develop intervention strategies.

There are two jobs that the sport psychologist may be called upon to engage in when it comes to crisis intervention. First, he/she may be required to provide those services himself/herself, and to recognize when and how a referral should be made to some other resource. Next, the sport psychologist may be asked to train coaches and athletes to provide crisis intervention services. This chapter has been written to assist the sport psychologist in providing both services. The first part of the chapter deals with the general theory and the implications the theory has for treatment and training of others. The second part of the chapter consists of a set of training materials that I use to teach others to provide crisis counseling.

In addition to being a loss of control, crisis situations are often seen as unexpected (although as some of the examples will indicate, some of them should be expected). Something traumatic occurs and it interferes with the athlete's ability to make decisions, to perform physically, or to concentrate. Examples would include events such as a death in the family. Howard Davis, a boxer for the U.S. in the 1976 Olympics, almost dropped out of the competition because of the death of his mother.

A diver who comes up to me just before the finals in the tower competition, telling me she can't think of anything except wiping out on her reverse-two-and-one-half somersault, is in crisis. The baseball player who feels socially isolated and suddenly leaves the team to go home to his family is also in crisis. The athlete whose marriage breaks up or whose love affair ends, often can't concentrate and is in crisis. Athletes who lose control over their own anger, yelling at people, charging the pitcher with a bat, risking ejection from the game, lawsuits, etc., are in crisis. Athletes who get angry at themselves and begin pressing too hard, or give up altogether are in crisis.

Depending upon the sport, the crisis may not need to last for more than a few seconds. Obviously, there is a difference between the situation in which an athlete's homesickness causes him/her to leave training camp, and the situation in which a momentary loss of concentration causes a severe injury. Given enough time, the athlete who is well put together will usually regain control. Bjorn Borg's performance in the finals at Wimbleton in 1980 provides a good example of this last point.

Borg got involved in an extended tie-breaker with John McEnroe in the fourth set. During that tie-breaker Borg had match point seven times before he finally lost the tie-breaker to McEnroe. At that point, as they went into the fifth and final set, Borg thought he had lost. According to his own report it took two or three games before he finally put the negative thoughts out of his head and went on to win the championship for a fifth consecutive time.

Unfortunately, most situations do not allow enough time for individuals to work themselves out of them. All too often, poor decisions resulting from the pressure make matters worse, digging a hole for the athlete that he or she may never get out of.

Consider the shooter in international skeet that hit one hundred and ninety six targets out of a possible two hundred to qualify for the Olympic team in 1972. Then, during practice he missed a couple of targets at one particular station. Because of the pressure of the competition and the knowledge that it was now or never, those misses became very important in the athlete's mind. He began to question his own ability to hit that particular target. As a result, he went into the actual competition "psyched out" by his own anxiety. He knew that he would need to shoot between 196 and 198 out of 200 targets to win the competition. He missed a total of eleven targets, eight of them on the station that had been upsetting him.

This athlete had lost control in that he could not maintain concentration or performance under certain conditions. The loss of control extended over several years before he finally began to regain his ability to hit the target with acceptable frequency from that particular station.

What happens during a crisis? Actually, it is not difficult to understand what is going on. Pressure in a situation mounts, affecting both physical and psychological functioning of the athlete. What it is that affects pressure can vary dramatically from athlete to athlete as the examples indicate. For Howard Davis a crisis was precipitated by his mother's death; for Bjorn Borg, it was the loss of a critical tie-breaker. As I discussed in chapter 4, the result is an increase in physiological arousal and alterations in concentration. The physiological changes that occur

124

include increases in respiration rate and muscle tension which can affect fine motor coordination and timing thereby affecting performance. With respect to concentration, the crisis results in a narrowing of attention. Often, athletes begin to attend to their own fears, worries and/or to the physical changes that are going on. Because they can't attend to important performance related cues, they begin to have difficulty.

As the situation worsens, attentional changes and physical changes feed on each other creating a downward spiral that results in further decrements in performance. The inability to concentrate and perform is upsetting to athletes, raising arousal even more and results in impairment in their ability to make decisions in logical rational ways. It is at this time that they are likely to charge the pitchers mound, or to take the first plane home. Their own attentional processes have become so controlled by arousal and by external factors, that they often cannot regain control on their own. At least, not until it is too late. If they are to survive and do their best, the coach or sport psychologist must intervene and help them regain control over their ability to concentrate and their level of arousal. The coach who calls time out to calm a player down before a critical free throw or an extra point or field goal is practicing crisis intervention. Whether or not the technique works will depend upon the athlete and the coach's intervention.

EFFECTIVE VS. INEFFECTIVE PERFORMERS

We can measure the physical and psychological responses that an athlete has to a crisis situation in terms of frequency with which they occur, the intensity of the responses, and the duration or length of time that they last. Although virtually every athlete will be in crisis from time to time, there are some very important differences between individuals in terms of the frequency, intensity, and duration of their reactions.

If we divide athletes up conceptually into three groups, those who choke, those who play well under normal amounts of pressure, and those who are extremely cool under pressure, we find the following differences. First, athletes who "choke" tend to have higher levels of trait anxiety. Since their overall level of anxiety is higher, they have less autonomic flexibility. For them, the difference in heart-rate, muscle tension levels, respiration rate, etc., is smaller than it is for the other two groups when measured in both low and high arousing situations.

A second difference that occurs involves the frequency with which athletes lose control over their own mental and physical processes. The higher the athlete's level of trait anxiety, the less capable he or she is of dealing with a large amount of external and internal information (the less flexible his/her attention), and the more complex his/her sport, the more frequent the problems. Some athletes are playing so close to the top of their potential under what would be considered nonstressful conditions for ninety percent of the population, that they have very little room for any distractions or increases in pressure. It is this group of

125

athletes that is seen as choking under pressure. The normal group of athletes has more flexibility and for this reason does not lose control nearly so often. The super athlete seems to be able to function even under extreme pressure. This ability is seen for a couple of reasons. In some instances, they have practiced skills to the point of those skills becoming reflexive. For these individuals, anxiety and pressure are still experienced, but performance continues almost without thought because of the incredible amount of training. For others, there seems to be a lower overall level of anxiety and a greater capacity to maintain control over concentration under pressure. Often, the attentional control remains because their processing capacity is great enough that it takes extreme amounts of pressure before it has been sufficiently reduced to affect performance.

A third difference that separates athletes involves the duration of the crisis experience. As my example with the skeet shooter illustrated, it is possible for a situation to continue to influence an athlete for years. Baseball hitting slumps, putting woes in golfing, free throw shooting, etc. are all long term reactions to pressure. In these situations, however, the athlete's reaction comes and goes quickly as the situation changes. The golfer may have putting interfered with, but then hit a great drive. The basketabll player recovers from the free throw miss in time to play great defense. Finally, the skeet shooter recovers in time to shoot adequately from the very next station. It is not simply the length of time that a problem continues or reoccurs that we are talking about when discussing duration.

Duration refers to the length of time that the individual is out of control in reaction to a single instance. Athletes who choke for example, tend to get overly anxious long before an event occurs and this anxiety interferes with concentration and performance sometimes for days prior to the actual competition. A great many athletes have difficulty carrying on a conversation with their spouses just prior to a game, or engaging in tasks that require thought. There are some for whom these disturbances begin days or weeks in advance.

For the super performer, arousal and disturbances in concentration peak prior to an event and then drop off rapidly just as the event is about to start. David Riggert, the Russian weight lifter provides a good example. An hour before a competition, and up to just a few minutes before he walks out to lift, measures of blood pressure and heart-rate indicate very high levels of arousal. It is as if the Russian is psyching himself up. Then, just before he actually lifts the weight, heart-rate and blood pressure drop dramatically. For the super performer, the crisis occurs prior to the event and, thus, is not a crisis at all. For the individual who chokes, disturbances in muscle tension and concentration continue well into and often through the entire competition. Average athletes fall someplace between these two groups. Typically, their performance is slightly interfered with early on, and then they begin to become involv-

126

ed in the competition and as a result gain control over attention and arousal.

Differences between athletes in the frequency, intensity, and duration of their losses of control have important implications for treatment. Generally speaking, the athlete who chokes has a much lower level of self-esteem and requires more external support and direction than the athlete who does not choke (frequently). Those individuals with high levels of trait anxiety require more extended treatment before they can make the personal changes needed in order to maintain control. Often, it is easier to make alterations in the environment (change the performance demands) than it is to change the athlete.

From a prognosis standpoint, the long term outlook for the choker is much worse than it is for the average and above average performer. At the same time, the short term prognosis is better. Since the super performers do not experience a crisis very often, when they do lose control the impact of the experience can be rather dramatic. These individuals are much more likely to engage in some impulsive emotional response that may be more harmful to themselves than is the case for the athlete who chokes. Failure to atheltes who are accustomed to falling apart is nothing new. They don't like it, but they have grown used to it.

Behavior during the crisis is often easier to manage in the case of athletes who choke than it is for super performers. The super performers are used to being in control and they will resist the help of outsiders even when they are coming unglued. Their pride and their need to be on top causes them to see any loss of control as a weakness, something that they cannot tolerate. When coaches or teammates try to intervene to calm them down, the anger that they have been directing towards themselves for losing control becomes directed at the helpers.

RECOGNIZING A CRISIS AS IT DEVELOPS

One of the obvious keys to prevention of a loss of control, is the early detection of rising levels of arousal and disturbances in concentration. There are several signals that the sport psychologist or coach can watch for:

1. Watch for any change in the athlete's normal level of arousal. A dramatically increased activity level, or the inability to sit still is often a sign of anxiety. Interestingly enough there are a large number of athletes who respond to increasing pressure with a parasympathetic response. These individuals become drowsy and even fall asleep just before competition. Often they will complain about not being up. They are defending against their own anxiety by physiological and psychological withdrawal. Obviously, the treatment for the two will need to differ dramatically, the second person does need to become more aroused.

2. Watch for increased tension in muscles particularily in the upper body and neck. You may see athletes working on their arms and

127

shoulders moving them up and down or swinging them to reduce the tension. In some instances you may literally see the shoulders raise up almost pinching against the neck. Should these changes occur, treatment may focus on reversing them since they will interfere with performance in a large number of competitive situations.

3. Watch for changes in breathing. The more anxious athletes become the more likely respiration rate will increase and breathing will become rapid and shallow. In addition, instead of breathing from down in the diaphragm, athletes will breathe from up in the chest. This acts to increase muscle tension and to create sensations of lightheadedness, dizzyness, nausea, etc. Note, this is not the deep gasping for breath that comes with extreme exertion or oxygen debt. This is more like a panting and athletes need to reduce the amount of air that they are taking in.

4. For many athletes increasing arousal is accompanied by small twitching movements in the face. Pay particular attention to the muscles in the chin and around the eyes.

5. Often there are increases in jaw muscle tension. We talk about the "set jaw" of an athlete. For some, this can be a sign that they are concentrating, for others it can herald a loss of control. In extreme cases, athletes may begin grinding their teeth (often at night before major competitions) and tension may be strong enough that they end up with headaches and neckaches. Because certain sports (e.g., luge racing) require positions that may lead to this type of problem, dentists have come up with mouthpieces to reduce this type of pressure and these have been associated with improvements in performance. (See *Sports Illustrated*, June, 1980).

6. Many athletes exhibit anxiety through alterations in their ability to shift attention. Some (those who are more analytical) become preoccupied, unresponsive to questions or things going on around them. Others (those with an external style of attention that dominates) tend to become highly distractable, unable to stick to a subject for any length of time. Watching the two groups you see one that is almost immobile, sitting quietly or walking into things because it is so lost in thought. In the other group, heads are in constant motion as their eyes shift from one thing to another. As with all of the changes being discussed, the sport psychologist is looking for a deviation from the normal behavior of a given individual, not for a deviation from the "average" person. The athlete is being compared to himself/herself under high and low stress conditions, not to others.

7. There are a number of responses like yawns, stretching, laughing and crying that are natural tension reducers. Increases in the frequency of these, increases in smoking, drinking, and eating are all associated with increasing arousal.

Every athlete has what is for him or her, a normal range for each of these behaviors. The differences between athletes in terms of the "normal" frequency of these responses is remarkable. Some individuals twitch all of the time and it means nothing, others almost never twitch. The sport psychologist must know the athlete well enough to know what the normal frequency of a given behavior is for him/her. It would be a mistake to attempt to assess an individual's level of arousal on the basis of some general population norm for jaw muscle tension, facial twitches, or respiration rate. What should be determined is when an athlete deviates enough from his/her own pattern that their performance begins to get interfered with. This deviation can only be detected through multiple observations under a number of different competitive conditions. This is one of the reasons that a coach may be in a better position to recognize an athlete's needs rather than a sport psychologist.

REGAINING CONTROL

The athlete, to regain control, must somehow break the feedback loop that has developed between attentional processes and physiological changes. Somehow he/she must free up concentration (getting out of his/her head and ignoring the physical arousal) in order to let arousal levels come down.

1. *Don't overload* the athlete with information. Under high levels of tension and in crisis situations, an individual's attention begins to narrow and to become less focused on task-relevant cues. Because the normal capacity to process information is reduced, it is important that the sport psychologist avoid providing too much information. Even if the athlete is requesting an analysis of what has happened, a discussion of the problem and all of its complexities should be avoided. "We'll talk about that later, right now you need to . . . ."

2. *Provide structure* and direction for the athlete. Give him/her one or two things to concentrate on and be very specific and operational. *Don't* give a general instruction like "concentrate."

3. *Get feedback:* To make sure the athletes heard what was said to them, ask them to repeat the instructions. It is a mistake to assume they heard. Often a blank stare (particularly when the coach or psychologist is also anxious) is interpreted as understanding. Likewise, nods of the head can be reflexive. A coach may ask "Do you understand?" and while asking the question the coach is nodding affirmatively. The athlete just nods along with the coach independent of what the coach says. If the coach shook his/her head no, the athlete would follow.

4. *Make eye contact and physical contact.* Look athletes in the eyes and make sure that they are seeing you. Nod your head to see if they follow in a way that makes sense, find out if they are responding to your words (by asking a question that requires a yes) or to your actions (by nodding no). Physical contact is important

129

because kinesthetic cues tend to dominate and grab attention. Put your hands on the athletes shoulders or their cheeks and grasp them firmly enough that they come out of their head. Often all that is required is a gentle shake. Don't make the mistake of slapping them around when they don't need it. There are times when contact is required (like a shake), but very rarely does it reach the proportions displayed in Hollywood where the actor slaps the hysterical actress.

5. *Direct attention to a couple of task relevant cues.* During the performance situation, the athletes attention should be focused on one or two performance related cues that set up an entire motor sequence. In diving, for example, concentration on the hurdle step may be all that is required to successfully execute a dive. If the diver knows the dive he/she is to do and then concentrates only on getting the lift out of the board (on a good hurdle step), the rest of the dive will automatically follow without conscious thought, including any corrections that need to be made because of problems with the hurdle step. The dive has been learned well enough that it is an automatic response. Likewise, hitters in baseball need to attend to the ball, they don't need to be thinking about other things in order to hit. Their swing is an automatic response given that they are attending to the appropriate cue (the ball). Other things can be thought about in practice and under less stressful conditions. During a tough competitive situation stick to the critical cue'(s).

6. *Distract the athlete:* During breaks in performance, if athletes are upset and preoccupied with their failure or their fear of failure, distract them. For those athletes who are low in self-esteem this means directing attention to neutral or pleasant cues, dissociating from the situation. For athletes who are high in self-esteem distraction can be accomplished by challenging them to think about what they are going to do to the other competitor or getting them to think about what is going on around them, rather than feeling sorry for themselves or getting down on themselves. "You are your own worst enemy, they won't beat you, you'll beat yourself. Stop crying and lets plan what you are going to do next." In contrast, with the low self-esteem person you might say "Don't worry about it, it will be okay. Lets get a drink and forget about it. Tell me what you are planning to do after this competition is over. Will you be seeing your girl friend? Where are you going to go?"

   The difference between these two types of responses is very important. To stay with performance relevant discussion, or to belittle the athletes who have low levels of self-esteem only provides them with additional material they can use to get down on themselves, it doesn't help.

7. *Legitimize the response:* Too often athletes feel that they are the

only ones who are having problems. They get down on themselves for being upset. Some support and statements like "The feelings you are having are normal," "anyone in your situation would be feeling the same things," can be helpful. It is also helpful if they know that you can really empathize with them because you have experienced similar things.

8. *Maintain some physical activity:* This does not mean wear the athlete out by having him/her run wind sprints. It does mean that some pre-game exercises could be helpful. Likewise, just getting the athlete to laugh and to get out of his/her head can be very helpful. The laughing is a tension reducer and the joke that he/she is responding to gets thoughts away from the anxiety inducers. Jumping up and down and yelling can also be methods for controlling tension.

Obviously, there are individual differences with respect to which of the above techniques will be most helpful. Likewise, there are differences in terms of what athletes see as funny. It will be important for the coach or sport psychologist to try out different methods and to be sensitive to individual differences.

The point of being sensitive to individual differences in terms of what arouses athletes and in terms of what calms them down cannot be overemphasized. Unfortunately, maintaining that sensitivity is not an easy task. This is especially true since crisis situations tend to be catching; they often increase the pressure on everyone. Let me use myself as an example:

I coached AAU age group diving and was fortunate enough to have a young diver with a tremendous amount of potential. Attentionally, this diver tended to have a narrow focus of concentration. He was extremely dedicated and practiced longer and harder than any of the other athletes. If he had a weakness, it was that he would over prepare. He was so concerned about perfection that he resisted any change in his list of dives. Even if I knew that he could execute a new dive in a competition and win, even if he blew the dive, he would resist taking the chance. I would be feeling that he needed some experience with a dive under competitive conditions and he would be fighting me. We both wanted him to win.

As a coach, my greatest attentional strength involved my ability to think analytically, to be sensitive to all of the technical aspects of diving, to the pressures of competition, and so on. The danger of this particular attentional style was that I was likely to overload athletes with technical information. This was especially true since I tend to express myself intellectually, enjoying discussions about the finer points of competition.

Both the diver I was working with and I had strong needs to be in control in competitive situations. This control-need meant that if there were any hint that we might lose control, our arousal levels would increase considerably.

Under the best of conditions (when both of us were relaxed), I had a

131

tendency to provide too much information to the diver and to push him too fast. This tendency would become worse in competition. Because I had a strong need for control, I would try and hang on to it as long as I could. When he would go up on the board to dive I would be stressed because I would be out of control.

One of the reasons attention narrows under stressful conditions is that there is a breakdown in the ability to shift from an external to an internal focus. Some individuals become caught up in their thoughts and don't attend as well to what is going on around them. For others, just the reverse holds true. Since my dominate attentional style involved being analytical, I had a tendency to go inside my head, to analyze, and to pay less attention to what was going on around me. I would be thinking of all of the things I wanted the diver to do and all of the things I didn't want him to do. At a time when it was all he could do to pay attention to one thing, I would be reminding him of eight or ten.

Because my diver needed to control, he would attempt to remember all of the things I was saying. The end result was he couldn't concentrate on anything. Out of my own anxiety and need to retain control, I was hurting more than helping.

For the coach or sport psychologist who has his/her identity tied up with the performance of an athlete, that person's loss of control can be very threatening. The coach needs the athlete to perform and the athlete needs the coach to retain control. When they perceive one or the other losing it, they both go down hill.

In succeeding chapters I will be discussing specific stress management techniques that can be used to both prevent and treat the problems associated with crisis situations. In the next few pages, however, I would like to present some of the materials that I use to train coaches to respond to crisis situations.

COUNSELING MANUAL

Over the years, psychologists have begun to move from the development of treatment approaches to sports-related problems, to the prevention of problems before they reach the point of requiring extensive intervention. A major part of this approach involves detecting potential problems at an early stage. In this way, treatment can begin before things get out of hand. Research has shown that in a relatively short period of time we can train coaches, athletes, parents, etc. to interviene and deal with most performance-related problems before they reach the point of requiring the services of a highly trained sports psychologist, or clinical psychologist. It is with this training goal in mind that the following manual was prepared.

This manual was written to be used by para-professionals. Any manual of this type should be backed by a training and supervisory staff that is available for consultation. Experience has indicated that minimal supervisory or consultative functions are necessary; however, those that are requested are usually indicative of a problem that is severe enough to demand immediate professional attention. In my own experience, I have found it productive to have an orientation session for coaches. During this session participants are encouraged to ask questions about the manual, we model and roleplay some of the counseling situations, and I provide a lot of support and positive feedback.

A major function of the orientation is to help the coach or athlete become aware of his/her own potential as a counselor. The level of his/her self-confidence (and ability to control his/her own arousal) in this situation is critical to his/her functioning. Generally speaking, the more confident appearing the coach the more effective is the counseling relationship. In the orientation session I attempt to increase the coach's level of confidence.

At a cognitive level, a sport psychologist can increase confidence by pointing out the fact that the coach has already functioned as a counselor in a great many situations. Athletes, friends, and family have come to him/her with problems and have asked for help. In most instances he/she has handled these requests very well. In addition, it can be emphasized that his/her sensitivity to the sports situation, to the pressures that performance places on the athlete, and to the demands of the competitive situation, places the coach in a much more helpful position than the sport psychologist who comes in as an outsider.

By being acquainted with the athlete, the coach already has established some trust and the "warm up" time required in establishing a helping relationship is eliminated. In addition, the coach or athlete counselor has an easier job of keeping the person he/she is helping, honest. The coach is more familiar with the individual and the particular situation and as a result he/she is less likely to be manipulated.

Finally, an orientation session with a group of coaches or athletes allows them to share their anxieties and concerns. Typically this results

133

in their becoming more supportive of each other. As they realize others have concerns (they felt they were the only ones before), they feel less alone. They recognize that often a calm front belies what is going on inside. They also begin to see that what is said is less important than how it is said. The end result is an increase in confidence as they see that they have a lot to offer.

INTRODUCTION

This manual is to acquaint you with some of the problems and procedures that you may encounter in "crisis" situations. The manual is at best a guide and cannot possibly cover all of the situations you will find yourself in. Hopefully these pages will serve two functions: First, they will help make you more comfortable and effective in dealing with out-of-control conditions. Finally, they will assist you in learning to discriminate between those problems you are capable of handling vs. those in which a trained professional should be involved.

THE PROBLEM SITUATION

Most of the problems that you will be asked to deal with can best be seen as acute, situational disturbances. That is, situations in which some immediate factor has created enough of an emotional and physical upset that it is interfering with the athlete's normal functioning. Some examples would include loss of a loved one, an injury, depression following a major competition, fear of failure, actual failure, homesickness, etc. Often, these stressful situations will lead to feelings of inadequacy and depression which then get attributed more broadly to the athlete's life. For example, failure in a competition may lead the individual to search for other failures in order to punish himself/herself. "I'm no good at anything, I let everyone down." In short, the athlete loses perspective and fails to be able to deal rationally with the real problem.

ROLE OF THE COUNSELOR

Most coaches or helpers enter a crisis situation with a strong desire to be of service — to help. If this is true for you, your need to be seen as a helping person, though an important asset, can also interfere with your ability to interact effectively with the athlete. It is important for you to take the time to look at your motivation, to analyze your reasons for becoming involved. The crisis situation is likely to arouse some strong feelings in you and you need to be able to anticipate how these will affect your behavior.

    1. An area in which you should keep a check on your feelings involves how confident you feel in a crisis situation. A moderate amount of anxiety is appropriate. Too much anxiety, however, will interfere. A major factor in the helping process is how confi-

dent you appear to the athlete. He/she needs to see you as capable of helping. If your own insecurity boils over it will be felt that your nervousness is a reflection of the severity of the athlete's problem, and as a result, he/she may lose hope.

Most of the insecurity you feel will be relieved by experience in providing crisis intervention services. In the meantime it would help you to remember that you have been attempting to deal with these problems already and in most instances have been able to do so with considerable success. Good counselors, teachers, coaches, and therapists share the ability to listen, to direct, and to motivate others. *You are capable.*

2. In the reverse direction, the motivation to help can be so strong and your own need for control can be so great, that you attempt to assume too many responsibilities. The misguided notion here is that you can be all things to all people. This "Jehovah" complex should be avoided and there are several factors involved here.

Occasionally, people in their eagerness to help and to reinstitute control create additional problems. When an athlete comes to you in trouble, you want to find a solution. Immediately the search begins for an explanation. Since we all have little quirks or behaviors that might be seen as unusual if attention were drawn to them, you can always find something wrong. I knew a coach who would immediately attempt to change a free throw shooter's style if he missed more than two free throw attempts in a row. He would inevitably find something which he felt would change things for the better. Too often he only made the athlete feel more awkward (he/she wasn't used to the changes and needed the rhythm provided by his/her little quirks). The athlete started out with no problem, or a relatively simple issue and the coach quickly complicated it. *Before making an intervention, think.* If at all possible, use the athlete to help you identify the difficulty. Above all, listen to what he/she has to say before you leap to conclusions. In a similar way, get the athlete to offer possible solutions.

Another problem that can occur as a function of the "Jahovah" complex is that athletes who need to learn to accept responsibility for their own behavior can avoid doing so by letting you accept it for them. A coach with a high need for control can find himself/herself making all of the athlete's decisions and this can rapidly become an overwhelming problem. Especially if the coach has several athletes with whom he/she must work.

YOUR JOB AS A COUNSELOR

By definition, a crisis in sport involves a situation in which the athlete is out of control. The athlete's ability to communicate effectively and to listen to what you have to say is dramatically affected by the pressure he/she is under. The more anxious and upset he/she is the greater his/her disability and the more difficult it will be for you to get the information you need to help him/her. Your job can be divided into three phases.

1. You must establish a relationship and obtain information. Even though you already have a relationship with the athlete, and even though a great deal of trust may exist, this can be affected by the loss of control. Individuals may find it difficult to let you down, to let you know what they are feeling. You will have to create the supportive acceptant conditions that will facilitate their self-disclosing. This means allowing them to talk and encouraging them. It means reflecting their feelings back to them and not offering solutions too quickly.
2. You must evaluate the severity of the problem. Do the feelings seem legitimate given the situation or is the athlete over-reacting?
3. You must decide upon or suggest a course of action.

ESTABLISH A RELATIONSHIP AND OBTAIN INFORMATION

Observe athletes talking and you will see that they tend to mirror each other. If one person talks softly so does the other, if one is excited so is the other, if one talks with long complicated sentences so does the other. This observation has great implications for crisis intervention. First, as a helper you need to make sure that you do not "mirror" the behavior of the individuals you are trying to help. At the same time, you can use this knowledge to control athletes. If they are anxious and talking rapidly you can modify that by talking slowly and softly. Here are some general rules to follow during your information gathering.

1. As has been mentioned, don't talk too much! Let athletes tell their story. Let them feel like they are being listened to. Pay attention to both what they say (the intellectual message) and how they say it (the emotional feelings). Try and respond to both what they think and how they feel.
2. Keep your sentences short, and ask only one question at a time. An anxious person is already confused. Long sentences, open ended questions, and multiple questions only make matters worse.
3. If athletes become distracted while answering a question gently remind them of where they were and ask them to continue. "Excuse me, John, I'm getting confused, you were saying . . . ." This will help you avoid becoming as confused as they are and at the same time will help them begin to sort things out.
4. In general, your tone should be "patient, interested, self-assured, optimistic, and knowledgeable."
5. Look at people when you talk to them. This helps them relax and it allows you to see if they are listening.
6. Respect the privacy of the individual. The amount of information you get from athletes will depend upon their trust in you. They

need to know that what they say will be kept in confidence.

7. Often it is easier for people to talk if they feel that you have experienced similar things and can empathize with them. If personalization of yourself is goal directed in that it can be used to assist the athlete in self-disclosing, or if it can be used to offer reassurance or support, then do it.

8. Finally, reflective statements can be helpful in getting athletes to talk and to clarify for themselves and for you, the nature of the problem. "Sometimes it hurts to talk." "You seem to be saying. . . ." "That must have made you very angry." "Do I have this right, if I were in that situation I'd be feeling . . . ."

In just listening to athletes you are already helping them in several ways: 1) You are showing them that you are interested in them and that you care. 2) They begin to feel that they are not alone, that someone else understands them. 3) You are helping them state a problem and it may be the first time that they have been able to clearly look at it. This may dramatically alter it's effect on them. Typically, they find out that things are not nearly as bad as imagined.

Once a problem has been stated you may need to gather more information to place it in the proper perspective. Typically, when athletes become upset and depressed, their whole outlook becomes negative. They inhibit any positive thoughts about their life. Suddenly it is not just raining where they are, but as far as they are concerned it's raining all over the world. *If you are to help, it is important that you be able to avoid adopting this narrowed perspective,* a perspective that keeps athletes from having hope or from finding solutions on their own.

There are some "sunny" spots in the world and these need to be discovered in order to place the crisis situation in perspective. The best way to obtain this balance is *not* by pointing out the good things. Instead, you should ask questions which will get athletes to relate the good things to you. As you ask questions you should be attempting to accomplish two things: 1) You want to widen the athlete's perspective so that he/she begins to see that his/her whole world or athletic future is not coming down. 2) The questions allow you to assess how serious the problem is. Depending upon the answers you will get a feeling for the resources that the athlete has available to deal with the problem. You will find out how many positive experiences he/she has had, how much success, how much support.

EVALUATE THE PROBLEM

There are several criteria that you can use to evaluate the seriousness of an athlete's problem as well as his/her ability to cope. All of us have problems at one time or another and all of us will act to at least some degree in the ways that will be mentioned. Thus, in evaluating a person on the basis of the criteria below you must consider the appropriateness of the behavior (tears are reasonable if an athlete has just failed in a competition for which they have been preparing for a year), as well as the intensity and duration of it.

1. *Mood or affect.* The emotions or affect of an athlete can be judged on two dimensions: 1) Appropriateness, is the person reacting to the situation as you would expect? Generally, the more inappropriate the emotions the more serious the problem. Example would include laughter instead of tears, or perhaps a total denial of feelings, when given the circumstances the athlete should be very upset. 2) Strength of feelings: If the athlete sounds tired, washed out, and depressed, the problem may be more serious than if they are in control. At the other end of an activity continuum, exuberance, rapid talking, confusion, irrational thinking yelling, etc. would be considered omnious. In this instance it would be important to get the athlete to a professional as quickly as possible.

2. *Acute vs. Chronic.* If the athlete has a chronic history of low self-esteem, or of one crisis followed by another, the long term prognosis for significant change is fairly poor. On the other hand, he/she is likely to get over the existing trauma without serious difficulty. He/she has had experience dealing with these problems in the past. For the athlete who has never experienced a loss of control or crisis the reverse is true. The long term prognosis is excellent, the short term prognosis however, is more guarded. This individual has more difficulty understanding what is going on and thus may be more upset by it.

3. *Resources.* If an athlete has no past successes to fall back on, or if athletics has been their total life and suddenly that life is taken away (retirement injury, etc.) adjustment can be very difficult. The athlete who is going through a depression following the end of their athletic career often needs some fairly long term counseling and support to find a new direction for his/her energy. The fewer the resources in terms of friends, personal options, family, religion, past accomplishments, etc., the greater the problem.

COURSE OF ACTION

1. *No action.* Most of the time the problems will be of such a nature that no action is required. Often, athletes will simply unburden themselves. They may need some reassurance that they are normal. Given this they will usually pick themselves up and find their own solutions to the problems. *Don't make the mistake of judging your effectiveness on the amount of energy or direction that you provide.* The less control you need to exert the more responsibility that the athlete can assume and the more effective your intervention.

2. *Action that involves your particular area of expertise.* As a coach you may see very clearly what mental or physical changes athletes need to make in order to be effective. Often this is simply telling them what to attend to, helping them relax certain muscles, etc.

When this is the case your intervention is obvious. Your role as a counselor then involves clarifying the problem for both of you and creating the conditions so the athlete can listen and follow instructions.

3. *Making a referral.* This is perhaps the most difficult and important responsibility you will have when attempting to deal with crisis situations. Referrals should be considered under the following conditions:

    a) Anytime emotional responses are extreme and inappropriate. Notice that I included both criteria. Extreme emotions alone if appropriate, may be dealt with by the coach or sport psychologist. If those extreme emotions seem unaffected by attempts to alter them or to calm the athlete down however, a referral should be made.

    b) When the solution to a problem seems obvious but when a treatment program is established, it keeps getting sabotaged. The athlete just can't seem to follow through. As soon as one solution is identified he/she redefines the problem. You begin to feel as if you are on a merry-go-round. This situation occurs when there are some underlying or dynamic factors that have not been identified, which are affecting the athlete's ability to follow through. Repeated failures in attempts to deal with what appear to be simple problems indicate the need for a referral.

    c) If a sudden and intense emotional involvement develops between you and the athlete. Most often the involvement is positive in that the athlete values what you have to offer. The difficulty is that he/she becomes dependent and the relationship between you (again because of underlying issues) becomes more important than the performance. He/she is not likely to admit this, but his/her behavior makes it obvious. He/she may engage in self-defeating behavior in an attempt to keep you involved to get the personal attention needed. They become jealous of your time this can interfere with the ability to coach and indicates a need for a referral. The trick here is to get the athlete to accept the referral and to not see it as a rejection. This is an issue that should be role played with an experienced counselor.

    d) Any time you feel yourself losing control over your own ability to be objective. Because your own attraction or anger towards the athlete interferes. Feelings may come out of your underlying or unconscious needs and may affect your judgement. You should be sensitive to this possibility and either check the feelings out in supervision an discussions with a professional, or make a referral to another coach or counselor.

    e) If there does not appear to be a logical rational base for the feelings the athlete is going through. Anytime you cannot justify the athlete's feelings you should question your ability to deal with them.

f) Anytime the athlete fails to be able to see or admit the obvious. You may immediately see that the relationship between an athlete and his/her parent is interfering with the ability to function, to listen to the coach, etc. If, when a very obvious fact is pointed out the athlete cannot listen, it is either because he/she doesn't trust you and your objectivity or because there are underlying issues you aren't seeing. In either case you should make a referral.

To clarify further when a referral might be made, let me present several examples. Consider the situation in which an athlete has just been told that one of his parents has been killed or died. This individual responds with considerable emotion. He talks about it and moves from crying and feeling alone and depressed, to being angry and feeling cheated by the fact that he has suffered this loss. "Why me; its not fair."

The coach in talking with the athlete can understand all of the feelings. Even though they are intense, they make sense. The athlete may not be able to concentrate without help, but that is to be expected. What the coach notices in talking with the athlete is that he is responsive to things that are being said. When the coach gets his attention and gets him out of his own head, he can listen. The coach sees that even though the athlete feels as if the whole world is coming down, when an attempt is made to remind him of other people who are left and who care, he can feel it. True, the feelings come and go depending upon the situation. When the athlete is alone he becomes more depressed, but with others around he can relate. The coach also notices that the emotions of the athlete can be changed by things said by the coach.

Under the conditions just described, a referral is not necessary. At this point the feelings are normal and expected. The athlete is not so out of control that he can't respond to others. He is able and willing to listen. It would be a mistake to insinuate that the athlete has problems by making a referral. If the athlete does not gradually begin to get more personal control (begin relying less on the coach to see the good things in life), or if he stops responding, or becomes incapable of changing his feelings, a referral would be in order. In this instance the referral might be made to a sport psychologist as an intermediate step if the sport psychologist already had a relationship with the athlete. If not, the referral should be made directly to a clinical psychologist or a psychiatrist.

A second example might involve the situation in which a very talented, artistic, temperamental skater comes apart just before a contest. This has happened in the past and the coach has usually been able to pull her together in time to get her to perform. On this occasion, the athlete does not "get it together" and she refuses to skate.

The coach attempts to talk with the athlete and finds that she is able to listen. The athlete recognizes her own loss of control, she is distraught by what happened, but she feels that she can handle it in the future. As the two of them discuss it, certain things come out which seem to in-

140

dicate that if various changes are made, the problem will be solved. In this instance, a referral is not made. Now consider a different type of response.

The coach attempts to talk with the skater and finds that she is so angered by the temperamental outbursts that she cannot control her own emotional responses. The coach is out of control and he is unable to listen to the athlete. The coach gives a lecture, swears and yells, and tells her that he has had it. He threatens to leave the athlete and he attacks the athletes personality, ability, and motivations.

In a situation where the coach loses control, a referral should be made. The sport psychologist would be helpful in working with these two to determine whether or not they should continue to work together. If they should, the sport psychologist may be able to provide assistance in finding ways to avoid these problems in the future.

A third possibility in the case of the skater might involve something like this. In talking with the athlete, the coach is unable to calm her down. She is crying and sobbing and doesn't know what is happening. She seems confused and is babbling about all kinds of things. She is not putting anything together, but is just talking in a meaningless kind of way. The one theme that keeps coming back has something to do with the fact that she feels as if she is hopeless, she can't do it, and she is no good. When this theme is addressed she does not respond but continues to babble.

In this instance a referral should be made. It might be made to the sport psychologist once again as an intermediary. Probably the simplest thing to do, given the lack of coherence on the part of the athlete, is to simply make a direct referral to a clinically trained psychologist or psychiatrist.

To summarize the examples that have been presented here, decisions were made on the basis of the following:

1. If the emotional and behavioral responses make sense given the situation, a sensitive, warm, empathetic coach, colleague, etc. can be helpful and a referral is probably not indicated.
2. If the coaches response to an event, or an athlete leads to his/her feelings interfering with effective communication, a referral should be made. In this instance, to the sport psychologist. In the skating example, the skater may have gotten angry at the coach and, as a result, refused to listen.
3. If there is a loss of control and the individual seems unresponsive to outside intervention. If the responses an individual makes to attempts to intervene are inappropriate or bizzare, a referral should be made to a clinically trained individual.

In conclusion, it cannot be over emphasized that adequate use of the material in this chapter requires the opportunity to role play many of the situations that have been presented. In addition, a review of the communication rules for providing feedback, presented in Chapter 8 would be helpful.

13

PREVENTION AND TREATMENT OF INJURY

In sports medicine there have been a number of questions relating to psychological factors and injury. Among these would be: Why do certain athletes seem more prone to injuries than others? What can account for the differences between athletes in terms of their tolerance for pain? Why is it that some athletes never seem to recover from an injury even though physical tests would indicate that they are fine?

It has only been within the past twenty years that we have started to get some answers to these questions. Prior to that time there was speculation that certain personality variables might be identified which would be associated with an "accident prone" individual. In addition, we knew that hypnosis could be used to alter an individual's sensitivity to pain and to increase endurance. In effect we had evidence suggesting that psychological factors played some kind of role, but we had not been able to identify what those factors were, nor did we understand the role.

In the 1960's we began to do research in the area of biofeedback. One of the most important findings to come out of this research was the substantiation of a link between cognitive or mental factors and physiological changes within the body. By providing feedback about different biological functions ranging from blood pressure to muscle tension, it was possible to show that alterations in thinking could result in significant biological change. Applied researchers began studying the effects of different psychological techniques on physiopathology. Biofeedback, in combination with psychological techniques like progressive relaxation, meditation, and various other concentration strategies was used in the treatment of a large number of conditions including problems due to improper or over use of certain muscles and tendons, chronic pain, and injury to the spinal cord.

As research continues, we become more and more aware of the dramatic effects attentional processes have on human functioning. What we concentrate on, and how we concentrate affects blood pressure, heart-rate, muscle tension, release of hormones and other biochemical substances that affect everything from sexual behavior to resistance to disease. In addition, it is our thought processes and attention that determine our perception of what is going on. By systematically altering what an athlete attends to, and by altering how he/she attends (e.g., actively, passively, associating, dissociating) we can increase or decrease the perception of pain and we can distort the perception of time. We can teach individuals to speed up and slow down the perceived movement of physical objects like baseballs, tennis balls and other moving targets.

The cognitive strategies that are used to modify attentional processes will be discussed in succeeding chapters. What I want to provide here is a conceptual understanding for how procedures like biofeedback, hypnosis, associative and dissociative strategies, etc. work to prevent and treat injury.

Without understanding the exact process involved, we do know that the systematic alteration of what an athlete is thinking about will have predictable physiological consequences. As already mentioned, we can monitor biological processes and teach athletes to use mental strategies to systematically alter arousal levels and concentration. Theoretically, we can explain a great deal of what goes on with the model that has already been provided. Figure 7 presents examples of two different situations commonly found in athletics. The first involves treatment of an injury that has developed due to excessive or improper practice. The second involves the development of an injury due to fear.

The tennis player described in Figure 7 is a professional. He developed tendinitis in his elbow following a change in racquets and an excessive amount of practice in preparation for a major tournament. This particular player had not been doing very well on the tour and had taken some time off to go back to his teaching pro for some help. He set aside several weeks to prepare his game for a major event and in his own mind this represented a major test. If he could not pull it together now, perhaps he didn't belong in tennis.

From a psychological point of view, there was a tremendous amount of pressure on the athlete. Tennis had occupied almost one hundred percent of his life. Both the athlete and his family had devoted everything from time to economic resources in the development of this individual's talent. Over the months, frustration had begun to build and the joy had gone out of tennis. He wasn't playing as well as he believed he was capable of, and he felt he was letting everyone down. He was being beaten by people that he shouldn't be losing a game to.

As the days passed, and the tournament came closer, pressure increased. He spent more and more time on the court and as a result began to experience some pain in his elbow. At this point the athlete should have gone to a trainer and/or a doctor for treatment. He did not, and it is at this point that we enter the figure on page .

The athlete had already injured himself and it is the awareness of this injury that is stressful. The injury is stressful because it represents a possible interruption in practice. The athlete is afraid to go to the doctor because he knows from experience that he will be told to stop practicing. With so much riding on his being able to perform well in the coming tournament, and with so much emotionally invested in what a failure

143

Figure 7
Prevention and Treatment of Injury

Situational Stressor

1. Joint pain in elbow due to improper backhand position in tennis.
2. Fear of hurting self on a reverse two-and-one-half somersault.

Physical Changes

1. Increased muscle tension in arm and rest of body from "bracing."

2. Increased muscle tension in neck and shoulders from "bracing." Lightheadedness from hyperventilation due to fear.

Psychological Changes

1. Attention narrows due to pain and to fear about the consequences of the injury. Focus of attention is on the injury.

2. Attention narrows due to fear of injury. Focus is on own anxious thoughts and on lightheadedness.

Performance Consequences

1. Feedback loop develops between attention and physical change. Result is chronic tension in effected area that aggravates the pain and impedes the healing process.

2. Feedback loop develops between attention and the increase in tension in neck and shoulders. With narrow attention and muscular stiffness, the dive is rushed, rotation is interfered with, and the diver hits the board.

would mean at this time, the athlete cannot let up.

The pressure placed on the athlete by the injury and the situation results in the physical and psychological changes outlined in the figure. Mentally, attention narrows and the athlete begins to monitor the injury.

He watches it closely because he can't stand to have it get worse. Each time he hits a backhand he feels the pain in his arm. Each time he feels the pain, muscle tension increases and anxiety goes up.

The increasing muscle tension acts to put more pressure on the joint and aggravates the problem. Very quickly the situation changes, as things go from bad to worse. Now the athlete's anxiety keeps him from letting up and seeking help, and as a result he runs the risk of permanent damage. In the case presented here, the athlete gave up tennis altogether.

For many very competitive individuals, the fear associated with having to give up practice for even a day can be quite high. In their own minds, their very lives depend upon their maintaining and upgrading their skills. As more and more money comes into the picture, the tendency to play injured or to risk permanent injury increases. Individuals in sports medicine, sensitive to the emotional concerns of athletes, have learned to grade the pain associated with problems like the one described. This grading then allows the individual to continue some practice (depending upon the intensity of the pain). At the University of Rochester we found that by grading the pain, providing pharmacological treatment for the inflamation, and by teaching individuals (via biofeedback) to relax the muscles in the affected area when they are not actually playing, we could greatly speed the recovery process and minimize time lost from practice. This combined psychological-physiological treatment procedure resulted in our seeing injuries earlier since athletes weren't so afraid to come in.

The second example presented in figure 7 involves a male diver competing in an international meet. This particular individual was under a great deal of pressure for several reasons. First, he had never won an international competition and going into this particular meet he had his best opportunity. He had been training specifically for this meet for several months.

From a competitive standpoint the diver felt that his would be his last chance as well as his best chance. He was getting older and there were a lot of good young divers coming up. He wanted very badly to retire as a winner.

To make matters worse, he had received a minor injury during practice about two months before the meet. He had been diving off the three meter springboard and had hit his hand on the board on a reverse dive. The injury itself was not that bad; he had only sprained two fingers. What hitting the board did, however, was to remind the diver of how close he was coming to it.

For the first few dives after the injury the diver didn't notice anything. Then, on a reverse dive he suddenly found himself go blank and stop in the middle of a hurdle step. He had made his approach, jumped up into the air and suddenly something kept him from continuing. He didn't know what made him stop, he just felt "funny" and came back down from the hurdle and stood there on the end of the board.

Puzzled, he turned around, walked back and started over. This time he executed the dive without difficulty. Over the next few sessions, however, he began to balk more and more on reverse dives and as a result began to think more and more about why he might be doing that.

As practice for the meet continued, the diver found himself avoiding doing reverse dives. He became aware of the fact that he was afraid of hitting the board. At one point he verbalized the fact that he was afraid he was "going to kill himself." What the diver was unaware of, and unwilling to admit, was the fact that he was under a great deal of additional pressure from the fact that this was a "do or die" meet for him.

It is as the diver enters competition that we pick up with figure 7. Because he has so much anxiety over his reverse dive, the diver has placed it last on his list. As he reaches the final dive the pressure has been mounting. He is in third place, but only five points out of first and with a good dive he may win. That fact, in combination with the fear associated with the reverse dive results in the psychological and physical changes presented in figure 7.

As attention narrows, the diver's perception begins to change. Since he cannot organize and deal with a lot of information at one time, his thoughts jump rapidly from one thing to another without any real integration. At one moment he is aware of the fact that he is standing on the board and the next instant he is in his head thinking about the dive. He jumps from thoughts of the dive to noticing that he has already started his approach. His attention is distracted from the approach by his beating heart and distracted from that by his breathing. Again, he directs attention outward to find that he is already at the end of the board, ready to take his hurdle step.

The effect of this jumping from an internal focus of attention to an external one in a rapid, uncoordinated way is to create the feeling that things are somehow speeded up. The diver is looking at the external world through the eyes of a 1920's movie camera. There are very few frames to the film and things seem jerky and speeded.

Because perception is altered and things seem to be coming faster, the diver has a tendency to rush to keep up. He doesn't feel coordinated, and he begins to get ahead of himself. It is the same kind of experience a person has when he gives a fifteen minute speech for the first time. The speech has been timed and practiced and it is exactly fifteen minutes long. Once the person starts the delivery, however, he rushes through and finishes in five minutes.

In addition, to the perceptual changes that are occurring, the diver finds the muscles in his neck and shoulder area become tense. Because flexibility in the neck area is critical to getting good rotation on a somersault, this tension will impair the diver's physical ability, slowing his spin. To make matters even worse, changes in breathing (hyperventilation) begin to make the diver feel slightly disoriented and dizzy.

As the diver is standing on the board feeling all of these things, they just feed on each other and begin to spiral. To get it over with, he forces

146

himself to go before he is ready. Instead of making a normal smooth approach, he almost runs to the end of the board. As he takes his hurdle step and goes up in the air he is already thinking about how fast he will have to spin.

His thoughts cause him to stand up a little straighter on the board and this means that he will come a little closer. As he comes down on the board, he normally waits for it to bend and spring back. Because things seem rushed, he fails to wait and trys to lift himself off the board too quickly. The result is that he kills his bounce and starts his spin too soon. He doesn't get the height that he needs and he is too close to the board.

In the case presented, the diver self-fullfilled his prophecy. He hit his head on the reverse-two-and-one-half somersault and was knocked unconscious. He ended up being pulled from the water and going to the hospital with a concussion. Although he recovered from the injury, his diving career was over.

The examples and the model that has been presented provide a basis for beginning to offer some answers to the questions with which this chapter started. What an athlete attends to, and his/her ability to direct concentration in task relevant ways has a lot to do with injury.

Apart from personality characteristics like hostility, aggression, etc. factors such as the level of an athlete's trait anxiety (which is associated with attentional and physical changes), and the pressure imposed by situational and emotional factors interacts with performance demands and attentional abilities to increase or decrease dramatically the likelihood of injury. Those athletes who are more likely to be stressed in general, to be stressed by certain situational conditions (e.g., a special competition, when performing in front of a certain audience, etc.), and those athletes with limited attentional control independent of arousal levels are much more likely to be injured.

With respect to differences in tolerance for pain, we now know that there are both physiological and psychological differences that account for what we see. Indeed, there are those individuals who, from a strict physiological perspective, have higher pain thresholds than others. At the same time, we know that pain perception can be augmented and/or reduced by psychological factors. It would be inappropriate to place a specific figure on the amount of pain that is due to psychological or attentional factors. We do know that when individuals are asked to rate their own pain on a scale ranging from 1 (no pain) to 7 (severe pain) before we intervene psychologically, and are then asked to rate it again after being hypnotized or taught to reduce the pain through attentional redirection, distraction, or strategies like association to the pain, or dissociation, we get large changes. Depending upon the study, the average drop in perceived pain is reported as ranging from one to five positions on the scale (14% to 70%).

As a result of the research on pain, sport psychologists are beginning to get involved in teaching athletes to push themselves farther, and to endure the pain of distance sports longer. There are some technical and ethical issues that become important as the psychologist attempts to modify perception of pain. These issues will be discussed presently. For the moment, the focus is on the fact that we can affect pain and the likelihood of injury through psychological manipulation.

A question often asked has to do with why some individuals never seem to recover completely from an injury. This failure is often seen in the case of knee injuries. The athlete is injured and has surgery. Tests of the knee's ability to withstand pressure, turning, twisting, etc. all indicate that normal strength, flexibility, and functioning has returned. In spite of this fact, the athlete still favors the knee and there are perceptible differences in the way the athlete runs and cuts.

What has happened for the injured athlete is that the pain and anxiety generated by the injury (fears of future injuries) result in his/her being more attentive and sensitive to this area. Attention is distracted from the usual cues to which the athlete attends. He/she begins to look for someone coming from the side instead of running with the same relaxed feelings he/she had prior to the injury. Performance is inhibited by the attentional distractions. In addition, muscle tension increases through bracing and a desire to protect the knee. As a result, flexibility on the playing field is reduced even though it isn't reduced in the lab or test situation. Given these changes the athlete doesn't perform as well and increases the likelihood of future injuries because of the reduction in flexibility.

There are many situations within which the sport psychologist might be used to prevent and treat injury. A few examples might be helpful:

1. Treatment of problems due to overuse. As mentioned earlier, this type of treatment should be done in combination with medical treatment for the physiological problems. The sport psychologist's role is to reduce anxiety and the muscle tension that might aggrevate the injury. Psychological techniques like teaching cognitive strategies for reducing perceived pain are often used. In addition, techniques like autogenic training, biofeedback, progressive relaxation, and meditation are often used to reduce muscle tension in the affected area.

2. Assisting in the psychological recovery from the trauma associated with previous injury. There are many examples where the damage athletes have suffered has been sufficient to create a fear that either kept them out of the performance situation entirely, or so altered their style that they could not perform effectively. These may be treated by desensitization.

   a. A skater who has had an ankle injury and has recovered performs poorly because he/she holds the affected foot in an awkward position on jumps. This keeps him/her slightly off balance and detracts from the beauty of jumps. In addition, on more difficult jumps it increases the likelihood of injury.

   b. The major league ballplayer who has been hit in the head by a pitched ball. He has recovered but now he has a tendency to back away from any ball even those over the plate.

    c. The gymnast who has injured himself/herself on a piece of apparatus and as a result won't practice.

3. Alteration in an athlete's tolerance for pain. There are many situations in which injury is not likely to occur by pushing harder. Distance runners, swimmers, cross country skiers, anyone involved in endurance events progresses by experiencing pain, and by pushing themselves to continue in spite of the agony. Many coaches are very fond of the saying "a day without pain is a day without gain."

    The sport psychologist can teach athletes techniques to break the feedback loop that develops between physical and psychological factors under stress. Consider athletes running a marathon. As they reach the "wall," they become acutely aware of their fatigue and pain. These are physiological cues in response to their extreme effort. The physiological cues, however, become stressors and can fit into the top of the diagram on page 207. Because the pain signals the athlete that they are in trouble, they become emotionally stressed as well as physically stressed. Attention focuses inward, on the pain and on the fear that they won't be able to finish or that their time will be poor, or that they will tie up. As these attentional changes occur, anxiety rises and so does muscle tension. The likelihood of developing a cramp or tying up is enhanced. The feedback loop has developed and performance is in danger of going downhill rapidly.

    By training an athlete to be able to either dissociate from the anxiety that is rising, or to attend to what is going on in an objective, unemotional way (requiring a high level of self-esteem) on the part of the athlete and considerable competitive experience), the feedback loop is broken. The addition of an emotional component which exaggerates normal physical symptoms is avoided. This does not mean that the initial physical pain or that the depletion of energy supplies is overcome or eliminated. It only means that the athlete does not add to his/her own downfall.

4. Prevention of injuries: The example of the diver who had considerable fear associated with a particular dive provides a good example for the use of psychological techniques from a prevention standpoint. What is involved is to identify those individuals who are likely to be stressed by certain situations, and/or those situations (e.g., learning a difficult and dangerous skill) that are likely to be stressful. Critical physical and attentional abilities are identified in these specific situations. For example, what muscle groups are involved and what are ideal tension levels? What performance relevant cues (e.g., the hurdle step in diving) should the athlete be attending to? Having identified those physical and psychological factors that need to be controlled, the athlete is then

149

taught to use cognitive techniques to exert that control. Biofeed-back, mental rehearsal, and attention control training can all be used to help sensitize the athlete to his/her level of muscle tension and to what he/she is attending to. At the same time, the athlete can be taught to attend in different ways in order to learn to raise or lower muscle tension levels as the situation requires. Finally, the athlete can be taught to reduce distractions and to improve task-relevant concentration (see chapters 17 & 18).

Obviously there are some concerns that sport psychologists must keep in mind when working in this area. First, unless they are trained in medicine and physiology, they are not qualified to treat the physiological aspects of injury. In fact, they should not presume to treat the psychological components unless they are sure that in so doing, they will not contribute to a physical injury. To be sure of this, the sport psychologist must maintain close contact with and supervision by a physician and/or trainer.

Athletic situations in general, and injury situations in particular, emphasize the very important interaction between psychological and physical factors. It is in this area that cooperation between the psychologist and the physician, trainer, and coach becomes absolutely critical. One of the primary ethical principles guiding behavior involves the recognition of the limits imposed by one's training and experience. Too often, psychological techniques can have a rather dramatic impact on the perception of pain. The examples with the use of hypnosis in chapter 16 emphasize this point only too well. There is a real danger, given a few successes to assume that psychological factors predominate and to eschew the need for medical consultation. This tendency should be avoided at all costs.

14

TREATMENT SELECTION

In the next few chapters I will be talking about a variety of psychological techniques that can be used by sport psychologists to enhance performance. Before making that presentation, it is worthwhile to use the theoretical framework that has been developed to understand why the techniques work, and to assist in determining which particular technique seems best suited to which problem, and to what situation.

As has been mentioned throughout this book, situational factors (e.g., competitive conditions, interpersonal relationships, etc.) affect both physiological arousal and the ability to direct and control attention. In sport, the level of an athlete's arousal and his/her ability to concentrate has direct relevance to performance and to each other. Excessive arousal and/or excessively narrowed attention can lead to poor performance and vice versa. It is when a feedback loop is created which sustains the physiological and attentional disturbances that the athlete chokes.

Figure 8 presents a number of different psychological and medical techniques that have been used to improve the performance of athletes. In essence, the techniques work because they act to break the loop that is sustaining inappropriate levels of physiological arousal (too high or too low), attentional disturbances, and poor performance. As can be seen in Figure 8 the intervention can take place at any point in the figure. For example, an athlete may report that muscle tension is causing him/her to cramp up and is interfering with performance and concentration. "If I could just stop the cramping I could perform." A medical technique that reduces the tendency to cramp (massage, quinine, etc.) also frees attentional processes because the cramps are no longer there to distract the athlete. As the athlete relaxes, attentional flexibility returns and performance improves. Because the athlete's own focus and complaint was on the physiological side of the diagram (he/she could have emphasized disturbances in concentration rather than the cramps), and because the attentional disturbances did seem to be secondary to the cramps, it was important to use a treatment approach that dealt directly with physiological issues. Had the cramps developed in response to attentional disturbances, it may have been more appropriate to select an intervention from the psychological side of the diagram.

Figure 8
Treatment Procedures

Situational Stressor

1. *Attitude change:* Implosion, Systematic Desensitization, Positive Thinking, Rational Emotive Therapy.

2. *Environmental Control.* (Avoidance)

3. *Selection and Screening.* (Prevention)

Physical Responses

1. Use of pharmacological agents (e.g., aspirin, valium, prednisone, etc.) to directly affect physical symptoms.

2. Biofeedback

3. Meditation

4. Progressive Relaxation

5. Breathing exercises ("centering")

6. Hypnosis

7. Autogenic Training

Psychological Responses

1. Use of pharmacological agents that focus on reduction of anxiety and thought disturbances (Tranquilizers, amphetamines, mood elevators, alcohol, barbituates).

2. External interventions by the sport psychologist or coach. These include the provision of structure, support, distraction, attentional redirection.

3. Mental Rehearsal and Discriminate Cue Analysis.

4. Cognitive Behavior Modification.

5. Attention Control Training.

6. Hypnosis-Self Hypnosis

Performance Problems

1. Getting the athlete to over-learn a response.

2. Developing accomplishable short term goals that lead to the ultimate goal or performance.

THE PLACEBO MYTH

As we talk about any treatment intervention, whether it is medical or psychological, we become concerned about understanding just what is the active ingredient. Often, it is our theoretical formulations that provide the basis for understanding rather than any hard incontrovertible "scientific truth." We need some theoretical construct in order to understand the mechanism by which a treatment works, to determine when, where, why, and how a treatment should be applied. We also need the theory to be able to improve upon the treatment or to make it more effective. If we cannot identify the active ingredient, we cannot alter the treatment's effectiveness.

When our ability to identify the active ingredient in any therapy is impaired and yet the treatment is effective, we fall back on a number of concepts to explain what has happened. We refer to the importance of uncontrolled for factors such as suggestion, distraction, etc. Often we talk about "placebo" effects. Somehow, something supposedly inert and intangible has entered the process. Too often, because we don't understand it or because we insist on physical evidence, we deny ourselves the benefits of very important and real treatment procedures. Two examples will illustrate what I mean.

A few years ago I remember reading a *Reader's Digest* article that was discussing the effects of aspirin. The author, a physician and pharmacologist was making the point that it was not understood how aspirin worked to relieve pain. The best that could be determined was that it seemed the active chemical ingredients could account for about ten percent of the effectiveness of the drug. He went on to report that he suffered from frequent headaches and that for many years aspirin had been a very effective drug. Now, since he had been studying aspirin and had found that pharmacologically he could not explain more than ten percent of his pain reduction, he retained ninety percent of his headache. Aspirin no longer worked as a complete pain reliever.

A similar story can be told about hypnosis. In this case, however, the failure to identify the active ingredient affected the entire medical profession and literally thousands of people.

The history of "modern" hypnosis dates back to Anton Mesmer a physician practicing in Paris in the late 1700's. According to Pattie (1967), Mesmer believed that disease was a result of the unequal distribution of nervous fluid in the human body. This disease process could be altered and cures could be effected by altering the magnetic fields which Mesmer believed surrounded the human body. Somehow, alterations in these fields resulted in corresponding alterations in the distribution of nervous energy.

In his practice, Mesmer used magnets and hypnotic techniques to alter the flow of energy surrounding the human body. The result of his procedures was quite dramatic in a large number of cases. Early in Mesmer's work, subjects for whom the treatments seemed most effective would evidence the changes that were occurring (according to Mesmer's theory)

153

by having a seizure. Presumably, the realignment of the magnetic forces was the cause of the seizure.

As Mesmer's reputation grew, so did the number of his patients. It was not long before he had to treat them in groups. He constructed a tub that had iron rods sticking out of it. Inside the tub were bottles filled with iron filings and supposedly "animal magnetism." Patients would surround the tub and take hold of the iron bars. Then, as soft music played in the background Mesmer would point his finger or an iron bar at one of the patients. He or she would begin to have odd sensations and before long would collapse having what looked like a seizure. Following the first patient's collapse, it was not long before many of the others would collapse also. Very often, the symptoms that brought the patients to Mesmer in the first place were removed upon recovery from the seizure.

Mesmer's practice created quite a stir in France and upset many important people in the fields of medicine and politics. The medical profession wanted him branded a charlatan. Finally, in 1784, the government established a nine man commission that included Benjamin Franklin and the chemist, Lavoisier, to investigate Mesmer's theory.

The commission designed a number of studies to investigate Mesmer's claims. They used all of the scientific instruments that they had at the time but failed to detect electrical currents and magnetic fields. They got one of Mesmer's disciples to magnetize a tree in an orchard. Then they took a boy who was highly susceptible to magnetism to the orchard and they had him touch a different tree which he was told was magnetized. Upon touching this tree the boy had a seizure. Following that, they had the boy touch the magnetized tree but told him that it was not magnetized and no seizure resulted.

Following their tests, the commission issued a report concluding that Mesmer's theory was unfounded and that Mesmer was a fraud. As a result of this report, the use of hypnotic techniques and suggestions fell into disrepute. For over fifty years the medical profession prevented any systematic use or investigation of "Mesmerism" or hypnosis. In effect, it had thrown the baby out with the bath water. Because a theoretical structure could not be identified that explained the phenomena, the medical profession eschewed the use of a very valuable therapeutic tool.

As is the case with aspirin, or any other technique, whether it is physiological or psychological in nature it is important to identify, if possible, the active physiological and/or psychological ingredient. The failure at this time to identify a specific physical or biological change that can account for one hundred percent of the changes that occur, should not cause us to cast away useful tools.

There is a tendency, even when looking at psychologically-oriented techniques, to want to identify a single observable site in the body that is affected by treatment. In the absence of such evidence, we talk about placebo effects. When we design studies in order to identify the "active"

154

ingredient and when we make comparisons between various psychological techniques, we find that nonspecific or placebo factors account for, by far, the greatest percentage of change. As with aspirin, it is possible at times to show that a percentage of the changes that are occurring may indeed be a result of some unique contribution of a particular technique. For example, biofeedback of muscle tension levels can facilitate greater muscle tension reduction than more general progressive relaxation instructions.

Because the vast majority of the effects of psychological treatments (and physiological treatments for that matter) cannot be attributed to specific physical factors, it is very important to attempt to identify the psychological factors that might be involved. As mentioned earlier, a theoretical framework is critical to the effective use and improvement of treatment approaches.

There does appear to be very strong evidence to show a link between changes in body physiology, hormonal balance and concentration or attention. It seems reasonable to assume that the "nonspecific" or "placebo" effects that are discussed result from a redirection of a patient's attentional processes. Let me take the case of aspirin as an example. An individual develops a headache and someone prescribes two aspirins. Let's assume that the headache developed as a result of increasing tension in the neck and shoulders. The patient had been driving on icy roads for a long period of time, hunched over the steering wheel. As the pain becomes apparent, the patient begins to experience some stress. In effect, the pain becomes the situational stressor in the Figures presented throughout the book. As the pain and stress increase, there are additional physical and psychological changes. Muscle tension continues to increase aggravating the headache and narrowing attention. As attention becomes more focused on the pain, the feedback loop mentioned previously is established.

When the patient takes the apsirin, she does so with considerable faith in its ability to help her. She has around her literally thousands of people who would testify to the effectiveness of aspirin when it comes to relieving the pain associated with headaches. In addition, her own past experience with the drug seems to support this notion. She has not been handicapped by reading the reports indicating that aspirin is ineffective for ninety percent of the pain.

It can be hypothesized that it is the patient's faith in the effectiveness of the treatment, and perhaps the ten percent reduction in pain, that allows her to relax and redirect attention. She no longer has to worry about the headache; she has taken something and she knows, that within fifteen to thirty minutes the pain will be gone. As a result, before the pain is gone, she redirects her attention to other things. She gets involved in something and momentarily forgets about the pain. As this happens, the feedback loop is broken and the muscle tension eases. With the easing of the tension the pain is gone. A few minutes later the subject stops what she is doing to check in on her headache and she finds it is gone. Mentally she makes a note to thank the aspirin and her faith in the medicine is strengthened. The increase in faith then increases the likelihood that it will have the power to allow her to make similar attentional changes in the future.

The placebo effect then can be seen as a result of an attentional shift. A shift which does indeed result in very real physiological changes within the body; changes that are directly related to the perception of pain and other symptoms or problems. Any technique then, psychological or otherwise that allows a subject to break the feedback loop that exists between physical and mental processes (and performance) will be effective in reducing, and in some cases eliminating, both mental and physical symptoms that are stress-related.

The critical variable from a treatment point of view involves the identification of an approach which is going to make sense to the athlete. If attention is altered, performance will be improved, but attention can only be altered if the athlete can place faith in the treatment process. The good sport psychologist or coach learns to develop that faith. Let me go back and explain how each of the treatment procedures in Figure 8 works and then I will discuss some of the specific factors related to the selection of treatments and the mobilization of faith.

The treatment procedures presented in Figure 8 are representative, but not exhaustive by any means. Undoubtedly it can be argued that some of them, depending upon how they are presented to the athlete (e.g., meditation, Attention Control Training, biofeedback), could be listed as being relevant to the treatment of both physical and psychological symptoms. What I have tried to do here is to place them under the heading that on the surface seems most logical and appropriate. For example, biofeedback as a treatment procedure focuses on the alteration of physiological variables. Subjects are taught to lower or raise muscle tension levels, to alter heart-rate, change skin temperature, and so on. Given the physical focus of the treatment, it would appear that this technique would most likely be successful in those situations where the athlete described his/her problem in physiological terms (even though attentional disturbances may be involved). Since faith in the treatment is such a critical variable, the athlete is more likely to be able to redirect attention and allow the feedback loop to be broken if the treatment approach responds directly to what he/she perceives to be the problem. Either that, or the sport psychologist must take the time to convince him/her that something else is really the problem — a task that is not easy to do with an athlete who has a high level of self-esteem and a strong need for control.

Beginning at the top of Figure 8, I have listed a number of treatment procedures that can be used to break the feedback loop by either altering the subject's attitude towards the situation creating the stress, thus making it no longer stressful and therefore, no longer resulting in the physical and psychological changes that interfere with performance. Or, the treatment removes the subject from or alters the situation itself.

156

Changes in attitudes towards situations and reductions in the destructive consequences of excessive arousal can be effected with clinical procedures like systematic desensitization, implosion, and rational emotive therapy. With systematic desensitization the sport psychologist teaches subjects to relax and then teaches them to be able to maintain that relaxation as the sport psychologist slowly and systematically increases the number of potentially stressful cues. This process is typically done by getting athletes to picture mentally progressively stressful scenes related to situations with which they wish to deal. Coaches use a live version of this technique. A gymnast who is afraid of a trick, or a diver who is learning a new dive will usually engage in what is called "lead ups." He/she starts out by doing only a part of the trick, for example, two somersaults instead of three. Another way of doing the trick is to increase the safety factor. A gymnast works with spotters, a diver has the coach call him/her out of a dive or executes it from a lower height. Slowly, in a systematic way, the athlete progresses towards the final accomplishment. As a function of these lead-ups, anxiety and attentional disturbances are kept under enough control that they do not reach the point of interfering with performance. The difference between what the coach does and systematic desensitization is that the coach doesn't train the athlete to relax first, and the coach doesn't rely primarily on mental rehearsal.

Implosion is a therapeutic technique that is similar to a procedure coaches use when they push athletes into performing in spite of their own fear. Again using diving as an example, the athlete may have wiped out on a dive off the tower. The coach will force him/her to go up and attempt the dive again. Once the athlete succeeds, and finds that he/she can survive, the situation becomes less stressful. The analogy to implosion holds with just a few changes. Once again, the sport psychologist relies primarily on the athlete using mental rehearsal to fantasize the worst possible consequences that could occur. In addition, the psychologist gets the athlete to exaggerate possible consequences. As an example, instead of telling the diver to go up and do a double somersault which is what he/she wiped out on, the coach says "go for three." Obviously, this would be foolish. Thus, with implosion, the treatment focus is typically on the fear that the athlete has over failing, rather than on physical injury. Implosion when it involves exaggeration should not be used with actual physical problems. When it is an emotional issue, and the athlete is placing too much importance on a feeling, then it may be instructive and useful to get the athlete to exaggerate in order to see that at his/her fantasized worse, the consequences are not all that bad. He/she can survive and having seen this, his/her attitude changes.

As an example I might have an athlete try to tell me all of the terrible things he/she believes will happen if he/she fails and in so doing lets his/her parents down. "Your parent's will look at you in disgust, they will disown you. They will be so upset by your failure that they will never admit that you are their child." Through implosion, the athlete works through the emotional blocks that are interfering and making certain situations excessively stressful.

Both implosion and desensitization involve altering the athlete's attitudes or beliefs. There are many times when changes in the athlete are either unwarranted, too costly in terms of time or money, or simply cannot be made because the individual lacks the capacity for change. When one of these techniques does seem appropriate, it should be selected on the basis of the needs of the athlete rather than the needs of the sport psychologist or coach. Too often, it is the sport psychologist's personality that determines the selection of a treatment approach. Selection factors like the level of the athletes' self-esteem are far more important. Individuals with low self-esteem need more support and are more likely to respond to a procedure like systematic desensitization. Athletes with a strong need to prove themselves, to be tough, etc. will respond well to implosion.

There is a general tendency in psychology and in athletics to place responsibility for change on the individual. In fact, we make it very difficult for athletes to accept the fact that it is often easier to accept a weakness, and to deal with it by altering the environment, than by demanding personal change. Somehow it is a sign of great weakness, a lack of courage, or masculinity, to give in to a problem and to admit that we can't handle it, or that there are easier ways of solving it than spending days, weeks, months, or years trying to change our attitudes or personality. Very often, the most important task a sport psychologist has involves teaching athletes to accept some of their limitations. Once they do this, they can take steps to minimize problems instead of placing themselves in situations in which they will fail. Then, having failed they become upset and frustrated and create the feedback loop that destroys their self-esteem and ability to perform in areas that they are quite capable of dealing with under less stressful conditions.

If there are questions about an athlete's abilities to meet the attentional or physical demands of a performance situation, it may be most cost-effective to alter the demands of the situation, rather than trying to change the athlete. This change can take place by allowing the athlete to avoid the situation entirely, or by team building, getting the athlete to work with someone else in a complementary way. In effect, the performance demands of the situations are split by the individuals involved so that a single individual does not have to be all things. An example of this complementarity would involve the situation where the coach takes on the responsibility of calling the plays in a football game. By doing this he frees the quarterback from the pressure of that responsibility.

Finally, the sport psychologist may be asked to engage in some type of selection and screening process to prevent the development of the types of problems we have been talking about. If we are able to identify the various performance demands and if we can assess the athlete's ability to meet these under different conditions of arousal, we can prevent the development of a destructive feedback loop.

The use of physiologically oriented techniques has already been illustrated through the aspirin example. It is the same basic process that occurs with the use of the other techniques listed under physical responses. To summarize the various procedures, there are certain medications that are known to have a specific physiological effect. As a function of that effect, and as a function of the confidence the athlete has in the procedure, anxiety and physical symptoms are both reduced. The ability to concentrate effectively returns. Biofeedback funcions in a similar way. Meditation, Autogenic Training, and Progressive Relaxation have been listed here because they are usually presented as techniques that have a direct effect on physiological processes including muscle tension, heart-rate, blood pressure, etc. As a result, these procedures have some face validity for the athlete who is complaining of physical problems interfering with concentration. Those physical problems may be fatigue (which meditation is advertised to deal with), muscle cramps, or dizziness.

The psychological techniques listed are usually selected when the athlete reports disturbances in concentration due to boredom, fear, anger, frustration, or a lack of energy. Like the physiologically oriented procedures, these techniques have face validity for dealing with the symptoms about which the athlete is complaining. When fear and anxiety get in the way, physicians often prescribe tranquilizers. If energy levels are down, medical treatments may involve administration of vitamins (e.g., stress tabs), amphetamines or mood elevators. Often, the actual physiological effects of the treatment are minimal. The vast majority of improvement can be attributed to the redirection of attention.

Techniques like mental rehearsal, discriminate cue analysis, attention control training, cognitive behavior modification, visuo-motor behavior rehearsal are all variants of the same basic process. They are designed to train the athlete to systematically identify and concentrate on task relevant information. At the same time, athletes may use techniques like "thought stopping" and "passively attending" to learn to deal with distractions in a way which allow for attentional redirection to task-relevant cues. Through this process, the feedback loop is broken, attentional control is regained, physiological arousal is reduced, and performance is enhanced.

An example of the attentional redirection process on the athletic field can be seen at the start of most games, particularly in contact sports. Athletes will hit themselves and each other, usually around the head, or they will yell together and the result of this process is that their attention gets directed to what is going on outside of them. Getting hit on the head gets one to focus externally. As a result, pre-game tension is reduced and performance errors due to concentration disturbances are reduced.

In addition to improving performance by altering attitudes, situational

159

demands, and the attentional and physiological responses of athletes, the development of negative feedback loops can be avoided by preventing performance problems from the beginning.

A technique that is often used in sports is to teach athletes to over-learn responses. They practice so much that the behavior they engage in becomes reflexive. Good boxers automatically execute a counter punch, they don't have to think about it. Responses that are over-learned are much more resistant to the effects of increasing arousal and attentional disturbances. In effect, in spite of the anxiety, the athlete performs at an acceptable level. In contrast, the athlete who has not rehearsed a particular technique as much, may be unable to perform.

As athletes over learn and they are able to perform in spite of their anxiety, the situation becomes less stressful and elicits fewer negative physiological and psychological responses.

Finally, Figure 8 indicates that by teaching athletes to focus on short term, task relevant goals, rather than thinking ahead to some "ultimate performance" it is possible to reduce the likelihood of developing a negative spiral. When athletes are accomplishing smaller short term goals they are attending to and receiving positive feedback. Frustration and concentration problems are minimized. In contrast, when the focus is on perfection, attention is directed towards failure rather than success. In effect, athletes have sensitized themselves to look for weaknesses (to overcome them, avoid them, etc.). Since athletes are not perfect they inevitably find things to be unhappy about, especially if their demands are too high. When they discover a weakness they focus on it and increase arousal and performance problems. They develop the downward spiral.

FACTORS IN TREATMENT SELECTION

Since almost all of the treatment procedures mentioned can be effective under the right circumstances, it is important to identify some of those circumstances that determine your choice. The ability to select presumes that as a sport psychologist or coach you have been able to define operationally the problem that the athlete is presenting. A specific problem and/or group of symptoms that are interfering with performance have been identified. You have been able to assess the physical and mental demands of the competitive situation, you have assessed the athlete's ability to meet these demands (under stressful and nonstressful circumstances), and you have identified the factors that raise and lower the athlete's level of arousal (what are the situational, personal, and interpersonal stressors).

1. As the symptoms are described, which ones seem to you to be primary? Is it the physical symptom that is leading to the disturbances in concentration or vice versa? If it is a physical symptom, are you competent to deal with it (has it been checked out medically)? Typically, a technique is selected that seems to be

most relevant to the primary symptom. This is especially true if the athlete sees the problem in the same way you do. On occasion the athlete may focus on the secondary symptoms and either deny or be unable to see what you feel is the primary problem. You may attempt to design a treatment that responds to both. Frequently, however, this will be your first indication that there are some larger underlying problems that may require some type of clinical intervention.

2. Where is the athlete's focus? The athlete may see that concentration is affected by physical symptoms, but feels that the physical symptoms are primary. In this case (because his/her faith and confidence in you and the treatment is critical) you would probably select an approach that has face validity for her/him.

3. Select a technique that allows for the most specific, operationally definable focus. An athlete may define the problem as being unable to concentrate on catching a pass because he is distracted by the sound of footsteps behind him. Telling him that learning to relax will help, might be true, but it does not provide him with a specific task-relevant focus. There is greater specificity, face validity, etc. in selecting a cognitive technique that trains him to improve concentration in this specific situation.

4. Identify personal psychological factors that are likely to affect the athletes' confidence in the procedures, in you, and in themselves.

   a. Athletes with low self-esteem need procedures that allow for more outside structure and support. They need someone else to take a more active role. They have difficulty believing in their own ability to implement a procedure. For this reason, they may have trouble with a technique like meditation that is less structured and leaves them on their own.

   b. Athletes with high levels of anxiety tend to become overloaded by their own thoughts and are easily distracted. They need fairly simple treatment approaches that provide a great deal of structure and gets them out of their head.

   c. Athletes with a high need for control are usually more responsive to procedures that allow them to assume more responsibility (e.g., biofeedback). Often it is helpful to use them as a consultant in the development of a treatment program.

   d. Athletes who are more analytically focused often need to understand the underlying theoretical constructs behind treatment. It will be important for you to select a procedure that can be defended on a logical, rational basis.

   e. Athletes who are more externally focused and who have a high activity level may need a technique that keeps them occupied both physically and mentally. Sitting quietly and meditating may be stress inducing rather than reducing.

161

f.   What attitudinal factors, religious beliefs, etc. are likely to influence the athletes' ability to respond. Hypnosis may be seen as mystical and may represent a loss of control to some thereby preventing them from responding. Meditation may turn others off because it emphasizes passive responding and their success and orientation is totally focused on taking charge, being active. Prayer can be a very good technique for helping some athletes redirect attention and lower arousal. Their religious faith allows them to attend to their prayers rather than anxiety. As a result, they can calm down.

5. Identify interpersonal factors that may have an influence on the process.

a.   What credentials do you have that will allow you to convince the athlete that you can make effective use of a given procedure? Faith in a technique may in some instances be secondary to faith in the individual. This is why many coaches can accomplish changes that sport psychologists are unable to when both use the same technique. Do you look like a hypnotist to the athlete? Do you sound like a hypnotist? Do you have the right title and the right experience to use this technique with this athlete in this situation?

b.   What resources are available in the form of other athletes, coaches, etc? Are there certain techniques that can be selected because they take advantage of available support systems? Perhaps the coach can be trained to provide follow-up, etc.

6. Identify the situational factors that have an important bearing on the selection of a technique.

a.   How much time is there for training? Do you have enough time to effect change in the individual, or do you need to modify the situation?

b.   Any treatment procedure must be cost-effective. How much money does the person (organization) have to spend? How broad and how far reaching are the goals of treatment? What services can be provided given the economic, time, personal, and interpersonal limitations imposed?

c.   How supportive is the general environmental situation? Is the atmosphere one which will support the use of hypnosis? Is it quiet, comfortable, etc.?

In the next few chapters I will be talking about a number of procedures that are used to facilitate performance. While doing this, an attempt will be made to point out some of the parameters of these approaches which are relevant to making decisions based on the factors identified above.

162

15

PREVENTION OF CHRONIC PROBLEMS

There are many stressors that an athlete faces which are fairly constant. These stressors are around day in and day out, whether the athlete is performing well, or poorly. Over time, the constant pressure wears the athlete down and ultimately leads to the development of chronic pressure that has come to be associated with excessive stress (e.g., hypertension, alcoholism).

The constant pressure of being on a tour, of traveling, can begin to wear down even the most free spirit. In sports like bowling and baseball, where the opportunity to drink is present, a large number of athletes become alcoholics. Individual's begin drinking to socialize and to ease the pressures associated with constant travel or the loneliness in being away from families.

Young athletes find that they are exposed to opportunities to experiment with a variety of drugs (amateurs and professionals alike), and there may be a great deal of pressure placed on the individual to go along with the group whether this involves sniffing cocaine, smoking marijuana, or engaging in homosexual relationships.

The athlete who needs privacy may find that he/she gets very little time alone. He/she travels with a team, sleeps with a roommate, and if recognizable to the public, he/she is constantly being approached by fans. The recognition that at first produces a very positive "high" can quickly become a burden.

Young players may initially find going out with the other members of the team to be fun and a great way to reduce some of the constant tension from the sport and from being alone. Unfortunately, drinking and chasing around can lead to serious long term problems including addictions. These outside difficulties, the emotional conflicts, marital problems, begin to add to the constant pressure that the athlete feels.

Following a group of athletes on tour can be a real experience. The pressures that individuals face make stress reducers or defenses of one kind or another absolutely necessary. Different individuals develop their own methods for coping and quickly become identified with one subgroup or another. There is a contingent that is extremely religious, having bible study groups and often placing greater emphasis on converting other athletes to the religion, than is placed on performance in the sport. For some individuals, these subgroups do indeed reduce

163

stress, for others they only increase the problem. It can be very difficult when the person you are rooming with keeps trying to convert you while you are trying to prepare for a match. It doesn't matter if the conversion is to a religious belief, or a sexual preference, the pressure is there.

Excessive drinking, smoking, eating, using drugs, sexual acting out, are all very effective *short term* ways of reducing the constant pressure than an athlete may face. Unfortunately, most of these short term tension reducers have drastic long term consequences.

Sharon is a professional golfer who must travel a great deal and who becomes more tense and anxious when she has to be away from her home and family for extended periods. She doesn't drink or smoke and she wouldn't use drugs, however, she finds herself eating a great deal. She will get away from the golf course and then go on an eating binge, stuffing herself. The act of eating helps to reduce the pressure, but almost immediately afterward Sharon becomes upset at her loss of control and at the fact that she might gain weight.

Concerns over weight gain raise Sharon's anxiety level considerably and it is not long before she finds herself throwing up after one of her eating binges. She again experiences a little relief from her tension as she throws up. Sometime later she goes on another eating binge but this time afterward she self-induces the vomiting. Again, the eating and the throwing up both reduce tension temporarily. Shortly after the experience, however, Sharon is upset and disgusted with herself. She is upset with the loss of control that led to the eating in the first place and she is beginning to feel that she is crazy or "sick" to go so far as to induce vomiting. The very behaviors she engaged in to reduce stress have reached the point of inducing more. A vicious circle develops (identical to the choking diagram outlined in previous chapters), with the anxiety leading to more eating and vomiting and the eating and vomiting leading to more anxiety. Sharon is now out of control and has developed a problem that will require the intervention of a trained clinician.

I believe that you would be surprised at the number of Sharon's there are in the athletic world. As with the alcoholic, this addictive behavior is just one more attempt at coping with constant pressure. Let me list some of the constant stressors with which many athletes have to contend.

1. A lack of personal privacy. This lack is especially difficult for those athletes who tend to be more introverted. The lack of privacy is caused by fans, fellow athletes, coaches, the medical profession (e.g., forcing female athletes to undergo sex identity checks), judges in the various sports, business demands, etc.
2. Loneliness and isolation. At first this seems a contradiction to the invasion of privacy mentioned above. Athletes have public lives and private lives. The public invades and puts pressure on athletes and doesn't give them personal space. At the same time, the

164

demands of the sport (e.g., the travel and time commitments) prevent athletes from having someone close by that they can share with. We all need someone, and not being able to be with that person, to share with them, can be very draining.

3. The demand to get "up" for the game each day, day after day through a very long pre-season, season, and post-season.

4. Injuries create a great deal of pressure for most athletes. Injuries, particularily those that sideline the athlete for several weeks or months are extremely stressful. The stress does not come from the injury itself, it comes from the interruption. Athletes are competitive and want to be on the field. They are afraid that they will be permanently replaced. They are afraid that they won't be able to catch up with the competition. They recognize that they aren't getting any younger and that their career is limited anyway. The stress that the injury causes can lead to chronic alcoholism, drug dependence, etc.

5. Retirement. Perhaps one of the biggest problems in sport involves finding ways to aid athletes in adjusting to their retirement from competitive athletics. Systems in North America do not provide for the vast majority of athletes once they have finished competing. Many athletes have invested their entire life in the development of a set of skills that they can no longer use after ten or fifteen years. Even if they have gone to school and gotten a degree that might prepare them for some other career, by the time they finish competition, their education is outdated. They either can't find a job or they start at the very bottom. Certainly there are exceptions, e.g., the decathlon champion who uses his recognition to build a career in television. Unfortunately, the vast majority of athletes do not have these opportunities. Athletes who have been the center of attention suddenly find themselves alone. At this point they have no useful identity, no focus for the future. They begin to feel used and they get frustrated and angry. Many of them, without some kind of assistance will live chronically unhappy angry lives, or attempt suicide.

6. Marital and family problems. Very often, young promising athletes are under constant pressure from their families. The parents have a need to live their own lives through their children. The demands from parents (coaches too can be guilty of this, as can sport psychologists) can create more pressure than the athlete is capable of dealing with. The vicious circle that we spoke about before develops in this situation also. Athletes may fight back against the pressure, or they may withdraw and get into the use of drugs, etc. In either case, the responses athletes make are often ones that at best provide some short term relief. It is not long before the temporary solutions become problems themselves.

Some of the problems presented here will require more than the substitution of a technique like progressive relaxation (to reduce stress) for alcohol abuse. When retirement is involved, or pressures involve others as well as the athlete (e.g., parents, spouses), counseling may also be required.

A point that I would like to make here is that we all need some defenses, or methods for coping with day to day pressure and stress. Habits like smoking, eating, drinking, etc. whether we realize it or not provide a great deal of relief from pressure. Unfortunately, the long term consequences of these stress reducers are very negative.

Publicly, the medical and psychological professions have worked hard to make people aware of the relationship between heart disease and smoking, drinking, eating, etc. We have sensitized people to the dangers of smoking and to the dangers of other drugs. We have told them what is wrong with what they are doing (increasing their stress), but we have not offered them substitutes. In some ways, we have behaved as if people should be able to get along just fine without any defenses. We seem to imply that only the weak and sick need defenses against pressure. Nothing could be farther from the truth, and nothing can lead to more problems than the misguided notion that "I should stand on my own. I don't need anybody or anything."

The techniques that are about to be discussed have been found to be useful substitutes for some of the other defenses we have been using. When used on a regular basis (e.g., every day) and practiced for twenty to thirty minutes at a time, they provide a much needed break from the constant pressure athletes are under. The techniques do not change the situation. They don't make the crowds disappear, nor do they fix a bad marriage. They do give the athlete a brief time out; a time out that breaks the feedback loop between mental and physical processes. That time out even though it is only twenty minutes long can provide a great deal of rest both mentally and physically. Research in the laboratory has shown that progressive relaxation, biofeedback, and meditation strategies allow for recovery from fatigue, reduce heart-rate and blood pressure. In addition, they help clear out some of the distractions and the overload that athletes feel mentally. As a result, they find it easier to get back to work, to go back into the pressure cooker.

When the sports psychologist attempts to get an athlete to use one of these techniques on a regular basis it will be important to remember that the motivation to follow through will only remain so long as the athlete feels there is an end in sight. A swimmer getting ready for the Olympics, even though it is two years away, may be motivated to use a relaxation procedure on a daily basis to cope with the pressure of practice. The swimmer will use the procedure because he/she knows that in two years it will all be over. The goal of competing in the Olympics is a strong motivator and he/she sees the technique as a means to helping accomplish that goal. If there is no end in sight however, motivation goes out the window.

Athletes who have severe marital problems or who have retired might be told that the technique will help them deal with the day to day pressure. To them however, there is no end in sight, life looks pretty bleak, why should they practice the exercise? Do they really want to do something that is going to prolong the agony? If the athlete is also being worked with to ultimately resolve the problem, then the promise of that resolution can be used to facilitate practice.

USES OF BIOFEEDBACK, PROGRESSIVE RELAXATION, & MEDITATION

1. These techniques can be used as substitutes for other more damaging methods for reducing constant pressure, pressure of travel, or injury.
2. These techniques can be used to teach athletes to control pre-start tension levels. By relaxing an hour or so before a competition an athlete can reduce tension. In addition, combining relaxation with visual imagery can be helpful in raising tension levels.
3. These procedures can be helpful to athletes by allowing them to fall asleep on the road, the night before a large competition, etc. Often, precompetitive anxiety interferes with sleep and the athlete makes matters worse by worrying about the effects the lack of rest will have on performance. The feedback loop develops and performance is affected. Use of relaxation strategies can break this spiral and can prevent its development.
4. Relaxation techniques are useful for conserving energy and for speeding recovery. Athletes can often use them to relax between races (if there are a couple of hours). In addition, if the athletes become skilled and can control the extent to which they relax, these techniques can be used to clear their minds during delays of twenty or thirty minutes between competitive efforts.
5. Relaxation techniques are used to facilitate the development of visual images, to speed learning, and to aid recall of information.

BIOFEEDBACK

At its simplest, biofeedback involves nothing more than providing an athlete with information about on-going changes in some biological function. Taking your own pulse or listening to your heart with a stethoscope are examples of biofeedback. It has been assumed that when athletes are motivated to learn to control biological processes, that simply providing them with information about the processes that they want to control is sufficient for them to be able to gain that control. There is enough reinforcement from learning and gaining control for most athletes to make it unnecessary to do anything other than provide them with on-going feedback about what is occurring in their body.

Early studies by Dr. Neal Miller at Rockefeller University suggested that even biological processes that were thought to be under only involuntary or autonomic control (e.g., blood pressure, heart rate, etc.)

could come under the voluntary control of the athlete. Research has shown that by feeding back information about various physiological processes, individuals can indeed gain some control over heart rate, respiration rate, blood pressure, muscle tension levels, blood flow, galvanic skin response, brain waves, etc.

Although it had been hoped that through biofeedback we would be able to learn to control autonomic functions, this does not appear to be the case. Ideally, we would like to be able to get a person who suffers from hypertension to bring his/her blood pressure down into the normal range. Studies with biofeedback indicate that the amount of control a person can gain over blood pressure, though statistically significant (that is we can reliably demonstrate a change), is clinically insignificant (the size of the change is so small as to be physiologically and pathologically useless).

For virtually every biological process there is some range of functioning that can be influenced by situational, interpersonal, and cognitive factors. That range of flexibility varies from person to person. With respect to blood pressure, the range seems to be somewhere between 2 and 10 milimeters of mercury. Thus, a person might be able to lower blood pressure from 160/100 to 155/95. Such a change, when it can be reproduced on demand, is statistically significant, but as has been mentioned is not clinically useful.

What biofeedback of involuntary processes like blood pressure, heart rate, and brainwave activity does, is to allow the person to discover for oneself what thoughts, bodily movements (muscle contractions), and situational factors cause fluctuations. By constantly monitoring one's own heart rate, an athlete can begin to observe which of his/her thoughts raise it and lower it (within a limited range). Having discovered the conditions which are affecting heart rate, the athlete is then in a position to control it by simply altering what he/she attends to.

A very important factor for the sport psychologist to keep in mind here is that although the amount of change an athlete achieves in attempting to control an involuntary process may be considered physiologically insignificant, it is not necessarily cognitively insignificant. As an example, consider the athlete who has just been told by the doctor that he or she is suffering from hypertension. That information serves as a situational stressor in the diagram that has been described so often. As a result, there are additional physiological changes. First, blood pressure for the athlete is likely to move to the high end of the athlete's scale. In addition, there are likely to be increases in muscle tension, increases that can cause other symptoms like headaches, backaches, and/or that can lead to performance problems. There are also psychological changes that will occur. Attention narrows, as the anxiety over having hypertension increases. The athlete will spend more time attending to his/her fears and less time attending to the performance situation. He/she will have difficulty shifting attention from an internal to an external focus and as a result will have problems organiz-

168

ing and thinking logically. The athlete will begin to feel overloaded, confused, and rushed.

Connecting the athlete to a piece of biofeedback apparatus and showing him/her that it is possible to get some control over blood pressure, no matter how small, helps him/her break the spiral that developed in response to being told he/she suffered from hypertension. The athlete used biofeedback to redirect attention towards neutral or positive cues that result in some lowering of blood pressure. Associated with this redirection of attention is a lowering of the muscle tension increases and a reduction in the feelings of being overloaded by information and rushed.

Since a great portion of any physiological problem is a result of the confounding of stress related responses with the basic disturbance, biofeedback like many other psychological techniques can be used very effectively to modify the stress-related component.

Any technique, whether it is biofeedback, autogenic training, attention control training, progressive relaxation, or meditation, will result in the changes just described (the breaking of the spiral) provided the athlete has enough faith in the procedure, and confidence in his/her own ability to follow the instructions, so that he/she can redirect attention to something else (e.g., the biofeedback signal, the mantra in meditation, the suggestions in progressive relaxation, etc.). The choice of a technique then depends upon factors like a subject's belief in the procedure, and cost effectiveness.

Biofeedback requires the use of equipment that may be difficult to bring out onto the playing field. Attempting to use biofeedback to help an athlete relax in an actual competitive situation is time consuming and likely to draw a great deal of attention to the athlete. Having people stare at him/her as he/she is attempting to relax can be stress-inducing rather than stress-reducing.

From a cost perspective, biofeedback equipment is expensive. Relaxation is usually taught by providing feedback about muscle tension levels (typically from muscles in the forehead). Electro myographic equipment (EMG) that will provide the required feedback ranges from $700 to $2000.

We have now had about thirteen years of experience in the use of biofeedback in the treatment of clinical problems. A review of the studies conducted over this period of time indicates that as far as the sport psychologist is concerned, there is little to be gained by spending money on equipment to provide continuous feedback about blood pressure, skin conductance (GSR), brain wave activity (EEG), or blood flow (skin temperature). These feedback devices have not been found to have any specific uses that would recommend them. They can be used to assist in teaching athletes to relax, but so can EMG feedback. Finally, most athletes can gain as much control over general muscle tension and concentration with other less expensive procedures.

There are two feedback devices that may have some specific uses in

169

athletic situations. Feedback of heart rate in a continuous fashion can be very useful in increasing an athlete's cardiovascular fitness. This will be discussed in a little more detail at the end of this chapter.

In addition, to its general relaxation application, equipment that measures muscle tension levels (a biological process that is under voluntary control) can have specific application in the prevention and treatment of injury. It was mentioned in chapter 13 that feedback of muscle tension levels (EMG) in the area surrounding a tendinitis could be used to teach the athlete to reduce the strain that excessive muscle tension places on the injury.

In a similar way, feedback of muscle tension from specific muscle groups can be used to increase an athlete's control over muscles that are critical to performance. Dan was a gymnast who was approaching the learning of a double back somersault with a great deal of anxiety. It was anticipated that his anxiety could result in excessive tension in neck and shoulder muscles thereby slowing his rotation and preventing him from successfully executing the trick. To reduce the likelihood of this possibility, the EMG was connected to the Trapezius muscles in the neck, and Dan was provided with constant feedback about the level of tension in these muscles.

He was asked to sit quietly in a chair and to very carefully image himself executing a single back somersault. As he was imaging the somersault, he was actually to make small muscular movements that would be associated with the trick. Throughout this imaging process Dan was aware, via feedback, of the level of tension in his shoulders. Next, he was asked to image the double somersault. Before he even began to develop the image, feedback from the EMG told Dan that the tension in his trapezius muscles had increased dramatically. He was asked to check the tension, to move his shoulder so he could see just how tight they were. As he moved around he reported that the tension level was too high for him to get the head movement he wanted. Just thinking about the new trick had increased tension that much in muscles critical to the performance (increased tension in irrelevant muscles would have little meaning).

Following that initial demonstration to Dan, it was a simple matter for him to then lower voluntarily the muscle tension level in his neck and shoulders. He was able within a few minutes of a single session to think about the double and to image it, without allowing his muscle tension to increase beyond what he considered an acceptable level. Following this learning, Dan had little difficulty getting the required rotation on his double back.

To summarize then, at the present time biofeedback of muscle tension may be a useful adjunct to teaching general relaxation. In addition, there are some specific uses that can be made of feedback of muscle tension in relation to treatment and prevention of injury. Research is continuing in this area and hopefully the future will see important additional developments. In the meantime, biofeedback is an expensive

170

procedure that is most likely to be effective with those individuals who have a strong need for a physiological and/or scientific approach to their problem. From a demonstration perspective, biofeedback has been extremely useful in showing athletes the inter-relationship between thought processes and what goes on in their body. It does help make them believers in the importance of mental factors. For more detailed information on the history, application, and research in this area you are referred to the suggested readings at the end of this chapter.

MEDITATION

There are a great many forms of meditation. The focus here will be on the type of meditation emphasized by Dr. Herbert Benson in his book *The Relaxation Response*. The procedure itself is quite similar and in many ways identical to transcendental meditation (TM).

1. The procedure is practiced once or twice a day for 15 to 20 minutes each time. According to Benson the ability to relax is a skill that is developed which requires regular practice. Without regular practice, the ability deteriorates.

2. Individuals sit quietly and reduce distractions by practicing in a place where they are not likely to be disturbed and by closing their eyes.

3. While sitting quietly with eyes closed, the meditators count one silently to themselves, each time they exhale. No attempt is made to control breathing or anything else. All that is required is that attention be directed towards counting one on each exhale.

4. Although individuals are attending to breathing and counting, it is important that these attentional processes be as "passive" as possible. This means that individuals do not fight to force attention. If they lose count, find themselves distracted, their mind wanders, that is all right. They simply react to each distraction by gently and unemotionally bringing their attention back to counting one on each exhale. It is very important that the individual learn to react in this rather passive unemotional way to distractions. In fact, that is one of the major benefits of meditation for athletes, because the negative spiral is broken by a passive attentional focus.

The regular practice of meditation allows individuals to relax and to recover some of the physical and emotional energy that may have been lost through work, pressure, etc. Typically, individuals report feeling comfortable, relaxed, yet more energetic and better able to think in a clear logical fashion following meditation.

A procedure like TM that has a certain amount of Eastern philosophy attached to it can be attractive to those athletes who are interested in and/or turned on by Oriental tradition and thought. Benson's procedure does not have the mystical associations and thus is less likely to turn on some athletes. By the same token, it is less likely to turn some of them off.

Because the meditative procedure that I have outlined is very simple, and because it requires that individuals assume control and responsibility (they are counting to themselves, no one is counting for them), the procedure is more likely to be helpful with individuals who have relatively high levels of self-confidence, low levels of anxiety, and a high need for control. As anxiety increases and as confidence and/or self-esteem decreases, it becomes important to provide more structure and external support. In these cases a progressive relaxation procedure may be better.

As has already been mentioned, meditation can be used on a regular basis to reduce the likelihood of chronic problems. It can be a good substitute stress reducer, replacing alcohol or drugs. There are some other specific indications in sports, and one contraindication that is worth mentioning.

It is not uncommon for some individuals to become very relaxed while meditating. For this reason, particularly in those sports that require quick starts and a higher level of arousal (e.g., boxing, football, etc.), it is a good idea to make sure that there is enough time between completion of the meditation and the beginning of the competition to insure that the blood is circulating again and that the athlete is alert and ready. This time factor will vary from athlete-to-athlete, but is something that should be considered.

Specific uses of meditation include teaching athletes to control anxiety by tuning out competitive conditions, and teaching them to prevent the development of the feedback loop by developing the ability to attend passively to distractions. Two examples can be used to illustrate these points.

Divers at the Spartakade games in Russia, who were tuning up for the 1980 Moscow Olympics, had to perform under very poor conditions. During the preliminaries there were a large number of divers and so each diver had approximately 20-30 minutes between dives. During this waiting period the divers were required by the Russians to go to a very small room and sit, literally, shoulder to shoulder in uncomfortable chairs with all of the other divers.

For the more introverted athletes being forced to sit in a room full of strange people, was a very stressful situation. The athletes could not talk to their coaches or to each other. They simply had to sit quietly with towels around them trying to stay warm and trying to concentrate in order to prepare for their next dive. Many of the competitors found those conditions so disturbing that they performed far below their capabilities. For a few, they coped by meditating. As they went into the room they just sat quietly in their chairs, attended to their breathing, and tuned out the conditions and their own concerns. For these individuals exposure to and the practice of meditation proved to be extremely valuable.

Meditation as a technique can be especially useful for those athletes who must depend a great deal upon their ability to maintain control

172

over fine motor coordination and timing. In these sports, athletes can function at lower levels of arousal than they might function at in sports involving short, intense bursts of energy (sprints, contact sports, etc.).

A certain number of external distractors are inevitable in any competitive situation. There isn't any athlete who can sustain such a narrow focus of attention that he/she fails to see, hear, or feel other irrelevant things going on around him/her. When an athlete is playing well, the distractions tend to be reacted to in a passive way. They come into consciousness momentarily, but because the athlete is so caught up in the game, the distractions drift out as quickly as they came in. Unless the athlete stops and takes the time to remember the distraction, he/she typically forgets about it. Because the interruption is so brief, it has very little influence on performance. A photographer's flash, a sudden yell from the crowd, the movement of an opponent drift in as they occur and drift out as they end.

Under pressure, the external distractors do not drift in and drift out. The athlete loses her ability to attend to distractions in a passive way. Instead, she prolongs the attentional disturbances by adding her own internal distractors. The photographer's flash provides her with an excuse for some of her problems and increases her fear that she will have more. As a result she gets actively caught up in thoughts like "Don't let that disturb you." "Damn it, don't those people have any more sense." As she begins to attend to these additional distractors, she destroys her concentration and her ability to perform. She creates the loop that has been spoken about and instead of making one error, she makes ten.

Regular practice of meditation requires the individuals to systematically learn how to avoid becoming actively trapped by their own distractions. Through learning to attend passively to the distractions, to bring attention gently back to counting the breathing, the athletes are practicing the same thing they need to be able to do when distracted in competitive situations. If athletes were to learn nothing more than to be able to respond to both external and internal distractions in a passive way during competition, that athlete would dramatically improve the average level and consistency of performance. They would perform much closer to their own optimal level most of the time.

PROGRESSIVE RELAXATION

Progressive relaxation as it was introduced by Dr. Edmond Jacobson in the 1930's, involved learning to relax by systematically tensing and then relaxing various muscle groups in the body. Over the past few years, however, the term progressive relaxation has come to be applied to any procedure that involves a regular, systematic relaxation of muscle groups. In most instances, tensing of muscles has been dropped from the procedure.

Initially, it was felt that tensing and then relaxing the muscles would

173

provide a contrast for the athlete and would also facilitate relaxation. Application of the techniques with non-neurotic individuals in preparation for actual competitive situations, however, seems to indicate that the tensing of muscles very quickly becomes distracting.

Most athletes do not have such chronically high tension levels that they have difficulty recognizing when they are relaxing. For these individuals, systematically attending to particular muscle groups and relaxing them seems to be a more efficient way to achieve control over level of arousal. In fact, the tensing of muscles tends to activate or arouse the athlete and results in prolonging the procedures. This fact is often used by athletes to raise their levels of arousal following relaxation, especially if they feel a need to "get up" for a competition.

As a technique, progressive relaxation is especially useful with individuals who have a need for structure. The dependency needs and control needs of athletes can be addressed by giving them more or less responsibility for the training. For example, tapes can be made which the athlete plays and listens to, in order to relax. This procedure tends to provide external support and structure for those individuals who have lower levels of self-confidence. In contrast, the techniques can also be taught to individual athletes and then he/she assumes responsibility for practicing them by saying them silently to himself/herself. This process comes closer to meditation, with the exception that the individual is systematically attending to muscle groups and actively attempting to relax these, rather than attending to a mantra and assuming that a natural by product of this "passive" attention will be relaxation.

Because progressive relaxation emphasizes the development of control over certain muscle groups, it has a great deal of face validity for those athletes who: 1) feel a need to assume an active role in accomplishing a goal; and 2) recognize the need for greater control over tension in specific muscle groups.

Progressive relaxation by itself can be used to simply relax or to provide that break from constant tension that allows the athlete to clear his/her thoughts and regain some physical energy. Many athletes use the procedure to get to sleep the night before a competition or to get back to sleep if they wake up frequently. More often, however, the procedure is used in combination with mental rehearsal and imagery techniques to facilitate performance.

Ron was an extremely dedicated athlete, with a strong need for control and a narrow focus of attention. He was disciplined and needed a regular training procedure and a great deal of structure. At the same time, Ron was a student of his sport. He was analytical enough that he wanted to understand the why's behind any technique or procedure he used. He wasn't the type of person who would try something just because someone else had and said it would work. He had to be shown that there was a logical reason for the technique.

In his junior year in college, Ron established the conference record in the shot putt. Through the off season Ron worked very hard on technique and improving strength. In spite of his dedication to physical development and training, he was unable to improve upon his own record. Ron's coaches felt that his dedication and development had paid off, but that Ron had simply reached his own maximal level of performance. He was considerably smaller than many shot putt competitors and as a result relied heavily on technique. The coaches felt his size limited him and felt his technique could not be improved upon.

Ron was very open to the importance of psychological factors in athletic performance. Discussions with him convinced him of the importance of increasing his control over muscle tension levels in his neck and shoulders. It was easy to show Ron that competitive situations and his own strong desire to improve upon his record were increasing his tension levels in neck and shoulder muscles. Thus, although he had made improvements in technique and in strength, these were being cancelled out by the increased bracing (generalized muscle tension) response and by attentional disturbances.

A progressive relaxation procedure was taught to Ron so that he could use it to become more sensitive to rising tension levels in neck and shoulder muscles and so that he could reduce the tension in those muscles that were antagonistic (flexor muscles) to putting the shot. Within two weeks of the beginning of training, Ron had improved his conference mark by several inches and he continued to improve through the remainder of the season.

A similar program was worked out for a female high jumper. Once again, the individual had reached a plateau in her performance. She was one inch away from qualifying for the collegiate nationals. Progressive relaxation was explained to her and the importance of being able to get maximal extension from the arms to assist in lifting the athlete off the ground was emphasized.

In this instance, the sport psychologist assumed more responsibility, taking the athlete through the relaxation and rehearsal processes. This external support was important because of the athlete's needs and confidence level. The psychologist would get the athlete to relax using the procedure that is outlined in the next few pages. Then, while she was relaxed he would have her rehearse her approach and jump, successfully clearing the national qualifying height. Through the rehearsal, the athlete was able to become sensitive to tension levels, and to be able to gain control over task relevant muscle groups. Relaxation facilitated the rehearsal process because it minimized anxiety and internal and external distractors. As a result, the athlete was able to concentrate more effectively. She cleared the qualifying height within a week of the initial training experience.

In Eastern Europe, they have been able to use progressive relaxation procedures to calm athletes and to facilitate their ability to concentrate on, and rehearse performance prior to the actual competition. Then, following the relaxation, they assist the athlete in developing task relevant imagery that will help them get aroused (particularly in sports requiring strength) and at the same time direct attention to appropriate task relevant cues. This "psyching up" process is supplemented by alternately tensing and relaxing muscle groups (e.g., tensing muscle in the forearms and upper arms and holding that tension for a few seconds, relaxing for a second or two, tensing again, holding it, relaxing for a couple of seconds, etc., for three or four times). This process helps the athlete achieve a more optimal level of arousal (for those that need to be psyched up) and at the same time facilitates mental concentration.

RELAXATION PROCEDURE

The procedure that is presented here, is the one that I use with athletes. There is actually very little difference between this progressive relaxation procedure and some hypnotic induction techniques. The primary differences involve the fact that the word hypnosis is never used, and that athletes are not led to believe that they are being hypnotized. As will be pointed out in the next chapter, these two small differences can be very important.

"I would like you to begin by sitting down and making yourself as comfortable as possible. Most people find that the procedure works best if they have their feet flat on the floor, and their hands and arms resting in their lap. If you feel that you would be more capable of relaxing in some other position, however, that's fine. Just make yourself as comfortable as you can.

"Now I would like you to close your eyes and begin by inhaling deeply from down in your abdomen, and exhaling slowly. That's fine, now as you exhale, I want you to relax all of the muscles in your right arm. Relax the muscles in your right hand, in the wrist, forearm, and upper arm. Notice that as you relax those muscles and as you exhale, your arm becomes heavier, sinking down against the chair, or against your body. Notice that as you exhale and as you relax the muscles in your right arm it becomes heavier, sinking down. That's fine!

"Now I want you to relax all of the muscles in your left arm. Relax the muscles in the fingers . . . hand . . . wrist . . . forearm . . . upperarm. Again notice that as you relax those muscles and as you exhale, your left arm becomes heavier . . . sinking down against your body, or against the chair. As you exhale, and as you relax the muscles in both arms, they become heavier . . . sinking down against your body or against the chair.

"Now, I want you to relax the muscles in your right leg. . . . Relax the muscles in the foot . . . ankle . . . calf . . . and thigh. . . . Just completely relax all of the muscles in your right leg and as you do, notice that as you exhale . . . your leg becomes heavier . . . pushing down against the chair . . . and against the floor. . . . That's fine!

"Now, relax all of the muscles in your left leg. . . . Relax the muscles in the foot . . . ankle . . . calf . . . and thigh. . . . Just completely relax all of the muscles in both legs and as you do notice that as you exhale your legs become heavier. It's a very pleasant heaviness as you feel your arms and legs relaxing and pressing down against the chair. Feeling very comfortable and very relaxed. . . . Relaxing all of the muscles in both arms . . . and both legs.

"Now, I want you to relax all of the muscles in your neck and shoulders. Just completely relax . . . let yourself go. . . . You will always be able to hear the things that I say and you will be able to enjoy the very pleasant feelings of being completely relaxed. . . .

"Now, relax the muscles in your face . . . and jaw. Relax the muscles around your eyes. . . . As you relax the muscles in your jaw, just let your mouth open slightly. . . . That's fine. . . . Just completely relax, relaxing all of the muscles in your arms . . . legs . . . neck . . . shoulders . . . face . . . and jaw. . . . Notice as you relax and exhale how much heavier your body feels as you sink down into the chair . . . always able to hear the things that I say.

176

"Now, relax the muscles in your chest . . . stomach . . . and back. . . . Just completely relax and let yourself go. . . .

"In a moment, I am going to count from one to twenty. With each count you will find yourself drifting down . . . becoming more comfortable . . . more relaxed . . . always able to hear the things that I say. . . . With each count you will find yourself drifting . . . floating . . . becoming more and more relaxed. . . .

"One . . . relaxing all of the muscles in your right arm . . . in the fingers . . . hand . . . forearm . . . and upperarm. . . . Noticing that as you relax and as you exhale . . . your arm becomes heavier . . . drifting down. . . . Two . . . relaxing all of the muscles in the left arm . . . in the fingers . . . wrist . . . hand . . . forearm . . . and upperarm. . . . Completely relaxing all of the muscles in both arms.

"Three . . . breathing deeply and slowing from the abdomen . . . relaxing all of the muscles in your right leg. . . . Four, relaxing the muscles in your left leg. . . . Five . . . Six . . . Seven . . . becoming more and more relaxed . . . relaxing all of the muscles in both arms and both legs. . . . Very comfortable, very relaxed. . . .

"Eight . . . relaxing the muscles in your neck . . . and shoulders. . . . Nine . . . relaxing the muscles in your face . . . and your jaw. . . . Just letting yourself go . . . becoming completely relaxed . . . always able to hear the things that I say. . . .

"Ten . . . half way there . . . drifting down . . . becoming heavier . . . and more relaxed . . . drifting . . . floating . . . in a very pleasant . . . relaxed state. Eleven . . . Twelve . . . Thirteen . . . Fourteen . . . down . . . down . . . down. . . . Becoming more and more relaxed.

"Fifteen . . . relaxing all of the muscles in your entire body . . . in your arms . . . legs . . . neck . . . shoulders . . . face . . . jaw . . . chest . . . back . . . stomach. . . . Completely relaxed . . . very comfortable. . . . Noticing that as you relax your muscles and as you exhale, you drift down deeper . . . deeper . . . still deeper. . . .

"Sixteen. . . . Seventeen. . . . Eighteen. . . . Nineteen. . . . Twenty. . . . Very comfortable . . . completely relaxed. . . ."

At this point in the procedure, I have several directions that I can take. If I simply want the athlete to continue to relax and to take over responsibility for directing what happens from this point I will instruct him/her in the following way:

"Alright, just continue to relax . . . while I talk to you for a minute. . . . I want you to continue relaxing, until you are ready to get up and to go back to preparing for the competition. . . . When you get ready to get up, it will be important to do so in a very systematic way. . . . You have been able to get very relaxed and as a result could get slightly dizzy or disoriented if you jumped up suddenly. To prevent this, just count three to yourself when you are ready to get up. On the count of one . . . inhale deeply. . . . On the count of two stretch your arms and legs . . . and on the count of three . . . open your eyes. Whenever you are ready . . . count one . . . inhale deeply . . . count two . . . stretch your arms and legs . . . and count three . . . and open your eyes. . . ."

If some rehearsal procedure has been worked out (see chapter 18), I typically have the athlete engage in that rehearsal process following the count to twenty. At that time I may direct the rehearsal process (depending upon the athletes dependence and need for control), or I may direct the athlete to rehearse. What is to be rehearsed will have been carefully worked out in advance.

"Just continue to relax and now I would like you to imagine that you are standing in front of the high jump pit. You have found your starting point and it is your turn to jump. . . ."

Following the rehearsal, I will either count to three and get the athlete to begin moving around in order to increase arousal to the desired point, or I will have instructed the person to do that for himself/herself.

Depending upon the individual athlete, how rapidly he or she relaxes, the entire procedure, including visualization will last not more than twenty to twenty-five minutes. The induction or relaxation part typically takes from five to fifteen minutes.

PHYSICAL EXERCISE

A final procedure that can be used on a regular basis to prevent or minimize the development of chronic emotional and physical problems is regular aerobic exercise. Research seems to indicate that regular physical exercise that elevates an athlete's heart rate to somewhere between 140 and 170 beats per minute and sustains that heart rate for approximately 20 minutes, results in increased cardiovascular fitness.

From a stress management perspective, running, swimming, cycling, etc., any exercise that sustains heart rate and is engaged in from three to seven times per week will result in a reduction of the symptoms associated with stress. This exercise has been found to be helpful in the treatment and prevention of depression, hypertension, and coronary heart disease.

On the face of it, we might assume that athletes who are currently active, are in good shape, and would not need some fitness program. Unfortunately, such an assumption is far from accurate. Most of the exercise athletes get, who are not involved in endurance sports, consists of short intense bursts of energy where speed, strength, and reaction time are emphasized. As a result, athletes may be very strong, but resting heart rate may be fairly high. Ideally, an athlete's heart rate when he/she is resting would be below sixty beats per minute.

The failure of many athletes to be physically fit from a cardiovascular and endurance standpoint can be highlighted by the experience of some professional teams. Off-season and pre-season training programs are worked out to help individuals in baseball, football, basketball, etc. maintain a fairly high level of physical conditioning. In spite of these training programs, at least one professional baseball team found that only six members of their entire squad were capable of running a mile in under six minutes at the start of spring training.

Regular physical exercise not only helps the athlete maintain cardiovascular fitness, but it provides a tension release and helps redirect attention to non-stressful cues. The athlete is too busy paying attention to his/her running, etc. to bother with all of the hassles. Thus, the exercise serves as a time out.

Earlier I mentioned the problems that a great many athletes encounter when they retire. They become inactive and they develop fairly serious depressions. Clinical studies have been able to show that physical inactivity and depression go hand in hand. In fact, if depressed individuals can be motivated to exercise, the resulting changes in biochemical processes result in a lessening of the depression. Athletes as a group are easier to motivate to exercise and for this reason the sport psychologist should consider this as a very important tool to use, especially with the older athlete.

178

HYPNOSIS AS AN ALTERED STATE OF CONSCIOUSNESS

There have been literally hundreds of books written about hypnosis. Probably no single psychological technique has been associated with more mysticism and fantasy than the use of hypnotic suggestions. As a tool, hypnosis has been used in a variety of medical situations to treat illnesses, reduce pain, and to minimize the likelihood of post-operative infection. Psychologically, hypnosis has been used to treat neurotic and psychotic conflicts. Hypnotic suggestions have been used to recall lost memories, to get people to forget traumatic incidents, to treat hysterical paralysis, blindness, and deafness.

Obviously, it is not possible to begin to cover the topic of hypnosis in just a few pages. The major emphasis of this chapter will be on understanding hypnosis as a tool for altering an athlete's perception or consciousness. What are some of the similarities and differences between hypnosis and relaxation techniques? How can hypnosis distort the passage of time, altering the athlete's perception of movement, slowing things down?

FOUR STAGES

Conceptually, it may be useful to think of hypnosis as consisting of four, more or less distinct phases. The first phase can be called the pre-induction stage. We often think of hypnosis as a state of hypersuggestibility. Athletes who are good hypnotic subjects seem to be able to respond to the suggestions of the hypnotist. The ability of the athlete to respond to suggestions, and how the athlete's own responses will be interpreted by him/her, depends upon his/her preparation for the experience. It is the preparation for hypnosis that is being referred to here, as the pre-induction phase.

Generally speaking, the sport psychologist will attempt to control and determine the athlete's attitudes and expectancies prior to hypnosis. Typically this control is accomplished by asking questions to determine what the person has been told, what experiences he has had, etc. Because so much has been written about hypnosis, and because a great deal of mystery surrounds its use as far as the general public is concerned, it is very difficult to be aware of and control all of the subject's potential expectations.

Since the subject can carry his own unverbalized expectancies into the hypnotic situation, it is very important that the hypnotist be aware of any unusual responses or concerns. Let me provide two examples to illustrate the importance of properly preparing subjects for hypnosis.

I was about to hypnotize a class one time, and asked the students if any of them had concerns about what might happen. One of the students told me that he had been led to believe that hypnosis might induce an epileptic seizure. I explained to him that although that had been Mesmer's experience (subjects when hypnotized appeared to have a seizure), it was a result of the subjects' expectancies and their suggestability. Research has since shown that seizures have nothing to do with hypnosis, and subjects no longer have seizures when they are hypnotized.

My response did not seem to satisfy the student. He mentioned that he was epileptic, and that he was afraid of losing control. To minimize his anxiety, I told him fine, that during the induction he would find he was in complete control. If, as he began to respond to suggestions he felt he was losing control, he was free to get up and walk out of the room. I told him that he would have no trouble doing this should the need arise. In effect, his concerns had forced me to give some pre-hypnotic suggestions. As a result of his own expectancies, he did begin to feel as if he was losing control. During the trance induction he got up and walked out of the room. He felt a seizure was avoided because of advance preparation.

A second example of the potential impact of pre-hypnotic suggestions or ideas came out of the development of committees for the protection of human subjects. I was conducting some research on the effects of hypnosis on relaxation and muscle tension. Routinely, all research projects at the University were cleared through a committee that had been developed to insure the safety of human subjects. Although the procedures that were being used, at least as I was using them, represented extremely little risk to any subject, members of the committee did not understand that. Two of the individuals on the committee did not understand hypnosis. All they knew about the subject was what they had read in the popular press, and what they saw on T.V. and in the movies. To them, hypnosis represented a potentially dangerous situation.

As a result of their concerns, it was determined that before I could conduct the study I would have to get the subjects to sign a paper saying that they "realized that hypnosis could be dangerous." The irony of the committee's demand was that the suggestion of danger implied in the consent form, so dramatically increased the likelihood of potential problems that we had to abandon what had been perfectly safe and acceptable research.

Because of the influences of prehypnotic ideas, suggestions, and

180

beliefs, the sport psychologist needs to take considerable time in preparing a subject. This is not only true in order to avoid problems, but it is equally important to maximize the potential effectiveness of suggestions. By using an induction technique and making suggestions that respond to the subject's expectancies, you can increase their ability to respond and to become hypnotized.

The second stage or phase of hypnosis is typically referred to as the induction. It is the induction that moves the athlete from a normal state of attending to one which allows him/her to respond to the hypnotist's suggestions.

There are probably as many induction techniques as there are hypnotists. These procedures vary from being totally nonverbal, simply pointing at subjects who have been properly prepared during the pre-induction phase (e.g., led to believe as Mesmer's subjects were, that when they were pointed at, certain things would happen to their bodies and minds), to making extensive suggestions about sleep and about entering a hypnotic state.

Some of the more popularized inductions involve the use of eye fixation techniques (getting the subject to strain the eyes by staring at a spot or object). The goal here is to pair suggestions of fatigue and tiredness with the strain the subject must endure in order to keep his/her eyes open. As he/she begins to respond to the suggestions to let the eyes close and enter a hypnotic state, the hypnotist has succeeded in capturing attention, and in getting the subject to respond in a more "passive," "observational" way to what is going on and what is being said.

Actually, there may be little difference between a hypnotic induction technique and the relaxation technique presented in chapter 15. In fact, I have had subjects become hypnotized when I used the progressive relaxation technique. The reason they became hypnotized was because they had seen a similar procedure used before and it had been called hypnosis. In spite of the fact that I was careful to avoid using the word hypnotized and that I told them they were simply learning a procedure they could use themselves to relax, they interpreted what was going on as hypnosis. I found out what was going on when they had difficulty waking up and asked me to "get them out of the hypnotic trance."

Although the induction phase may be identical to a relaxation procedure, and although the attentional changes associated with the development of a trance occur in the two states, the two experiences are usually seen as dramatically different by the subject. These differences can be attributed to the pre-induction expectancies. Once again, a couple of examples will help illustrate the point.

Alpha waves are an 8 to 13 cycle per second electrical discharge given off by the human brain. Research as far back as the 1930's indicated that when subjects were in an alpha wave state, they tended to be relaxed, and to be attending in a passive, non-focal way.

If we take naive subjects and monitor their brain waves, and then ask them what they feel like when they are in alpha, they will describe themselves as slightly bored, but relaxed. Their minds are kind of wandering from one thought to another without much direction. The state will not be described as unpleasant but it will not be seen as anything special.

On the other hand, if we get a number of individuals who are enthusiastically exploring Eastern philosophies, we are likely to get different results. For these people, passive attention may be a highly desirable goal. They have learned that most Westerners have a difficult time relaxing and attending passively. Their study of the Eastern mystics and gurus has led them to believe that non-focal attending is a means of beginning to achieve "enlightenment" or "oneness with the universe." When these individuals are hooked up to the EEG and asked to describe what it is like to be in Alpha, they describe it as a highly desirable state and often equate it with religious enlightenment. For this group, the experience of being in alpha can have a prolonged impact on their behavior. Because they describe it as an altered state, as something very special, they may actually alter major aspects of their life in order to spend more time in a state that someone else would refer to as boring.

Research on the effects of hallucinogenic drugs like LSD reveal similar findings. Individuals who take LSD and who view the drug as little more than a recreational experience, simply "get high" and forget about it. On the other hand, there was a group of drug users who were led to believe that LSD was a chemical sacrament, a way to achieve enlightenment. For these people, the alterations in consciousness that resulted from ingestion of the drug were interpreted as highly significant.

In all of the cases mentioned, something happened which altered the individuals' normal way of attending to the world (their consciousness was altered). We all experience alterations in awareness from time to time. Sleep, dreams, exposure to sensory-deprived conditions, or to excessive stimulation (e.g., light shows and rock concerts), smoking marijuana, etc. all induce alterations in awareness. Hypnosis and progressive relaxation are methods of altering normal attentional processes. Just how these alterations will be interpreted will depend upon pre and post induction factors.

The third stage of hypnosis can be referred to as the trance state within which the actual hypnotic work occurs. The induction technique has been used to help the subject focus attention on the suggestions being made by the hypnotist. Once the proper attentional state has been established (a state in which the subject is responsive to suggestions), and the trance has been achieved, the hypnotist usually offers some goal-directed suggestions.

A wide variety of suggestions can be made that good subjects will respond to. For the most part, these suggestions involve getting the subject to experience alterations in perceptions, thoughts, and feelings. By getting the subject to attend in certain ways (e.g., focusing in more intently on a particular feeling or thought, or by attending to non-threatening cues rather than threatening or painful ones), the hypnotist can enhance and/or minimize the subject's sensitivity to pain, emotional events, the passage of time, etc.

Generally, the sport psychologist uses hypnosis to assist athletes in recalling and rehearsing specific performances. Often, suggestions are used to increase motivation and self-confidence. Under proper supervision, suggestions can be used to increase endurance and to minimize pain. The effectiveness of hypnosis in pain reduction is truly remarkable. Hypnosis not only acts to reduce pain (being used as the only pain reducer in many surgical situations), but it appears to have some antiseptic properties as well. During the 1800's, hypnosis was used in conjunction with major surgery in India. In over 150 cases of surgery for the removal of scrotal tumors, the mortality rate dropped from the typical fifty percent for that time, to a mere five percent. In addition to it's antiseptic and anesthetic qualities, hypnosis is also used as a crisis intervention technique, as a means of calming an athlete down and helping him refocus attention.

The final stage to be discussed, is the post hypnotic phase. Following the preparation of the subject, the induction of the trance, and the suggestions designed to modify behavior or attitudes, the athlete is awakened. At this time, he or she may begin to respond to the post hypnotic suggestions that the hypnotist has made. These suggestions may involve feeling increased confidence or less anxiety. They may involve being capable of sustaining performance under pressure. The actual impact that the suggestions will have on behavior will depend upon the depth of the trance and on how the person interprets the whole experience.

To facilitate the effects that hypnosis can have, the sport psychologist should debrief the subject. After he or she has come out of the trance, the experience should be discussed. The realness of it, and the relevance it can have for the athlete should be emphasized. In many instances, the subject will be looking to the sport psychologist for reassurance that he/she was really hypnotized. On these occasions, profound perceptual changes have not been experienced. This lack of this experience may be because the subject was incapable of responding as completely as some other individuals, or it may be because the subject experiences alterations in what most others would consider "normal awareness" fairly frequently. In either case, the sport psychologist can help by providing reassurance and support for the things that were experienced. The subject may need help in seeing the subtle changes that did take place. The confidence that the hypnotist has in what happened can infect the subject, even when the psychologist has his own doubts about whether or not the athlete was hypnotized.

There are those individuals who have difficulty responding to suggestions when they believe they are hypnotized because the hypnotic situation represents a loss of control. As a result, they resist during the formal part of the experience. Then, after "awakening" they relax and can become very caught up in the suggestions and interpretations offered by the hypnotist. In effect, they are in a state of "waking hypnosis." They became more responsive and suggestible following the experience than they were during it.

DIRECT VERSUS INDIRECT SUGGESTIONS

How suggestions are made in order to induce a hypnotic state, and to facilitate the trance work of subjects, can be categorized on the basis of the directness. Generally speaking, it is assumed that direct suggestions (e.g., "your pain will go away.") have little lasting effect on neurotic conflicts and problems. Presumably, the patient or athlete's difficulties cannot be solved by "conscious" processes. If they could be, the individual would have found a solution earlier. Instead, indirect suggestions must be used to allow the patient to get around the blocks and resistances that are preventing them from solving their own problems.

Sarah was a thirteen-year-old diver who was competing in local meets. She was diving off the one meter board, and although she had a great deal of promise, she still had a great deal to learn. On the surface, Sarah had a great deal of desire and motivation to become an elite diver. Her intense drive, however, was confounded by an underlying fear of failure. At a conscious level she was driven to achieve and she pushed herself to the point of tears and frustration. At an unconscious level she was keeping herself from really finding out how good she could be. She was so afraid of failure that she would find little problems that kept getting in the way. Given her conscious competitiveness and desire, there was no way she could accept or admit her own underlying fear.

Approximately two weeks before a key meet, Sarah suddenly lost her ability to do a forward somersault with a full twist. She had been doing the dive and began to have a little trouble deciding when to start the twist. She began to build up her own fear of the dive and the problem to the point that she could not even begin to throw the dive. She started looking for reasons and pointed out conflicting suggestions from different coaches, she talked about being lost (not knowing where she was in the air), she emphasized that she was thinking too much during the dive, and so on.

In an attempt to deal with this, Sarah was relaxed and direct suggestions were made to increase confidence and to allow her to execute the dive. "You will get on the board and feel confident. You will find that you know how to do the dive. You will take your approach, find yourself going up in the air, you will feel good and strong and you will complete the best full twisting somersault of your life." The suggestions, given Sarah's underlying fears, failed to work. She was unable to place confidence in the procedures as they were presented to her.

A second attempt was made to use hypnosis to help Sarah with her problem. This time, however, it was decided to follow the format of-

184

fered by Erickson and Rossi in their book, *Hypnotherapy: An Exploratory Casebook*. Indirect suggestions were used to get Sarah to break through her own unconscious resistance. The following suggestions were made: "Sarah, you will find that *if you want to,* you can let yourself complete the forward somersault with a full twist. When your mind and body are ready you will allow it to happen. You can talk without thinking of forming the words, you can walk without thinking about the steps you are taking, those processes are controlled by your unconscious. When you wish you can allow your unconscious to take over. When you are ready you will do the dive."

Following the suggestions, Sarah went out and executed the dive with only minor difficulty. Within a few minutes she had regained control over herself and the dive. The difference in the suggestions involved the fact that no pressure was put on Sarah in the second case. "You will do the dive when you are ready." In addition, the conflict of thinking too much was removed by suggesting that the unconscious would handle the problem. Because Sarah had been able to execute the dive before, it was reasonable to assume that she would be able to do it again, if she could just stop the interfering thoughts.

The difference between direct and indirect suggestions can be a very important one. In a great many athletic situations, the sport psychologist is not dealing with serious underlying conflicts and can make direct suggestions. In fact, treatment may proceed more rapidly by being direct. Even so, a knowledge of the issues underlying the choice of words that a hypnotist uses is very important. The use of indirect suggestions is, or can be, a highly refined art. I would recommend Erickson and Rossi's book very highly.

HYPNOSIS AND ATTENTION

Hypnotic suggestions can have a rather profound effect on the athlete's perception of time and pain. Frequently you will hear athletes talk about "highs" in which they believed they achieved some super level of performance. They went out and everything seemed to fall into place. Perceptions were slowed down, and it was as if they were in complete control of everything. The athletes knew what was going to happen almost before it occurred. They could anticipate their own moves and those of their opponents. They felt "suspended" in the air, almost as if they were floating. If they were trying to hit a ball or a target, the object they were aiming at seemed to be slowed down, and to be larger than life. Baseball and tennis players report being able to "read the label on the ball." Quarterbacks like John Brodie report knowing when they are going to throw a touchdown pass even before the ball finishes leaving their hand. They sense the developing play and everything "feels right." At times it seems as if athletes are sitting above and behind their own bodies, they are outside themselves, watching everything as it unfolds around them.

This type of alteration in awareness is one of the most sought after experiences in sport. Athletes have the feeling that if they could just reproduce those moments, if they could just increase their frequency, or develop these "highs" whenever they wanted to, they would be unbeatable. Because similar states can occur when hypnotized, hypnosis is often looked to as a procedure that may be useful in training individual athletes to alter awareness on demand.

Although we have still not gained the type of control we would like over attention and thought processes, it is currently possible to shed some light on what is happening. Although I will be talking about these alterations in awareness within the context of hypnosis, it is important to remember that a formal hypnotic induction is not required. As mentioned earlier, other procedures like progressive relaxation, meditation, etc. can be used to alter normal awareness. Hypnosis is often seen as more effective, because the athlete's pre-induction preparation has increased his/her ability to let go and to attend in the desired way.

In chapter 4 I discussed several dimensions of attention that are relevant to being able to perform effectively. The dimensions include the width of an athlete's attentional focus (broad to narrow), and the direction (internal vs. external). Under normal conditions athletes shift and move along these two attentional continuum. Although we all differ with respect to the frequency and direction of shifts, individually, we have our own regular or normal patterns. Any experience that disturbs our normal pattern, results in an altered state of consciousness. Figure 9 presents the attentional dimensions and indicates how various experiences alter normal attentional processes.

As an example, hypnosis is seen as a process which affects attention in two ways. First, attention is narrowed and the amount of information that a person attends to is dramatically reduced. This shift occurs because the athlete focuses on the suggestions of the hypnotist. Typically, external distractions are reduced by having the individual close his/her eyes, and by selecting a quiet place for the hypnosis to take place.

In addition to narrowing, hypnosis results in a breakdown in the frequency with which a subject shifts from an internal focus of attention to an external one. The athlete learns to attend to the hypnotist's suggestions and pays progressively less attention to his/her own analytical thoughts or questions. In effect, he/she trusts enough to stop second guessing and simply responds passively to whatever is suggested.

Earlier it was pointed out that the perception of movement depended upon the attentional processes of the athlete. The more anxious they were, the more likely internal distractions like worries or self-instructions, were to distract them. If they were supposed to be attending to a ball that was being thrown at them, each of their internal distractors seemed to cut a few frames out of the movie they were watching. In effect, the ball seemed to come towards them more quickly and they felt as though they had less time to respond. Anxiety distorted perception by making things seem as if they were happening more quickly than usual. In contrast, hypnotic instructions and the hypnotic state can help the athlete focus more completely on an object. The difference in this instance is in the opposite direction. Now frames are added to the film because there are even fewer distractors than there are in the normal state. As a result, the athlete feels as if they have more time, things have slowed down, and they can "read the label on the ball."

The farther an athlete is pushed along any of the attentional dimensions (and the more shifting is reduced), the greater the perceptual alterations, and the more profound the impact of the experience. When something very dramatic happens to our normal attentional processes we quickly attempt to find an explanation. It is here that our pre-induction expectancies and our post hypnotic or post experience explanations become critical. The sport psychologist who is capable of maximizing an athlete's expectancies and of manipulating attention, can dramatically alter an individual's faith in himself/herself, in the psychologist, in psychological techniques, and in his/her own ability.

By altering attention, pushing an athlete to attend to task relevant cues, or not to attend to pain, the sport psychologist can improve performance, increase endurance and/or break the feedback loop that develops under pressure.

Figure 9
Attentional Processes and Alterations in Consciousness

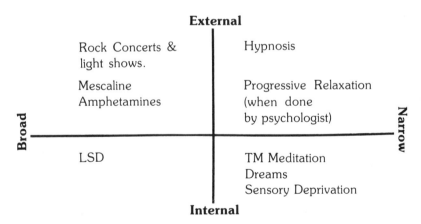

To clarify this process further, consider some of the other techniques that are used to alter awareness. Sleep, is seen as an altered state. The passage of time is distorted, emotional responses can be dramatically altered as can perceptions. During sleep, there is a dramatic reduction in the amount of external stimuli to which we attend. Under waking conditions, we shift back and forth between our thoughts and interpretations and physical reality. When this shifting breaks down, so does our ability to think rationally and logically. Images become distorted by our imagination, and are not brought back into focus because we don't compare them to external reality, to see what is really there.

Consciousness is altered in another way by drugs like LSD. Presumably, LSD acts to reduce our ability to inhibit the input of information to the brain. As a result, we get overwhelmed by all of the things that we see, hear, smell, or think. Somehow the drug has moved us out along the width continuum and as a result, normal consciousness is disturbed.

APPLICATIONS OF HYPNOSIS TO SPORT PSYCHOLOGY

As I have already mentioned, hypnosis has been found to have a large number of medical and psychological uses, especially in the treatment of abnormal and/or pathological conditions. For those with medical expertise and/or expertise in clinical psychology, an exploration of the ways in which hypnosis can be applied would be most useful. At the present time, I would like to focus discussion on the use of the procedure to reduce anxiety and improve concentration and to enhance motivation and confidence.

I would like to emphasize that prior to using hypnosis for the purposes outlined, sport psychologists should ask himself/herself the following questions.

1. Do they and the athletes have clearly operationalized goals?
2. Do they have a clear understanding of the athlete's expectancies and beliefs concerning the effects of hypnosis?
3. Are they qualified to use the procedure for the particular application they have in mind? Do they know enough about hypnosis, about the athlete, and about the demands of the athletic situation to use the procedure in a safe way?
4. Do they have enough of a feeling for the types of problems that can develop as a function of excessive dependency, and/or underlying conflicts, so that they know when to make a referral?
5. Do they have the capacity for dealing with unexpected events in a cool, rational fashion?
6. Is expert supervision and/or back-up available should it be needed?

Larry was a world class sprinter and national record holder in the hurdles. Throughout his competitive experience Larry had seemed almost unflapable. His concentration during an event was almost total and if you asked him if he were ever distracted during a race he would say no.

As the time for qualifying for the Olympics drew nearer, Larry began to find himself becoming distracted during races and even in practice. Because he had never been aware of the distractions before, he became concerned. His times in tune up meets were below what he had hoped they would be and this, in combination with the increased distractability,

188

caused him to begin questioning his ability. An athlete who had always been confident was in danger of choking.

Larry knew that the Olympics represented his last chance. Not only was it the culmination of his athletic career, but a win could mean a great deal financially. Whereas before Larry was relatively unencumbered by worries (there was always another meet, if he didn't win this one, he would win the next), suddenly things had changed and he wasn't used to it.

Larry approached a sport psychologist and asked for help. He knew that the psychologist had helped other athletes on the team with the use of hypnosis and was hoping that a similar procedure would work for him. Larry appeared to have a great deal of faith in the fact that hypnotic suggestions could be used to remove the distractions that were interfering with his ability to concentrate.

In talking with Larry it was obvious that his expectancies were not unrealistic. He really did not expect the hypnosis to allow him to do anything that he had not already been capable of doing. What he hoped would happen was that the suggestions would help him regain an ability to concentrate.

Larry proved to be an excellent hypnotic subject. His ability to narrow attention and to concentrate, the same ability that led to the development of his athletic skill and world class ability, facilitated the development of a deep hypnotic state. Following a standard induction procedure, it was suggested that Larry would visualize himself going through a race from start to finish. He would see himself approaching each hurdle, he would be aware of exactly how many steps he took between hurdles, he would know the positions of his legs. The entire race would be run in slow motion and would feel effortless. He would watch as he breezed to a new world record time. During the race his concentration would be totally caught up in his own movements. He would be able to passively observe as his body would naturally respond to the demands of the race. He would feel great, on top of the world and would find that his ability to concentrate in such a total way during the hypnotic state would generalize to practice and to races.

Larry had no difficulty at all in visualizing the race, or in maintaining total concentration. Upon coming out of the hypnotic state Larry was amazed at his own response. He was surprised at the depth of his relaxation and at the vividness of his imagery. Discussions with the psychologist following the session reinforced the fact that hypnosis has simply helped Larry to regain his old confidence. "From this point on you shouldn't have any problems. If any distractions do occur they will float in and out quickly and will not interfere with your race at all."

In Larry's case, without any direct mention of it, hypnosis was used to reduce anxiety. By lowering anxiety, concentration could be improved and the athlete's confidence could be re-established. The fact that Larry was not expecting hypnosis to allow him to do anything that he hadn't already demonstrated he was capable of was important.

Another use of hypnosis involves increasing motivation and confidence. This process can become more complicated when athletes are expected to perform in new situations. On these occasions, they don't have past experiences that they can use to fall back on. The task of the hypnotist is to use suggestions to redirect attention in order to break away from negative self-defeating thoughts. One of the best ways to do this is to get the athlete to focus on some past experience that was both pleasant and successful.

The following procedure worked very well with a group of little league baseball players. For many of the kids on the team, this was their first competitive experience. Confidence was not high and there was a tendency to put a lot of pressure on themselves and on each other. No one wanted to let the team down.

Hypnosis was introduced to the team as a "special procedure" that they could use to feel better about themselves. They were told that everyone makes mistakes and that it is important for them and for the team that they be able to forget about them during the game. They need to be able to support each other and help each other out.

Each day prior to a game the team would get together before warming up. At that time they would all lie down and the coach would take them through an induction procedure that is very similar to the relaxation procedure presented in chapter 15.

Once the players were relaxed the coach would have them all visualize getting a hit and then making a good fielding play. The athletes would be told to experience the feelings of excitement and enthusiasm as they performed well. Following this procedure, the coach would ask them to imagine a very tough situation in which the ball would take a bad hop, or they would lose it in the sun, or they would strike out. The coach would help them get into some of the feelings that they would have but at the same time remind them that everyone on the team makes mistakes and they need to pull together. The coach would suggest that when a mistake occurred they would respond by helping each other forget about it. "It's okay Tommy; we'll get the next one."

Through these suggestions the coach was able to get the players to be more sensitive to each other's feelings and to their own. The coach was able to develop a team spirit and a lot of support. The confidence of the players in themselves and in each other grew dramatically. The coach prevented the downward spiral and eliminated much of the pressure that many little league players feel, without dampening their desire to win and without reducing their performance.

When hypnosis is used for confidence building, motivation, and anxiety reduction, there are no absolute rules to follow in terms of the type of suggestions that should be offered. Some general considerations are important.

1. Typically a goal is to redirect attention. Help the athletes avoid attending to negative cues by providing them with a positive focus.
2. Suggestions should be explicit and in a language that the athletes

can understand and relate to. The suggestions should fit in with the athlete's expectancies regarding the types of suggestions hypnotists are supposed to make.

3. Suggestions help the athlete focus on both the attitudinal and performance changes that are to occur. "You will feel good." "You will feel totally in control." Words like, "boss," "Mr. Cool" etc. can be used and should be if the athlete relates strongly to them. Behaviorally, suggestions focus on specific cues to which the athlete should attend. "You will find your thoughts locking in on the ball. You will attend so closely to the ball that you will be able to see it in the pitcher's glove as he holds it behind his back and above his head."

4. Suggestions should be designed to help the athletes develop greater confidence in themselves as opposed to greater confidence in the hypnotist or in the power of the hypnotic state. "You will find that you will be able to . . ." "Hypnosis will help you develop your own power. . . ." "Hypnosis will allow you to do what you really want to, you will find the strength inside yourself."

5. Suggestions designed to alter perceptions, to slow down various events should be limited to the rehearsal process. Help the athletes use the special conditions of relaxation and concentration to gain greater control over rehearsal and then suggest that when they are ready they will be able to exert the same control over themselves in actual performance situations. "You will find that you can see everything as if it was occurring in slow motion. You can follow your own movements and you feel as if you are in complete control. As you get better and better at controlling your thoughts you will find that you begin to experience greater control on the field. When you are ready and have rehearsed enough, your mind will take over and you will be able to create this feeling of total control for yourself."

SETTING THE STAGE

When we go out and use standardized tests of hypnotic susceptibility to measure who will and who will not respond to hypnotic suggestions, we find that about ten percent of the population develops a very deep trance and responds to all of the standard suggestions. Another ten percent of the population does not become hypnotized and refuses to respond to any suggestions. The remainder of the population falls someplace in between.

At first glance, these statistics would appear to indicate that hypnosis is a limited technique. The use of standardized suggestions, administered under controlled conditions to groups of subjects, however, is not the best way to determine what percentage of the population will respond. Because expectancies and trust play such a large role there are tremendous differences from situation to situation.

191

I have already spoken about some of the athlete variables that are important. The athlete must have some trust in the situation and in the hypnotist. The athlete must be able to concentrate and to sit still for a period of time. Typically, quiet comfortable situations are facilitative. It is easier to become hypnotized when reclining in an easy chair than it is to become hypnotized when sitting in a straight backed wooden chair.

I was asked to give two guest lectures on altered states of consciousness in an introductory psychology class. There were about four hundred students in the class and as it turned out, my appearance in the class followed an appearance on a network T.V. show (The *Tonight Show*).

The university had provided a lot of publicity for my appearance on Johnny Carson's show. As a result, virtually all of the students in the psychology class had either seen it or heard about it. On the show I had used suggestions and special instructions to help Carson concentrate in ways that increased his tolerance for pain. An electric shock apparatus was developed which would administer an increasingly large shock. Carson was able to use attentional training procedures to alter his pain threshold. In addition, and more dramatically, I got him to break a one inch board (the type used in karate demonstrations) with his head.

As I went into the class the students were ready to see me as someone special. I spent the first day talking about fantastic feats evidenced by masters of the martial arts and individuals capable of developing altered states of consciousness. The stories were stimulating and exciting and I ended them with the promise that I would hypnotize the entire class during the next session.

When I came back to deliver the second lecture there wasn't even standing room in the auditorium. The word had gotten out and the place was packed. My own credibility couldn't have been higher. I hypnotized the class and got them to respond to a variety of suggestions. Then, just before awakening them I gave them a post hypnotic suggestion. I told them that they would be unable to move out of their chairs until I said so.

Under normal circumstances I might have expected 10 to 15 percent of the students to respond to the post hypnotic suggestion. You can imagine their surprise and mine when better than fifty percent of them failed to move at the end of the period.

The confidence that the hypnotist has and the confidence that he or she can instill in subjects along with the conduciveness of the general atmosphere and the support of the environment for responding to suggestions are all critical elements in the successful use of hypnosis. This is a tool that has great promise, but requires a great deal of skill to use in an ethical and responsible fashion.

17

ATTENTION CONTROL TRAINING

In chapter fifteen I talked about a variety of psychological techniques that can be used on a regular basis to deal with chronic pressure. In competitive athletics, however, there are a great many situations that are acute. Unanticipated things happen and suddenly in spite of the distractions or problems, the athlete must pull it together and perform.

Consider the plight of the diver who after coming to attention at the top of a ten meter tower suddenly has his/her concentration disturbed by a gust of wind or something else. He/she cannot back down nor even step back momentarily. To do so would result in a penalty and the deduction of points from the dive.

In the *Inner Athlete,* I described a situation in which a swimmer was psyched out by one of his competitors. The individual in the lane next to him purposely false started. As he entered the water he ducked under the lane rope and slowly swam back in the other swimmer's lane. As he climbed out of the pool he whispered to his opponent "I just pissed in your lane." The information proved distracting enough to the swimmer that he got a slow start when the gun finally sounded. He had his concentration disturbed by thoughts about what he was diving into.

Athletes don't need to be psyched out by others; more often than not they let their own performance psych them out. A tennis player who misses a point and then lets the fact interfere with subsequent concentration is psyching himself/herself out. There are a tremendous number of situations in sport where the individual must either recover from a distraction to prevent a problem to begin with, or where he/she must recover from a mistake in order to prevent additional problems and the development of a spiral I have spoken about so frequently.

In the situation just mentioned, in fact in most competitive situations, athletes do not have time to employ the types of techniques that have been discussed thus far. The diver on the tower cannot take fifteen minutes out to meditate, nor can the tennis player call time out. Somehow the athlete must be able to deal effectively with the unexpected. The athlete must be able to quickly get control over his/her own arousal and concentration.

As a student of Aikido and Karate in Japan, I was often amazed by my instructors' ability to retain control over their minds and bodies under extremely stressful conditions. I had watched them retain their

193

composure when being attacked by several people at the same time, both in demonstrations and in real life situations. I had watched my Aikido instructor retain control even in the face of the unexpected. On one occasion he had made a mistake while attempting to take a knife away from an opponent. He grabbed the knife blade instead of the attacker's wrist. As a result when the attacker jerked the knife back he sliced open the palm of my instructor's hand.

As I watched what was occurring my instructor showed no awareness of the mistake. He simply reacted by automatically moving to another technique which allowed him to get behind the opponent and to then disarm him. Following this, he took a brief time out to wrap a dirty rag around his hand and then completed his demonstration. Through the remainder of the demonstration there was no indication that the injury bothered him, or that it had even occurred. Several minutes later he calmly went to the hospital to have the wound sewn up.

When I would ask my instructor how he could remain calm and able to respond under extreme pressure he would tell me that it was by "concentrating on the one point." The one point was a spot just below and behind his navel that was the center of gravity in his body. He suggested that if I could learn to let my mind rest there I would remain calm and undisturbed.

My instructor was continually telling us that thought and movement were related. If we thought about being defeated we would be. He would illustrate how our own thoughts defeated us by testing our ability to concentrate on the one point.

To begin with, my instructor would challenge two of us to lift him off the ground. The first time we tried he would cooperate in that he would "think about being lifted." What we would find is that under these circumstances we had no problem lifting him. He weighed about 160 pounds and the two of us weighed at least 180 pounds a piece. We would stand on either side of him and with our two hands grasp one of his wrists. I would grab the right wrist and my friend would grab the left. My instructor would keep his arms stiff and then as he thought up, we would be able to lift him off the ground.

Following our successful lift, my instructor would think about the one point, he would "center" his concentration on this spot and challenge us to lift him. To our amazement we were unable to budge him. We could not even raise him an inch off the floor.

Then it would be our turn to be lifted. The instructor would select another student and the two of them would try to lift me. The first time, as I thought up, they had no problem. The second time, as I tried to think about the one point, they also had no problem. My instructor would look at me, shake his head and shout "you are not concentrating on the one point."

At the time, I thought my instructor was crazy. I had been concentrating but what he was saying made no sense. There must be some other explanation that he was unaware of. For several months I tried to

194

find that other explanation without success. Then, several years later as I was studying psychology and the relationship between physical arousal, concentration, and performance, my instructor telling me to concentrate on the "one point" began to make sense.

My instructor's challenge, his expectancy for me to perform, and my own desire to be able to accomplish the kinds of things that he could do, caused the lifting test to be a stressful situation for me. As a result, I was unable to concentrate in the way I needed to and I was unable to control physical arousal as well.

I would be standing there trying to concentrate on the one point, yet my mind would be distracted by thoughts like: "What if this doesn't work?" "This is silly, you can't let your mind rest in your navel." "I hope I can do this." "What will my instructor do if I fail?" "Won't I ever be as strong and confident as he is?" "There must be something else." Along with these attentional distractions and concerns, there would be increases in my neck and shoulder muscle tension. These muscular bracing responses in combination with a tendency to breathe from up in my chest (you hyperventilate as you get more anxious), would result in a raising of the center of gravity of my body. Tension literally would cause me to straighten up a little more, raising the center of gravity from .5 to 2 inches. This would make the task of lifting me much easier. In effect, my anxiety was causing me to help the people on either side of me.

Under conditions of increasing tension, the changes in general muscle tension and breathing cause athletes to feel uneasy or unstable. Standing on the ground, you don't feel as solid and as in control as you normally do. This is because of the alteration in the center of gravity and the hyperventilation.

For me, the increased tension and the concentration disturbances would feed on themselves. As I felt myself wavering, and it looked as if I might be moved, mental distractions would occur. Instead of attending to the one point I would start attending to "Oh no, they are lifting me. What do I do now? This shouldn't happen." Those thoughts would cause further muscle tension increases and, zip, up I would go.

What I discovered some years later was that if I prevented the change in the center of gravity in my body by not becoming tense and by maintaining concentration, I could not be lifted. It wasn't that I couldn't be lifted because I had somehow magically changed the weight in my body, I still weighed the same. I couldn't be lifted because without raising the center of gravity of my body, individuals as large or larger than myself could not get beneath my center of gravity in order to lift me. this meant they had to lift me by using smaller muscles in their forearms that simply did not have the strength.

Since that time, I have learned to concentrate effectively enough to keep two people from lifting me off the ground. Actually, that type of concentration is quite simple for the average athlete to learn. Once you know what to attend to, and how to attend, control can be quickly learned.

The importance of learning to concentrate in this way is not to be able to keep someone from lifting you off the ground. Although that can be a good test of your ability and can be a motivator to get you to learn to attend to the one point. *The really important aspect of this type of concentration is that you can use it to break or prevent the downward spiral I have spoken so much about!*

Research examining the inter-relationship between thought processes, centering attention, and physiological arousal indicates that the average person can learn to very quickly redirect attention and lower tension levels enough to regain control over attention. In effect, the centering procedure is a quick time out that allows the athlete to regain control. It is a time out procedure that can be used during an actual competition (e.g., while the diver is at attention). It is a time out that takes only a few seconds to do. The trick involved in successfully using the centering procedure to regain control consists of: 1) Recognizing when to apply it. This means detecting situations in which you are in danger of losing control and then finding the time to go through the procedure. 2) Knowing where to redirect attention in order to begin coping effectively with the situation. At the same time preventing yourself from falling back into the negative focus you just got out of. A great deal more will be said about this point in the next chapter.

The actual centering procedure is quite simple and is presented below. For additional information on this process you might read: *A.C.T.: Attention Control Training*, Wyden Books, 1978.

CENTERING PROCEDURE

The centering procedure is something that can be rehearsed mentally as well as physically. Often, I have athletes rehearse various aspects of actual performance situations (mentally) and during that rehearsal, I have them rehearse the incorporation of the centering procedure. This technique is illustrated in some of the case material that follows.

To center concentration on the "one point," athletes need to directly counter the natural responses that they tend to make in stressful situations. Typically I teach them to be able to do this from two positions. One position is a standing position and the other is a sitting position. The position that they will use, will depend upon the position they are in during the actual competitive situation.

INSTRUCTIONS FOR THE STANDING POSITION

1. Have the athlete stand with feet slightly apart and knees slightly bent. Weight should be evenly distributed between the two feet. This can be tested by having the athlete lean forward, backward, and side to side so he/she can see what his/her body feels like when the weight is evenly balanced. The knee bend is important and should result in the individual being able to feel the tension in

the muscles in the calves and thighs. This bend counteracts the natural tendency to brace and to lock the knees.

2. The athlete should consciously relax the neck and shoulder muscles. This is checked by making slight movements of the head (forward, backward, and side to side) and arms (gently shaking them to see if they are loose).

3. The mouth should be opened slightly to reduce the tension in the jaw muscles.

4. The athlete then breathes in slowly, from the diaphragm. He/she inhales slowly and as he/she does, attends to two set of cues. First, he/she notices that he/she is extending his/her stomach in breathing. Second, he/she consciously maintains the relaxation in his/her chest and shoulders. He/she avoids allowing the inhale to cause the chest to expand and shoulders to rise. This breathing counters the tendency to brace the muscles in the neck and shoulders, and it prevents hyperventilation.

5. As the athletes exhale slowly, they attend to the feelings in their abdomen, they notice stomach muscles relaxing. At the same time, they consciously let knees bend slightly attending to the increased feeling of heaviness that develops as they exhale, and as their body presses down toward the ground. The exhale counteracts the natural lifting caused by breathing in and as a result the athlete's body actually begins to feel steadier. This attentional break counters both the physical responses to stress, and the attentional ones. As the athletes attend to these relaxing physical cues they cannot attend to the negative distractions and fears that have been creating problems. The spiral is broken and they recover enough control to become capable of reminding themselves of some constructive action or focus that they should take.

6. Where or what to attend to, will be determined by the problem and by the demands of the performance situation. As mentioned earlier, some advance preparation to identify the critical cues to attend to following the centering process, is an important part of attention control training. Centering allows for a quick recovery of attention, and for a brief lowering of arousal. To be used effectively, however, the breathing procedure must be followed by attentional changes that lead to a task relevant focus. The chapter on rehearsal techniques describes how this can be accomplished.

The actual process of centering does not take long. The first few times athletes practice these procedures they are slowed down by the fact that they must take time to remind themselves of all the things to attend to. After a few practice sessions however, the whole process becomes automatic. At the same time they are inhaling, they are checking muscle groups to see that they are relaxed, knees are bent etc. Very quickly, the athlete learns to center in the length of time it takes to inhale and exhale slowly, one time.

INSTRUCTIONS FOR THE SITTING POSITION

The basic instructions for the sitting position are very similar to those for standing. Athletes can also learn to center while laying down.

1. The athlete consciously checks to make sure that neck and shoulder muscles are relaxed. Arms should be loose and the athlete should move his/her legs to reduce any excessive muscle tension in calves or thighs.
2. The mouth should be opened slightly to reduce tension in jaw muscles.
3. The athlete inhales slowly from down in the diaphragm. As he/she does, an attempt is made to feel the stomach muscles expand and avoid any increase in the tension in neck and shoulder muscles.
4. On the exhale, the athlete (is sitting) attends to the feelings in buttocks and stomach. He/she feels the stomach muscles relax and notices how the buttocks press down against the chair or the ground. If the athlete is laying on the ground, he/she attends to the fact that the entire body begins to press down against the ground on the exhale. This position is an important position for some rifle shooters, drag racers, etc.

CENTERING CASE HISTORIES

In chapter nine I discussed the case of a professional tennis player who came to me to get some help in controlling her attention and attitude. She was a serve-and-volley player, who among other things was having problems with her serve. Since her whole game worked off her serve, difficulties in this area were particularly stressful.

This particular athlete had sustained an injury to her shoulder that had interfered with her ability to serve for a while. Following the recovery from the injury, however, she found that she was still having trouble with her serve. In a game, if she would fault, she would begin to get up tight. This would result in an increase in neck and shoulder muscle tension which would interfere with her serve. She would double fault and then begin to get down on herself, only adding to the problem.

For C., centering seemed like a natural, easy way to break the self-destructive spiral. The centering procedure would help her focus directly on countering the increasing neck and shoulder muscle tension that was interfering with the serve. What became important was to help C identify when she needed to use the procedure, and to help her find something to direct her attention towards following centering.

In this particular case, it was decided that it would be best to use the centering where C felt that she was beginning to get tense. It was agreed that following the centering process, C would direct her attention to the toss of the ball. Her goal at this point was to maintain her attention on the ball and to simply allow the serve to happen. She had learned her serve and didn't need to thing about that anymore.

198

A second example involved a drag racer. This individual had been doing fairly well until he noticed that he had begun to lose consistently in the third round of competition. He began to develop a block and could feel his own tension levels rising as the third round approached. In his particular sport, there was a handicapping system that would allow slower cars to compete against faster ones. Prior to a race, each driver would "dial in" the fastest time of which he thought he was capable.

If one driver dialed in 8.0 seconds for the quarter of a mile and the other driver dialed in 8.5 seconds, the slower driver would be given a .5 second head start. Should the driver who estimated his best time at 8.5 seconds go faster than that, he would be disqualified for "breaking out."

The ability to know your own abilities and the capability of your car, to select a time that you think you will run, requires good concentration and analytical ability. The ability to make these kinds of judgments gets interfered with as tension increases. This was one of the factors that was contributing to the problems that the drag racer was having.

As we spoke about the problems in the third round, it became apparent that the athlete was beginning to attend to inappropriate cues. If he had the faster car, he would attend to the sound of his competitor's engine, or to the position of his competitor on the track, instead of attending to his own starting signal.

To counteract these problems, the racer was taught to use the centering technique just after burning his tires and just as he settled in at the starting line. As he completed the breathing he would remind himself that he had only one thing to attend to, and that was the starting light. This procedure though quite simple, took his mind off of the increasing tension and the fact that this was "the third round." As a result, he broke out of his "slump" in the very next competition.

A third example involved a figure skater. This individual was attempting to pass a particular test; a requirement she must meet to qualify for senior women's competition. Since she competed in pairs as well, her progress was doubly important because success had a lot to do with her ability to find a good partner. Male partners are very hard to find.

As time for the test grew closer, the skater became progressively more anxious. Her coach was getting frustrated at the emotional outbursts that were occurring and in addition was disturbed by the fact that the skater was not getting enough "flow." Flow in this instance refers to the power that the skater appears to get out of a stroke. For this particular individual there would be times when she would seem to glide easily and effortlessly across the ice. A stroke seemed very powerful, propelling the skater. This flow is critical because it sets up difficult tricks, and because when a skater has it she isn't working as hard. As the competition was approaching, the flow was diminishing.

With this particular skater it was a fairly simple matter to illustrate the relationship between what she was calling flow and the muscle tension changes that occur under pressure. She learned the centering procedure as a means of counteracting these changes by lowering her center of gravity she found that she immediately experienced increased flow. By looking at her routine, it was a simple matter to identify those places where she was making a transition from one trick or more to another. In these spaces she could attend to breathing and to centering. This helped her avoid attentional distractions and gave her the power she needed to move into succeeding tricks. She could actually do the breathing on the ice.

It is important to point out here that the skater's routines were rehearsed to the point where they did not require a great deal of thought. She knew almost instinctively what move followed and how to execute it. Concentration then could focus quickly on breathing and at the end of the centering she would immediately direct attention to the take off for succeeding tricks.

There are literally thousands of situations in which athletes can use the centering procedure. Typically, these situations can be categorized into two general classes.

The first class of situations involves the prevention of a performance error. In these circumstances, something unexpected has happened which is stressful to the athlete (e.g., having someone "piss" in your lane). To be able to retain control the athlete must somehow inhibit a strong emotional reaction: he or she must prevent the tendency to let anger and outrage get the best of him/her, or avoid allowing fear and anxiety to interfere. "I may be angry if someone urinates in my lane." "I may be frightened if I see the competitor in front of me split their head open on the same dive I am about to do."

Within this class of situations, the athlete attempts to use the centering to inhibit the build up of tension long enough to allow him/her to respond to the immediate situation. Following that response, however, it may be necessary to bleed off some of the tension that has built up. The sequence then involves being sensitive to a possible problem and to one's own possible loss of control, briefly regaining control, performing effectively, then finding an acceptable way to relieve tension.

Consider the baseball coach who is in a very tight game and who has a chance to reach the playoffs. The umpire makes what the coach considers to be a bad call. The situation is so stressful to the coach that he runs out yelling insults and ends up getting himself kicked out of the game and perhaps even out of the series. If that is not enough, he may be fined a sum of money. The coach in a basketball game who gets a technical is in a similar situation. Because of the coaches's loss of control, the team loses.

To prevent being kicked out of the game, the coach attempts to use the centering procedure to calm himself down enough to deal in a more effective way with the situation. That may mean that he is capable, after centering, of talking with the umpire and of making his point. It could mean that he recognizes as a function of the centering that he is not going to be able to deal effectively with the umpire. His breathing calms him down enough to realize that he doesn't like the guy and given the situation he will blow it. As a result, he delegates someone else to talk to the umpire.

In this situation the coach used the breathing to maintain a certain amount of control. That may have allowed him to get through the immediate situation, but it may not have allowed him to bleed off the tension. The umpire may refuse to back down and now the coach walks back to the dugout still angry. At this point the coach needs to find an acceptable way (one that won't interefere with the game) of letting off some of the tension. This may involve throwing things around in the dugout, going into the washroom and yelling, complaining to an assistant coach etc. The point is, in spite of preventing a problem and perhaps instituting some control, he still needs to let go.

The second type of situation involves those times when a mistake has already occurred. The athlete or coach was not sensitive enough to rising pressure and they blew it. He may have lost concentration on a pitch and it was hit for a home run. He may have screamed at the official and been called for a technical. He ventilated some of his anger, fear, or frustration and now is confronted with the consequences. In these situations the centering procedure is used to regain control once it is lost to prevent things from going from bad to worse.

Once athletes or coaches make the type of mistake we are talking about, they usually have one of two responses, either of which can compound the problem. Those with high levels of self-esteem and confidence tend to get angry and to blame others. They react to being kicked out of the game by yelling more. If they have made a mistake in their own performance they become angry at themselves. Athletes who have lower levels of self-confidence tend to react by feeling guilty. They get down on themselves becomeing anxious, increasing arousal and concentration disturbances. They too, continue to have problems.

For athletes with these difficulties, the centering procedures are used to get them to break that loop. Once the mistake is made it serves as a cue, reminding them to center. Having centered, they attempt to remind themselves and to get others around them, to remind them that its okay to make a mistake. Everyone does. The challenge now is to direct attention to task relevant cues. What those task relevant cues are will depend upon the situation. How they are identified will be discussed in the next chapter.

18

COGNITIVE REHEARSAL TECHNIQUES

Psychologists, coaches and athletes have been advocating the use of mental rehearsal techniques for years. It has been suggested that through mental rehearsal, athletes can change attitudes, motivate themselves, speed the learning of new skills, increase the overall level of performance, and identify problems they may be having in a particular performance situation. In spite of a mass of anecdotal information testifying to the potential benefits of some type of mental practice, it has only been in recent years that we have had strong scientific evidence for the utility of these practices.

With research in the area of psychophysiology and biofeedback leading the way, we have begun to provide a wealth of experimental evidence supporting the importance of thought processes in developing all of the skills or abilities listed above. In the rush to emphasize the importance of mental factors, we have come up with a list of catch names to emphasize some important aspect of the rehearsal process. As a preface to this chapter it would be helpful to provide a brief definition for some of the terms that are in vogue.

MENTAL REHEARSAL

This is a global term applied to any thought process that involves systematically rehearsing some behavior. A basketball player who mentally replays every aspect of a game he/she has just completed is engaging in mental rehearsal. In a similar way, a coach who mentally rehearses the thought processes that he/she went through to reach a decision about whether or not to play a certain athlete is engaging in a mental rehearsal. The term is global in that nothing is specified about what is to be rehearsed, or how. At times athletes may rehearse motor behavior, thought processes, emotional experiences etc.

PSYCHOCYBERNETICS

This is a term introduced by Maxwell Maltz and is the title of his book. Psychocybernetics is a sophisticated term for mental rehearsal where the primary focus is on the rehearsal of the successful completion of some activity. The idea presented is that mentally rehearsing a particular activity can result in a more rapid increase in skill than simple physical practice alone, or no practice. As an example, basketball free throw shooters are instructed to visually rehearse the process of shooting a free throw. Research on the effectiveness of the procedure seems to indicate that athletes who rehearse mentally, but have the same amount of actual physical practice as those who don't rehearse, sink a higher percentage of free throws on a test of ability.

POSITIVE THINKING

In psychocybernetics, the focus tends to be on altering physical behavior, like free throw shooting. With positive thinking, emphasis is placed on altering attitudes that an athlete has towards himself/herself. It is believed that we are no better than we think we are. Positive thinking is based on the assumption that all things are possible if we only believe in ourselves and our own power to accomplish them. The idea is to get the athlete to alter negative self-talk. By force of will, the athlete attempts to convince him/herself that he/she is a winner. Presumably, as attitude changes, performance changes will follow.

DISCRIMINANT CUE ANALYSIS

This is a mental process that involves getting an athlete to compare two similar experiences. In one experience he/she should have been successful, performing at a very high level. In the second experience, the athlete experienced failure. By mentally re-experiencing the two situations and by contrasting them, the individual identifies those mental and physical cues that interfere with performance as well as those that support effective performance. This information is then used to help the athlete develop the mental and physical abilities he/she needs to perform at a high level more consistently. The "discriminant cues" are those factors that differentiate between the two situations.

VISUO-MOTOR-BEHAVIOR-ANALYSIS (VMBR)

Visuo-motor behavior analysis is a term coined by Richard Suinn, a sport psychologist at Colorado State University. As with the other rehearsal techniques, subjects typically relax first, in order to facilitate the rehearsal process. Following the relaxation, however, the athlete focuses in on rehearsing every aspect of a performance, with special emphasis on the development of the physiological cues and feelings that should be associated with the actual competition. The idea here is that the actual rehearsal of motor responses will speed the learning processes and improve the athlete's control and efficiency.

COGNITIVE BEHAVIOR MODIFICATION

Behavior modification involves the manipulation of reinforcement contingencies in order to control actual behavior. As an example, if increasing an athlete's practice time is a goal, reinforcers are identified that when provided following an increase in practice time, result in positive feelings, and thus increase the likelihood that the athlete will increase practice time on subsequent occasions. At the same time, the reinforcers for avoiding practice are identified and they are either removed (e.g., a girlfriend has been distracting the athlete. Without knowing it, her attention has been reinforcing his avoidance of practice) or made contingent upon practice. The athlete in the example could only see the girl after practice. Her attention becomes a reinforcer for practice under these conditions.

Behavior modification can be seen as focusing in on the physical side of the figure that shows the relationship between physical processes, mental processes and performance. Theoretically, by altering actual physical behavior, changes in attitude will follow. In contrast, cognitive behavior modification tends to focus on the mental side of the figure.

The term cognitive behavior modification was introduced by Donald Meichenbaum, a psychologist at the University of Waterloo. Emphasis was placed on identifying those thoughts that controlled behavior and attitudes. The goal was to reinforce the individual for substituting coping thoughts (e.g., "I must go slowly") for more self-destructive thoughts (e.g., "I can't do this"). To provide reinforcement, it was first necessary to sensitize an individual to the conditions that triggered certain thoughts and to then train him/her to make substitutions and to reinforce him/her verbally, physically, etc. for any positive change.

Each of the procedures presented has some overlap with the others and each has been found to have value in altering athletic performance and in increasing the effectiveness of athletes. By examining the procedures collectively, it is possible to point out several factors that should be considered by the sport psychologist in developing any rehearsal program:

1. A rehearsal program should recognize that *both* attitudes and actual behaviors are important. Some attempt should be made to identify appropriate behaviors and attitudes.
2. Comparison of success and failure experiences is a good way for finding out what to attend to.
3. What is rehearsed is important. Some rehearsal procedures emphasize visual rehearsal, others emphasize kinesthetic rehearsal. Both may be important, especially when learning a new skill or increasing the consistency of performance is the goal.

    A decision to rehearse successful experiences vs. failure experiences would depend upon the goal of the rehearsal process. To identify problems, rehearsal of failure would be needed. To alter self-concept, failure experiences may be avoided.
4. How the athlete rehearses is important. VMBR requires that the

204

athlete view what is going on from inside their own body in order to facilitate motor learning. That part of a discriminate cue analysis that involves rehearsing a failure experience can often be better carrried out if some parts are rehearsed as if athletes were viewing themselves on film. This allows them to remain more relaxed and emotionally uninvolved and they can comment more easily on what is happening.

5. What are the reinforcers for an individual. Often, we assume that success is reinforcement enough. If we simply make athletes more successful they will continue a behavior. That is true only so long as competition in the sport is number one on their personal hierarchy. Take time to identify as many positive reinforcers as you can.

ROLE OF THEORY

As the sport psychologist begins to develop a rehearsal program the theory that underlies his/her understanding of athlete behavior becomes very important. The athlete needs direction with respect to where to look for problems, where to look for task relevant cues, etc. It is the sport psychologist's theory that is going to determine where they both look.

DEVELOPMENT OF A REHEARSAL STRATEGY

The following steps outline the general progression I follow in attempting to develop a rehearsal program for an athlete.

1. First, I attempt to operationally define a specific problem and/or goal. By operationally define, I mean that we identify the behaviors and attitudes that we want to change and/or we identify the specific goal we want to accomplish.
2. I gather information about the performance situation. I need to find out what the mental and physical demands are. What skills are required? To gather this information, I need to have a theoretical framework that guides where I look. In addition, I need to have a great deal of information about the sport. I cannot help athletes identify what they should attend to if they don't already know (many times they don't), and if I don't know the requirements of the sport. It is here the sport psychologist must recognize limitations and be prepared to call in an expert (e.g., a coach, or a highly skilled competitor who can evaluate the situation).
3. I identify two situations that relate to the performance goal. In one, athletes have been successful, in the other they have not. I pick situations that athletes have actually experienced as opposed to ideal situations or as opposed to using other athletes as examples for two reasons. First, the athlete provides a better model for himself/herself. He/she may not be able to relate to the ideal (never having performed that way) and may not be able to relate

205

to another model. Research indicates that to develop coping behaviors it is important that athletes have someone they can identify with, someone like themselves. The second reason is that by looking at a success experience and a failure experience I can get an idea of their own best level under optimal conditions. I can see what it is they are really capable of and we will not set our expectations too high.

4. Next, I take athletes through a progressive relaxation procedure and get them to rehearse the two situations with me calling their attention to those factors that my own theoretical notions indicate are important.

    a.   I get them to attend to differences in terms of their ability to control and direct attention. I find out what they are attending to in the success experience and I find out what is distracting in the failure experience. Are they distracted by external cues, and/or internal ones? When distracted in either situation, how do they react emotionally? Do they become upset, what do they think, what do they feel, what do they attend to?

    b.   I get them to identify situational differences that might be expected to contribute to differences in arousal level. How important is the contest? Where are the two contests being played? How good are the competitors? How large is the audience? How well did they prepare? Were they surprised by anything?

    c.   I get them to attend to personal and interpersonal differences. Who was in the audience? Were they in control? Were they feeling confident? What had happened just before? Did the coach or another player say something that set them up? How were they introduced?

5. Having identified the cues that discriminate between the two experiences I use them to help athletes understand what is happening and what must be controlled in order to perform effectively. Together we work to identify the ways that anxiety can be controlled.

    a.   We identify those situational, personal and interpersonal factors raising anxiety and see how many can be removed.

    b.   We identify techniques that they can respond to which will help them relax prior to the competition, and help them rehearse disattending from negative thoughts and cues, and attending to positive ones.

    c.   I help them identify methods that they can use to regain control in the actual situation. Where can a centering procedure be introduced in the competitive situation? What should cue the athlete to center? Where should the athlete attend after centering, and/or what step should he /she take to allow others to help him/her regain control.

6. The next step involves working with the athlete to determine what to practice and where to rehearse. Generally speaking, any extensive rehearsal must be engaged in either during practice, or away from the competition. There simply is not time in most competitive situations to engage in a thorough systematic rehearsal of all aspects of a performance.
   a. I attempt to get athletes to confine their analysis of errors to practice and post competition sessions.
   b. I emphasize the use of centering techniques and passive attending as ways of coping with pressure and mistakes during the competition.
7. I attempt to determine the amount of support and encouragement athletes will need in order to follow through on prescriptions. The lower the self-esteem and the more severe the problems, the more I will have to be involved to provide structure and support. Tapes will be used and emphasis will be on positive experiences and on learning to accept some failure as a means of preventing further problems.
8. I get them to establish intermediate, short term goals as well as a long term goals. This allows us to evaluate and *positively* reinforce progress. It helps maintain a high level of motivation. These goals must be realistic.
9. I develop a very specific rehearsal process that athletes engage in every day. They do this by relaxing and then rehearsing successfully coping with the identified problem.
10. I provide a follow-up usually within a week of development of the program. At this time I can provide support for any success the individuals may be having. At the same time, I may find that they are not practicing or have managed to destroy a perfectly logical program. When this is the case, I alter my theoretical perspective so that I can pay more attention to possible underlying conflicts. If these seem likely, I make a referral.

CASE HISTORIES

Hal's stepfather contacted me by phone and after telling me he had read my book, said that he would like to have me help his stepson. He indicated that Hal, who was twenty years old had joined the professional golf tour eighteen months before. It was costing a lot of money to support Hal on the tour but he "didn't mind that," he just wanted him to be able to play up to his potential. The stepfather indicated to me that in practice Hal could shoot tremendous scores, but somehow when he would get into tournaments he would develop problems. As a result, Hal had not even qualified for several tournaments that he should have had no problem getting into. I asked him to have his stepson contact me.

Hal did contact me and an appointment was made. I told him to bring his golf clubs and indicated that in addition to giving him some tests and asking him some questions, I would like to get out on the course and see "what kind of a golfer he was."

During our first appointment Hal was quiet, and seemed shy. He answered all of my questions and indicated that golf was the most important thing in the world to him. He did not volunteer any information and instead waited for me to ask questions. He was very thorough in answering my questions.

According to Hal, he was golfing well enough to be winning money on the tour. In competition, however, he would "choke." He would get out on the course and things would go alright for a while and then he would make a mistake or a bad shot. Once this happened, it would be all over; he would not recover.

Testing revealed that Hal was overloaded by his own thoughts, that he had a tendency to worry and ruminate about things. His self-esteem was low and he was feeling as if he was not in control. He was introverted, staying to himself and this made it more difficult for him to get out of his own head when something started to go wrong.

He went out on the golf course and Hal demonstrated to me (without wanting to) all of the things he had been talking about. He played the first hole fairly well (par) and then became aware of me. For the next five holes he played some of the worst golf of his life. Finally, after the sixth hole I told him that I had seen enough and I thanked him. Then I told him that as long as we were out there he could give me a lesson. He agreed and quickly got into helping me with my swing. He offered some good advice and then when I had trouble he would hit the ball to demonstrate.

Before Hal realized it, we were playing a round together as if we were old friends. He was playing super golf. After this went on for a few holes, I decided to alter the situation again. I stopped playing and told him that I would like to observe him again. Immediately, his playing fell apart.

We had identified the problem that we wanted to work on as helping Hal avoid falling apart after that "first mistake." We went back to my office and I had Hal relax and rehearse a successful experience and an unsuccessful one. In this case, since we had been on the course and since we could see both experiences right there, I got him to focus in on the attentional and interpersonal differences in those two situations.

By comparing the two situations we were able to come up with a lot of discriminating cues. When we had first gone out on the golf course, Hal had been very concerned about performing well for me. He "wanted to show me how good he could be." He became very aware of the fact that he was being observed and started thinking thoughts like 'I wonder what he is thinking." "He probably thinks I'm sick." He became very sensitive to his own performance and he could feel himself tightening up, especially in the upper body. He became afraid that he wouldn't hit the ball well and began trying to talk his way mechanically through each swing. He was literally trying to remind himself of everything he should do from start to finish, while he was actually doing it. At the same time, he was getting flashes saying "don't raise up," or "bring your hips through," or "your shoulders are too tense."

When he rehearsed the part of the round where we were playing together, he became aware of the fact that he had forgotten about his own game. His attention was directed toward my shots. He was so busy analyzing what I was doing that he didn't have time to think about himself. As he thought back, his neck and shoulder muscles had been relaxed. He was able to keep his attention on the ball when he hit it. He felt loose and his swing was natural; he wasn't thinking about it. Once he had selected his club and lined up the shot, all he did was concentrate on the ball. As he thought about it, I had changed from being a critical audience to just being an average person. In fact, I was just one of those guys trying to break ninety.

It was no problem for Hal to translate the things we were observing in order to relate them directly to his performance in tournaments. The identical processes were going on. Following our discussion, we worked out a set of procedures to help Hal reduce his anxiety. We made a tape that he would use to relax about an hour before a competition. As part of the tape, he would rehearse a few holes of golf. He would rehearse playing well for a couple of holes and then making a mistake. He would then feel himself beginning to tighten up and he would rehearse using a centering procedure for lowering arousal and redirecting attention. It was decided that he would redirect attention to the ball. In addition, between shots we decided that he should attempt to attend to things other than his own game. His self-esteem was low enough that trying to simply pick himself up and order his anxiety away was very difficult. Instead, he would attempt to analyze the swings of other golfers, to look at the scenery, etc.

A follow up with Hal revealed that he had two tournaments in which he had a lot of success. After these experiences, however, he became unglued. Performance under pressure was as bad as ever. At this point I decided that I had better expand my theoretical notions to include the possibility of some underlying problems. Hal's success had simply not been reinforcing.

In a long session with Hal it came out that he really didn't want to be on the tour. He felt that he owed it to his mother and stepfather since they had invested so much in him, but he really didn't want to be there. He had a girlfriend back home that meant everything to him. She was the only person he felt close to and trusted. He was afraid to be away from her and he was lonely. He had started drinking to deal with the loneliness and his anxiety and had experienced several black outs. Hal didn't know where his insecurity and unhappiness were coming from and he was upset when he thought about his dependency on his girlfriend. Although he thought he trusted her more than anyone, he was aware of his increasing anxiety when he would leave her alone. I ended up referring Hal to a clinical psychologist who could help him work through some of his fears and insecurity.

The second case I would like you to consider involved a competitor in the decathlon. This individual contacted me and asked for help after I had provided an introductory talk about sport psychology to a group of competitors.

When he came up, Steve indicated that he had a "bad attitude." He said that he would like me to help him overcome the problem. Since bad attitude wasn't too operational, I asked him what he meant. He told me that lately he kept having self-defeating thoughts. He noticed these especially in relation to two events: the 1500 meters, and the pole vault. He felt as if he wasn't competitive in these events and had been avoiding practicing them. In effect, he had been treating the anxiety that the two events generated by avoidance. When he didn't practice them he wasn't so anxious and he didn't have so many negative thoughts. Now, however, a competition was approaching and he would suffer for the lack of practice. We agreed that he would attempt to develop a program that would alter his attitude toward the two events, and increase his practice time.

Testing revealed that Steve had a tendency to become overloaded and distracted by things going on around him. It was his tendency to be tuned into the external environment that caused him to be especially sensitive to the performance of the other athletes around him. When these individuals performed at a higher level than Steve, he would begin to feel anxious and get down on himself.

Rehearsal of all of his events indicated that the key differences between the 1500 meters and the pole vault had to do with how Steve evaluated his own performance relative to the other competitors. He was extremely attentive to their technique and performance and he was constantly comparing it to his own. Whereas he felt he could hold his own in the other events, when he would make comparisons in these two he came out on the short end.

As a result of the tendency to make comparisons, Steve would begin to get down on himself. He would start to have the feelings of wanting to give up and he would lose his motivation. His performance would drop below what he was capable of, becoming even worse. Thoughts were "What's the use," "I'm no good at this, why don't I just give it up?" "I'll never make it." "How can I win if I can't be competitive in these two events?"

Further analysis revealed that Steve didn't just want to be competitive, he expected to win. The mark that he was shooting for in each event was the winner's time or height. This goal seemed so far out of reach that Steve couldn't possibly motivate himself to accomplish it. He was thirty seconds behind the winning time in the metric mile and three feet below the best competitor in the vault. Steve's "attitude problem" had reached the point of affecting performance in all events.

Looking at those situations in which Steve did well, it was apparent that he motivated himself by believing he could win, and by challenging himself to beat the other competitors. He would use imagery of winning to increase his arousal level and improve his ability to narrow attention and concentrate. On these occasions he would do well. The audience didn't bother him — it "psyched him up."

Steve's problem proved fairly simple to deal with. After looking at what was happening, it was easy to point out that his tendency to look at other's performance and his own unrealistic expectancies were self-defeating. He was reminded that to win the decathlon he did not have to actually win a single event. He earned points for his performance in each event. It was emphasized that in the two events he was having trouble with he should learn to attend to his own performance, to identify a personal best, to set a small goal that was independent of what the other competitors were doing, and to challenge himself to meet that goal.

In the pole vault instead of thinking about the three feet he had to make up, Steve focused his attention on his own technique. He decided that with some practice he should be able to increase his personal best by six inches within the next few weeks. Success was the primary reinforcer for Steve and the simple cognitive change, getting him to attend to his own performance independent of others, resulted in his getting positive feedback (he was winning against himself), rather than continual negative feedback.

In the 1500 meters it had been Steve's habit to stare at the backs of the athletes in front of him and to then begin a whole lot of self-defeating thoughts. He was instructed that when he looked up and noticed his position he was to redirect attention to his breathing. He was to make sure that he would take a breath from the diaphragm and following this he would remind himself of the pace he wanted to set for himself. He would then concentrate on that pace which was designed to improve upon his own best time. In this way it didn't matter if everyone else in the race ran a world record time. Steve was concerned with his own time.

One final step in the process was to teach Steve to use mental imagery to get himself up. Prior to events he would go through them in his head. He would "psych himself up" by seeing the crowd and by reminding himself of the time he wanted to establish. He would then visualize running the race, hearing the splits, pushing himself to keep the pace, and experiencing the joy of establishing a personal best. This rehearsal process would increase his enthusiasm and involvement. For Steve it was not a matter of learning to relax. He needed to become more involved and to avoid withdrawal and apathy.

Follow up revealed that Steve had experienced a turn around emotionally. He was enjoying the competition and had managed to establish personal bests in five of the ten events.

19

THE MAKINGS OF A GOOD SPORT PSYCHOLOGIST

In concluding this book I can only hope that the material has pointed out the variety of opportunities, the tremendous challenge, and the great need for professional responsibility within the field of sport psychology. Many of the functions that a sport psychologist can fill have been discussed, but most certainly there have been some that have been left out. An attempt has been made to show the complexity of the relationship between physical and psychological processes and performance. At the same time ethical concerns and issues have been raised.

At the very beginning of the book the fact we do not have a unified program to train applied sport psychologists was pointed out. Although an integrated curriculum and internship training experience may be developed in the future, I think that is a long way off. The variety of experiences that the sport psychologist finds himself/herself in draws upon a number of different areas. It will be very difficult to get people to agree on a "best" curriculum. I do think that we can begin that process, but the completion of it is several years off. This future date is especially apparent if we hope to train individuals to meet all of the needs and to be able to provide all of the services described in these pages.

In the meantime, what do we do? Sports governing bodies and various professional associations can make recommendations regarding certain specific services. We can, for example, describe the experiences that we feel individuals who use biofeedback or assessment should have. These experiences need not be tied to any particular program. In fact, I think it would be a mistake at this point to suggest that training in one particular area is a prerequisite to functioning as, or calling one's self a sport psychologist. Given the inadequacies in existing programs in terms of being able to provide supervised applied experiences in athletic settings, and in terms of being able to provide relevant courses (we need them from physical education, physiology, psychology, sociology, and education), it is every important that we assess competency on an individual basis. This is not to say that we shouldn't move towards the articulation of a basic or core curriculum for the sport psychologist, I believe we should. What is being said is that we are now in a position to establish how we want to identify those people who are currently qualified to teach and practice?

As a partial answer to the question of qualifications, I have listed some of the personal and interpersonal skills that I feel are important to effective functioning. I would add to these abilities or characteristics the obvious fact that the person has learned (through some means, whether it is formal course work or on the job experience) the technical skills and theoretical constructs that are important to effective functioning.

SELF-AWARENESS

I believe it is important that relative to the average person, sport psychologists have a great deal more self-awareness. This means that they understand what motivates them, why they are doing what they do? They know what their "reinforcers" are, what are they working to obtain: They have good insight into themselves, into their own personality characteristics and abilities. They know what situations are stressful to them, and how are they likely to respond? They know what their own needs for control are. They understand what their level of self-esteem says about their ability to listen: They can be supportive and/or confrontive. They can set limits. They know what situations interfere with their ability to perform and why.

In line with the ethical standards that were discussed, it is the self-aware individuals who are much more likely to be in touch with their own limitations. They will be more likely to recognize what they are qualified to do, and assuming they have integrity, will set limits on themselves to prevent taking advantage of their position or of the athlete.

COMMUNICATION SKILLS

Sport psychologists must have the ability to relate to athletes in the athlete's own language and on the athlete's terms. They must be able to translate their theoretical constructs into words and examples that the athlete can relate to. They must have the ability to be clear, well organized, and concise in their thinking.

MOTIVATOR

It is very important for sport psychologists like teachers or coaches, to be able to instill confidence in the athlete. Athletes should have confidence in the sport psychologist and the sport psychologist should be capable of motivating the athlete. This ability to motivate means that they will be sensitive to the athlete's needs, to what the athletes want to hear. They will understand the athletes and what motivates them well enough to be able to provide the support and/or challenge that is needed at the right time.

DEDUCTIVE AND ANALYTICAL ABILITY

Sport psychologists must have the capacity for developing a broad internal focus of attention. They must be able to take in information and to then ask themselves the "what if" question. They should be able to think about the past and the future in order to anticipate the consequences of their actions. They need their planning ability to be able to develop treatment programs.

ABILITY TO EMPATHIZE

Sport psychologists need to have had the experiences and the personal sensitivity to be able to "walk in the athlete's shoes." It is the ability to empathize with the situation as the athlete describes it, to place themselves in the athlete's position, feeling what they feel and thinking what they think that allows them to use their analytical ability to develop appropriate responses. It is the ability to empathize that will be used to establish a relationship with the athlete that can lead to the athlete believing the sport psychologist does understand, and can help. It is this ability that is critical to the sport psychologist being an effective motivator as well.

PROVIDE BALANCE BETWEEN SUPPORT AND CONFRONTATION

Sport psychologists need to be able to express positive feelings and negative ones. They must be sensitive to the athlete's needs in order to walk the thin line between being too acceptant and supportive (crippling the athlete and making them too dependent), and being too confrontive (destroying the self-confidence and/or driving the athlete away). They must be able to recognize that there are individual differences in terms of athlete's needs and they must be capable of responding to these.

ABILITY TO DEPERSONALIZE

In line with the rules for communication presented in chapter eight, sport psychologists must be capable of expressing criticism in a way that does not appear to be a personal attack. To facilitate the athlete's ability to listen they should be able to find ways to introduce emotionally charged material so that it will not interfere with the athlete's ability to listen.

ABILITY TO SELF-DISCLOSE

Sport psychologists should be capable of reducing the distance between themselves and the athlete, when that distance is interfering with the athlete's ability to respond to suggestions. To do this, the sport psychologist must be able to be human, to admit weakness, to be humble, and to recognize the expertise of others. These characteristics are communicated to the athlete through self-disclosure. It is important, however, that sport psychologists not self-disclose out of their own need for closeness. In this case they are using the athlete. Instead, self-disclosure comes only so long as it facilitates the successful completion of the service contract.

ABILITY TO OPERATIONALIZE

Sport psychologists understand the need to be able to develop a very clear, attitudinally and behaviorally operational service contract. They have the interviewing skills necessary to ask questions in a way which will lead to the development of specific contracts.

TRUSTWORTHY

Sport psychologists are honest and open. They are trustworthy because they are self-aware, they know what affects their behavior and they own it. In addition, the underlying factor in their relationships to others is the fact that their contract implies that they will place the athlete's needs above their own. This fact, and behaving in a way that is consistent with this principle is what makes them trustworthy.

ATTENTIONAL FLEXIBILITY

Sport psychologists have good control over attentional abilities. They are able to shift from one types of attention to another as the situation changes.

ABILITY TO FUNCTION UNDER PRESSURE

Ideally, sport psychologists are above average when it comes to being able to maintain their attentional flexibility under pressure, in a crisis, or when something unexpected has happened. This self-control is especially important because athletes need the sport psychologists' support when they are confronted by their own anxiety. The athletes must feel that the individuals who are providing help are capable. This does not mean that sport psychologists must be as good at the athlete's sport as the athletes are. It does mean that athletes can expect the sport psychologists to be able to maintain their composure and their ability to think and problem solve, when things aren't working, or when the pressure is on.

Ideally, the sport psychologist would be all things to all people. Obviously this is not possible and in fact, very few people will be able to live up to all of the ideals presented here. Don't expect perfection; you can only be frustrated by your inadequacies and suffer the same fate that awaits the athlete who is disturbed by his or her own performance. Do take a personal inventory. Ask yourself how you fare in terms of some of the characteristics mentioned. Take a good hard look and don't be afraid of what you see. If there is room for improvement and you have the ability and motivation, great. If motivation and ability are lacking, then use what you have found to set limits for yourself — limits that will allow you to function at maximum effectiveness and limits that will protect those you would serve. Don't ask yourself to do the impossible, but rather model the self-awareness, acceptance, and self-discipline you would like the athlete or coach to develop.

STUDY QUESTIONS

Chapter One
1. Identify some of the problems associated with attempting to function both as a clinical psychologist and as a sport psychologist.
2. Identify and define the roles that a sport psychologist may be called upon to assume.

Chapter Two
1. Legally who can call themselves a sport psychologist?
2. Why is it necessary to develop ethical standards for sport psychologists?
3. Ethical standards serve as guidelines to the professional, they are not absolute laws. What are some of the factors that determine how a given standard will be interpreted within a particular situation?

Chapter Three
1. Why do sports psychologists need a theoretical base?
2. Is there a need for more than one theory? If so, under what conditions might you shift from one theoretical approach to another?
3. What are some of the theoretical constructs that determine your behavior in relationship to others and to competition? What is it that allows you to understand, predict, and control?

Chapter Four
1. What attentional characteristics seem to be related to performance?
2. What is the effect of increasing arousal on attentional abilities?
3. Pick a sport and identify the different attentional demands placed on the athlete who is competing in that sport. Draw a diagram to illustrate which behaviors require which attentional abilities.
4. Outline and describe the inter-relationship between increasing pressure, physical arousal, attention, and performance.
5. What is the relevance of interpersonal and situational factors to attention and to predicting performance?
6. What interpersonal factors do you think should be considered in assessing an athlete's strengths and weaknesses?

Chapter Five
1. What rights does the athlete who is being tested have, with respect to the test data?
2. What are the sport psychologist's responsibilities and what requirements should they meet in order to be able to administer psychological tests?
3. Define the term objective as it is used in reference to tests.

4. What are some of the problems that occur when psychologists begin to equate objectivity with a lack of bias, and with validity?
5. Define a correlation.
6. How do you determine the strength of a correlation, its predictive utility?
7. What factors determine the statistical significance of a correlation?
8. Under what conditions might we want perfect correlations?
9. Under what conditions would we expect and desire less than perfect correlations?
10. Why is the sport psychologist concerned with consensual validation?

Chapter Six
1. What knowledge is required of test users?
2. What are the effects of response styles on the use of tests for selection and screening purposes, and for counseling purposes?
3. Define within subject interpretations.
4. When are response styles of concern? List some of the conditions that are likely to lead to "faking good."
5. What are some of the steps the sport psychologist can take to control response styles?

Chapter Seven
1. What is meant by the statement "operationalize the referral question?"
2. How would you go about attempting to help athletes operationalize their problem?
3. What influence does your theoretical orientation have on your ability to operationalize the problem?
4. What are the goals behind taking a history, making behavioral observations, and testing?

Chapter Eight
1. What might some of the effects of being referred for testing, as opposed to requesting testing, be on the athlete's response style?
2. Describe some of the things you might do to maximize cooperation when introducing testing to a group of athletes.
3. Identify and define the communication "rules" suggested for providing test feedback.
4. How might you balance feedback when an athlete's scores on the attentional sclaes on the TAIS indicate that he/she is overloaded, out of control, and has a very low level of self-esteem?
5. What are some of the things you can do to show your respect for the person you are providing feedback to?

Chapter Nine
1. What are some of the patterns you might look for in error scores

to determine if anxiety is interfering with performance?

2. What information do you think can be gained from the assessment of your own feelings in response to the athlete's success and/or failure in following your program)

3. How is it that tests which may be inaccurate for making cross subject comparisons can still be useful for counseling?

Chapter Ten

1. What are some of the ethical problems a sport psychologist is likely to encounter when team building?

2. What are some of the things the sport psychologist can do to insure that a clear contract is established and maintained?

3. What things can you do to keep the roles of coach, sport psychologist, and clinical psychologist separate?

Chapter Eleven

1. List some of the advantages to both the coach and the sport psychologist for having the sport psychologist function as a program developer, trainer and supervisor.

2. What are some of the ethical responsibilities of the sport psychologist when functioning as a consultant, trainer, and supervisor?

3. How can the sport psychologist avoid becoming and/or training, "true believers?"

4. What are the dangers inherent in being a true believer in the power or utility of a particular technique (e.g., hypnosis)?

Chapter Twelve

1. What happens to attentional processes during a crisis?

2. How can you recognize when an athlete is anxious?

3. What are some of the things you can do to re-establish contact with the athlete and develop control?

4. When one person loses control in a crisis situation why does that increase the likelihood that others (e.g., the sport psychologist) may lose control too?

5. In a crisis, are there differences across athletes with respect to: a) the intensity of the emotional and physical changes; b) the frequency with which control is lost; c) the duration of the loss of control? This assumes that every athlete is in crisis from time to time.

6. What are some of the signs that would indicate the necessity for making a referral to a clinically trained person?

Chapter Thirteen

1. How might biofeedback be used in the prevention and treatment of injury?

2. Describe the interaction between physical and psychological fac-

tors that can lead to increasing or decreasing the length of time it may take an athlete to recover from muscle or joint problems.

Chapter Fourteen
1. Identify at least one treatment approach, and describe how and why it might be effective, when intervening at the level of: a) the stressor; b) the physical response; c) the psychological response; d) performance.
2. What is the placebo myth?
3. How does attentional redirection affect physical and psychological functioning?
4. What effect do factors like the athlete's level of self-esteem and need for control have on the selection of a treatment?
5. What influence does theory have on your treatment selection?

Chapter Fifteen
1. What are some of the chronic stressors that athletes face?
2. List some of the uses for progressive relaxation, biofeedback, and meditation.
3. How can physical exercise be helpful to the athlete?

Chapter Sixteen
1. What are the four stages of hypnosis?
2. Why are the subject's expectancies prior to being hypnotized so important?
3. What effect does hypnosis have on normal attentional processes? How can these attentional changes explain alterations in the perceived passage of time?
4. What are some of the factors the sport psychologist should consider before hypnotizing an athlete?

Chapter Seventeen
1. What does the process of "centering" do for the athlete?
2. Describe the standing position. In a step by step fashion, describe what the athlete is expected to do?
3. How can thought and movement be related in a way which makes it more difficult for an athlete to be lifted?
4. Where could you use the centering procedure to increase the consistency and control you have over performance?

Chapter Eighteen
1. Define the following terms: Mental Rehearsal, VMBR, Discriminant Cue Analysis, Cognitive Behavior Modification.
2. List some of the factors that should be considered in developing a rehearsal program.

SUGGESTED READINGS

Sport Psychology Overview
1. Straub, W. (Ed.) *Sport psychology: An analysis of athlete behavior,* (Second Edition) Mouvement Publications, Ithaca, N.Y., 1980.
2. Morgan, W. *Contemporary readings in sport psychology,* Thomas, Springfield, Illinois, 1970.

Applied Books
1. Nideffer, R. *The inner athlete: Mind plus muscle for winning,* T. Y. Crowell, New York, 1976.
2. Klavora, P., & Daniel, J. (Eds.) *Coach, athlete, and the sport psychologist,* University of Toronto School of Health Physical Education and Recreation, Toronto, 1979.
3. Suinn, R. (Ed.) *Psychology in sports: Methods and applications,* Burgess, Minneapolis, Minnesota, 1980.
4. Orlick, T. *In pursuit of excellence,* Coaching Association of Canada, Ottawa, 1980.

Assessment
1. Nideffer, R. M. *Predicting human behavior: A theory and test of attentional and interpersonal style,* Enhanced Performance Assoc., San Diego, 1979.
2. Nideffer, *An Interpreter's Manual for the test of attentional and interpersonal style,* Behavioral Research Applications Group, Rochester, New York, 1976.
3. Nideffer, R. M. Test of attentional and interpersonal style. *Journal of Personality and Social Psychology,* 1976, *34,* 3, 394-404.
4. Morgan, W. P. The trait psychology controversy. In M. J. Safrit (Ed.) *Research Quarterly of Exercise and Sport.* Volume 50, 1980.
5. Martens, R. *Sport competition anxiety test,* Human Kinetics Publishers, Champaign, Illinois, 1977.
6. Maloney, M. & Ward, M. *Psychological assessment: A conceptual approach,* Oxford University Press, New York, 1976.
7. Cone, J., & Hawkins, R. (Eds.) *Behavioral assessment: New directions in clinical psychology,* Brunner/Mazel, New York, 1977.
8. Mischel, W. On the future of personality measurement. *American Psychologist,* 1977, *32,* 246-254.
9. Rotter, J. The future of clinical psychology. *Journal of Consulting and Clinical Psychology,* 1973, *40,* 313-321.
10. McClelland, D. Testing for competence rather than for intelligence. *American Psychologist,* 1973, *28,* 1-14.

Attention and Performance
1. Nideffer, R. M. Knute Rockne, John McKay and Arnold Schwartz, *Coaching Review*, June, 1980.
2. Wachtel, P. Conceptions of broad and narrow attention. *Psychological Bulletin*, 1967, 68, 417-429.
3. Easterbrook, J. A. The effect of emotion on cue utilization and the Organization of behavior. *Psychological Review*, 1959, *66*, 183-201.
4. Nideffer, R. M., & Shapre, R. *A.C.T.: Attention Control Training*, Wyden Books, New York, 1978.
5. Landers, D. Arousal and attentional factors, in *Sport Psychology: An analysis of athlete behavior*, Straub, W. (Ed.), Mouvement Publications, Ithaca, 1980.

Stress and Physiological Arousal
1. Selye, H. *Stress without distress*, J. P. Lippincott, New York, 1974.
2. Whatmore, G., & Kohli, D. *The physiopathology and treatment of functional disorders*, Grune & Stratton, New York, 1974.
3. Kamiya, J., Barber, T. X., Miller, N. E., Shapiro, D., & Stoyva, J. *Biofeedback and self-control*, An Aldine Annual (1971; 1972; 1973; 1974; 1975; 1976/77), Aldine Publishing Company, Chicago.
4. Cooper, K. H. *The new aerobics*, Bantam Books, New York, 1970.
5. Nideffer, R. M. Brain thrust — stressing the truth about biofeedback, *Gentleman's Quarterly*, April, 1977.
6. Nideffer, R. M., & Hessler, N. Controlling performance anxiety. *College Music Symposium*, July, 1978.
7. Blanchard, E., & Epstein, L. *A biofeedback primer*, Addison-Wesley, Menlo Park, 1978.

Statistics
1. Young, R. K., & Veldman, D. J. *Introductory statistics for the behavioral sciences.* Holt, Rinehart and Winston, N.Y., 1965.
2. Hays, W. L. *Statistics for psychologists*, Holt, Rinehart and Winston, N.Y., 1963.
3. Nunnally, J. C. *Psychometric theory*, McGraw-Hill, N.Y., 1967.

Ethics
1. *Ethical Standards for Psychologists*, American Psychological Association, 1200 Seventeenth St., N.W., Washington, D.C.
2. *Standards for educational and psychological tests*, American Psychological Association, 1200 Seventeenth St., N.W., Washington, D.C.
3. Ogilvie, B. C. Walking the perilous path of the team psychologist. *The Physician and Sports Medicine, 5,* 4, April, 1977.

4. Kidd, B. Athlete's rights, the coach and the sport psychologist. In Klavora and Daniel (Eds.), *Coach, athlete and the sport psychologist,* Human Kinetics Publishers, Champaign, Illinois, 1979.
5. Tutko, T. The identity of the sport psychologist. In Klavora and Daniel (Eds.), *Coach, athlete and the sport psychologist,* Human Kinetics Publishers, Champaign, Illinois, 1979.
6. Ogilvie, B. C. The sport psychologist and his professional credibility. In Klavora and Daniel (Eds.), *Coach, athlete an the sport psychologist,* Human Kinetics Publishers, Champaign, Illinois, 1979.
7. Tutko, T., Butt, D. S., Pressman, M. D., Suinn, R. M., Ogilvie, B. C., & Nideffer, R. M. Who is doing what: Some viewpoints on psychological treatments for athletes. In Klavora and Daniel (Eds.), *Coach, athlete, and the sport psychologist,* Human Kinetics Publishers, Champaign, Illinois, 1979.
8. Salmela, J. *The world book of sport psychology.* Mouvement Publications, Ithaca, N.Y., 1981.

Meditation
1. Carrington, P. *Freedom in meditation: Getting the most out of meditating.* Doubleday, 1977.
2. Benson, H., & Klipper, M. *The relaxation response,* Avon., 1976.
3. McCluggage, D. *The centered Skier.* Vermont Crossroads Press, Waitsfield, Vermont, 1977.
4. Gallwey, T. *The inner game of tennis.* Ramdom House, New York, 1976.
5. Forem, J. *Transcendental meditation,* E. P. Dutton, New York, 1974.

Behavior Modification
1. Meichenbaum, D. *Cognitive-behavior modification.* Plenum, 1977.
2. Franks, C. M., & Wilson, G. T. *Annual review of behavior therapy: Theory and practice.* Volumes 1 through 5. Brunner/Mazel.
3. Wolpe, J., & Lazarus, A. *Behavior therapy techniques,* Pergamon Press, New York, 1968.
4. Stuart, R. B. (Ed.) *Behavioral self-management: Strategies, techniques and outcomes,* Brunner/Mazel, New York, 1977.
5. Martin, R. A., & Poland, E. Y. *Learning to change: A self-management approach to adjustment,* McGraw-Hill, New York, 1980.
6. Watson, D. L., & Tharp, R. G. *Self-directed behavior: Self-modification for personal adjustment,* Brooks/Cole, California, 1972.

7. Maltz, M. *Psycho-cybernetics*, Wilshire Book Company, Hollywood, 1960.
8. Nideffer, R. M. & Sharpe, R. *How to put anxiety behind you*, Stein & Day, New York, 1978.
9. Nideffer, R. M., & Sharpe, R. *A.C.T.: Attention control training*, Wyden Books, New York, 1978.

Hypnosis and Altered States
1. Barber, T. X. (Ed.) *Advances in altered states of consciousness and human potentialities*, Volume 1, Psychological Dimensions, New York, 1976.
2. Barber, T. X. *LSD, Marijuana, Yoga and Hypnosis*, Aldine, Chicago, 1970.
3. Tart, C. (Ed.) *Altered states of consciousness*, Wiley, New York, 1969.
4. Marcuse, F. L. *Hypnosis fact and fiction*, Pelican Books, Baltimore, 1959.
5. Gordon, J. E. (Ed.) *Handbook of clinical and experimental hypnosis*, Macmillan Company, New York, 1967.
6. Erickson, M. H., & Rossi, E. *Hypnotherapy and exploratory casebook*, Irvington, New York, 1979.
7. Hilgard, E. R. *Hypnotic susceptibility*, Harcourt, Brace, and World, New York, 1965.
8. Murphy, M., & White, R. A. *The psychic side of sports*, Addison-Wesley, Menlo Park, 1978.

APPENDIX A

The Test of Attentional and Interpersonal Style (TAIS) was developed in response to some of the criticisms of traditional assessment instruments (Rotter, 1973; McClelland, 1973; Jackson, 1971). The goal was to construct an instrument that would measure the attentional and interpersonal variables that it was hypothesized were important for: 1) predicting performance across a wide variety of life situations; 2) developing programs to improve an athlete's ability to control mental and physical processes, especially under pressure.

To accomplish the goals established for the test it was important to construct an instrument that was behaviorally relevant, that is, useful as a descriptive tool, with a broad range of performers. It was hoped that the TAIS would be useful as a feedback and training tool with poor performers, average performers, and "super-stars." Obviously constructs measured would have to be relevant to performance, they would have to be face valid to the athlete, and they would have to be relatively non-threatening. An athlete's scores on the test would then have to be operationalizable in the sense that they would lead to specific behavioral recommendations regarding performance.

Since the attentional and interpersonal characteristics we wanted to measure had been clearly articulated, it was decided to follow Jackson's suggestion and use a rational approach to test construction (Jackson, 1971). This approach was accomplished by systematically writing behaviorally anchored items that reflected the specific attentional and interpersonal characteristics we wanted to measure. For example, to measure the ability to develop a broad-internal focus of attention, we might ask the athlete to describe how frequently the following statement described his/her behavior: "I am good at organizing and analyzing a large number of thoughts and ideas." The athlete would respond by answering never, rarely, sometimes, frequently, or all the time.

After items had been written to reflect all of the subscales described in Table 1 of the main body of this book, the items were administered to a large number of subjects. Item analyses procedures were then used to refine the scales (Nunnally, 1967). This process resulted in the development of a 144 item self-report, paper and pencil inventory, that takes an athlete approximately twenty-five minutes to complete (Nideffer, 1976).

There were several important basic assumptions that were either explicitly or implicitly made when constructing the TAIS. Each of these assumptions has important implications for the use and interpretation of the test.

1. It was assumed that attentional abilities have both state (situationally influenced) and trait (trans-situational) components. This assumption has not been empirically validated at this time.

225

Clinically and practically, the assumption has been found to have a great deal of utility. There is considerable anecdotal support for the validity of this assumption.

2. In contrast to earlier studies of personality traits, it was assumed that the attentional characteristics being measured by the TAIS had direct relevance to performance. That is, attentional characteristics are not just reflecting a need or preference, they are also reflecting a performance related ability. Correlations between performance on attentional tasks and scores on the TAIS, as well as correlations between coach's ratings of athlete behavior and attentional characteristics provide some validity for this assumption (Nideffer, 1979).

3. It was assumed that there are individual differences in attentional abilities. Some individuals by virtue of birth and/or learning have greater control and attentional flexibility than others. Some athletes are more internally focused, others fail to broaden, or to narrow. Studies comparing large groups of homogeneous subjects (e.g., police with business executives, etc.) provide some validity for this assumption and also indicates that certain performance skills are correlated with certain attentional skills (DePalma & Nideffer, 1977).

4. It was assumed that the ability and/or inability to shift from one focus of attention to another could be inferred from subjects' self-reports of their tendency to make mistakes because they attend inappropriately. This assumption has received some empirical support through correlations with other measures of cognitive confusion (e.g., the schizophrenia scale on the MMPI).

5. It was assumed that the influence of response style characteristics could be minimized by looking at within subject scores on the test. Thus, the athlete's scores, though of questionable validity when making between subject comparisons, are usually quite valid for counseling purposes. At the present time this assumption is lacking empirical support. Nevertheless, there is a great deal of clinical and anecdotal support for the utility of this assumption.

6. On the basis of clinical observations, it was assumed that one of the reasons attentional flexibility is reduced under pressure is that athletes stop shifting their attentional focus. Initially, they begin playing to their own greatest attentional strength, or attentional style. This assumption has been found to have a great deal of support in applied situations. Once again, clinical observation and anecdotal information provide ample evidence for the utility of this assumption and its relevance to performance improvement.

7. As pressure increases even more, reaching the point of creating obvious changes in heart rate, blood pressure, etc., it was assumed that attention would begin to involuntarily narrow and

become more internally focused. Through correlations with measures of anxiety and arousal this assumption has received some empirical support (Nideffer, Wolfe, and Wiens, 1979).

8. It was assumed that interpersonal characteristics would provide valuable information for determining the types of situations that would stress athletes, thereby affecting arousal and mental control. This assumption has been found to be clinically and practically useful. In addition, factor analysis studies of the predictive utility of factor scores derived from the TAIS subscales are providing some empirical validity for this assumption.

9. It was assumed that interpersonal characteristics would indicate how individuals would be likely to react to pressure, who would withdraw, who would become aggressive, who would act impulsively, physically, analytically, etc. To date, only single case studies have been conducted to illustrate the validity of this assumption.

10. Finally, it was assumed that the interaction of two or more individuals (e.g., coach and athlete) attentional and interpersonal styles would provide the information needed to develop effective communication and team building programs. This assumption has been repeatedly justified in actual performance situations.

Research has provided considerable evidence for test-retest reliability for the TAIS. The mean two week test-retest correlation for the seventeen TAIS scales is .83. It has also been demonstrated that inter-rater and interpreter reliability can be established for the test. In fact, decision rules have been made which allow for computerized interpretations of TAIS results.

Evidence has been provided which indicates that the test has good construct, predictive, and concurrent validity. Attentional characteristics appear to be affected in predictable ways by alterations in arousal levels. There are predictable relationships between attentional abilities and/or deficits and performance on several tasks. There are predicted between group differences where groups differ in terms of some chosen vocation or overall level of performance.

It can be argued that the TAIS has as good, or better, validity and reliability for the purposes it was designed, as the majority of psychological instruments. Nevertheless, as the ethical standards for test providers would indicate, every test is limited. The responsible and effective use of any instrument requires considerable knowledge on the part of the test administrator and interpreter. These individuals must:

1. Understand the constructs of validity and reliability.
2. Know their own limitations and be able to determine how appropriate material measured by the test is to their particular population and problem area.
3. Understand the concept of measurement error and the absolute necessity for consensually validating any interpretations.
4. Be aware of and responsive to the athletes' rights.

227

In the next few pages I have provided some information about interpretations that are often made in response to certain scoring patterns on the TAIS. The goal here is to provide you with some idea of the types of problems you might expect an athlete to have and to sensitize yourself to some of the techniques that can be used to minimize these problems:

It should be emphasized that the frequency with which the types of problems indicated will occur, cannot necessarily be assessed on the basis of the elevation of the athletes' test scores. Response style characteristics, and situational factors, influence absolute elevation of scores and minimize the validity of between-subject comparisons. Although there may be some validity established when making comparisons based on large groups of athletes, interpreters would be advised to use great caution in making between-subject interpretations. Interpretations *must* be consensually validated.

The pattern of an athletes' scores (within-subject variation) does provide information about relative strengths and weaknesses and allows us to predict the types of mistakes that are more likely to occur (however frequent or infrequent). This information is then used to develop training programs to minimize identified weaknesses and to maximize identified strengths.

Those who are interested in more information on the Test of Attentional and Interpersonal Style should consult the references at the end of this appendix. In addition, material about the test as well as the test materials themselves can be obtained by qualified individuals, by writing to: Behavioral Research Applications Group, 19 Cambridge St., Rochester, N.Y. In Canada write to: Behavioral Research Applications Group, 75 Perkell Place, Kitchener, Ontario. Information can also be obtained from Enhanced Performance Associates, 12468 Bodega Way, San Diego, California.

BET is the highest attentional scale:

1. These athletes may be too stimulus-response oriented. They may not use reflection (analytical thought processes) to modify behavior.
2. Athletes may have difficulty sticking with a problem over a long period of time. In practicing they want to try new things too soon and may fail to stick with the basics. Their sensitivity to external cues makes them distractable and more likely to become psyched out by others.
3. These athletes are good at reading others and are usually more sensitive to others' motives and feelings than they are to their own.

Recommendations:

1. Get the athletes to develop a subvocal strategy that helps them mentally count ten before acting. The centering procedure em-

phasized in attention control training can provide this function.

2. Get them to be willing to use others and the environment to help keep them task oriented, focused and thoughtful. They can leave notes for themselves, have others remind them, or give them signs.

3. Reduce the number of distractors in the environment. This can be done mechanically by putting on blinders, getting ear plugs. Stress management techniques should involve some stimulus reduction.

OET is higher than BET:

1. These athletes may try to shy away from busy situations because of their relative difficulty in dealing with large amounts of information. They may feel more comfortable in one-on-one situations.

2. If athletes have a tendency to express negative feelings they may have difficulty because they behave impulsively when they get confused and overloaded.

Recommendations:

1. Learning to relax by any method will help these individuals to broaden attention and reduce the tendency to become overloaded.

2. Relaxation that requires eye closure and an internal focus of attention is most likely to be effective.

3. It will be important for these athletes to learn to respond passively to external distractors. Mental rehearsal procedures can be developed which will help them react passively to distractors. The procedure involves rehearsing both the distraction, and the passive response.

4. It may be helpful for the coach or a sport psychologist to help these individuals conduct a discriminate cue analysis, to help them determine what to attend to. By identifying important task relevant cues athletes can keep anxiety from making them feel as if they must attend to everything.

5. Arrange the practice situation so that distractions are minimized. At competitions, find ways to help individuals isolate themselves and avoid being distracted.

BIT is the highest attentional scale:

1. These athletes may be so inclined to engage in analytical thinking that they forget what is going on around them. They psych themselves out.

2. In interactions with others they have a tendency to listen to the first part of what is said and to then tune the rest out. They may drift off on their own.

3. If these athletes are also high on intellectual expressiveness, they can confuse others with all of their thoughts and ideas. In attempting to help, they end up overloading others.

Recommendations:

1. Use any technique that will help hold attention on external cues. Get the athletes to talk. Get the athletes to reflect, or repeat what has been said.
2. These people have a tendency to psych themselves out because they can become overly analytical. At times they will need to be able to respond passively to internal distractions.
3. Physical exercise can be a good way of getting these people out of their heads, and more externally focused.

OIT is higher than BIT:

1. These athletes are overloaded by thoughts to the point of interfering with their ability to function, to attend to what is going on around them.
2. When they verbalize their associations, they often confuse others with their rambling, disorganized and often repetitive thinking.
3. Often these individuals have high levels of trait anxiety.

Recommendations:

1. Relaxation training can assist in getting these people to broaden attention and reduce overload. This training typically requires an external focus (someone else directing it). Progressive relaxation on tape, hypnosis or physical exercise.
2. Mechanically, these athletes can make use of outlines to help them organize their own thinking.
3. A tape can be made that directs the individuals to rehearse becoming overloaded by their own thoughts, centering, and then redirecting attention to external task relevant cues.

NAR is the highest attentional scale:

1. Athletes and coaches dominated by this attentional ability are dedicated and disciplined. They may make mistakes because they are seen as too narrowly focused as rigid and inflexible.
2. Emphasis may be on perfecting a particular aspect of performance to the point of boredom for others. Time deadlines and the imposition of multiple demands are typically very stressful.
3. These athletes may have difficulty generalizing what they learn from one situation to another.

Recommendations:

1. Support will have to be provided, and reinforcement will have to be given, to any attempts these athletes make to develop hierarchies. They need to be able to let things go; they can't perfect everything.
2. Meditation as a technique, can teach the athlete to relax and to

passively attend. The athlete's narrow focus of attention may be well suited to a procedure like TM.

3. Rehearsal procedures would focus on getting these people to broaden their perspective by learning to view situations from other positions.

RED is high:

1. These athletes are the ones who are most likely to be described as "choking" under pressure. They fail to switch attention from an external focus to an internal focus or vice versa. They make mistakes because they end up being inattentive to important task relevant information. Their attentional focus is excessively narrow.

2. Often these people are anxious and have difficulty listening to, or following instructions, especially in highly competitive situations.

Recommendations:

1. Relaxation is critical for this group. They are likely to need a technique that provides some support since very often high scorers on this scale have low levels of self-esteem.

2. It will be important to enlist the help of others. Often these athletes' problems are added to by the tendency of coaches, athletes, friends, etc. to give them too much information. Outsiders need to help them focus and to provide structure. They need to help the athletes maintain a task relevant focus.

3. During competitions and just before, when the anxiety level is high, it is often helpful to distract these individuals in order to get them to relax. This may be done by telling jokes, talking about the weather, giving them a simple mechanical task that is unrelated to the competition but requiring their attention.

CON is high (above the 90 percentile):

1. These athletes tend to be leaders, at the same time, their competitiveness and need for control can lead to authority conflicts. This tendency is especially true if their coach has a strong need for control as well.

2. For young athletes who have to work with controlling individuals, problems can occur. The way in which these individuals go about getting control can make others feel incompetent. There may be a tendency to put others down.

3. Often, very high scorers on this scale are seen as manipulative by others and this can elicit anger, especially in team situations.

Recommendations:

1. The hardest thing for these athletes to learn may be that there are those occasions where the only way to regain control (or to keep

231

from falling apart completely) is to admit that they are out of control.

2. Work with the individuals to identify situations where their own demands and desire to win get in the way. Get them to help you design a program to find ways of easing up. Get their permission for you to be able to tell them that they are losing it and to remind them that they agreed to allow you, to briefly take charge in order to get them back on the track.

3. Where ever possible allow them as much control and direction as possible. At the same time, let them know that this is something you are agreeing to because you feel it is best, not something that they are forcing on you.

CON is low (below the 10 percentile):

1. These athletes may enter situations convinced that they will lose before they have even started. As a result they tend to create a self-fulfilling prophecy.

2. They are anxious and will tend to avoid leadership situations. They are not likely to volunteer to take the last shot, etc.

Recommendations:

1. Assertiveness training is often helpful.

2. Identifying goals that can be accomplished and then gradually increasing these and providing support and reinforcement can help these people develop.

3. The coach and/or sport psychologist needs to be careful that he/she does not foster a dependent relationship. Gradually, the athlete should be pushed to assume more and more repsonsibility.

High SES (above the 90 percentile):

1. These athletes may have difficulty hearing constructive criticism. Their response when criticised may be to ignore it entirely, or to attack the person making the criticism. In this instance they get defensive and see any problem as someone else's.

2. These athletes and coaches can appear condescending and egotistical to others.

Recommendations:

1. These people are often very difficult to deal with because they don't feel that they have any problems. They may have to be confronted by someone who is very sharp, or by some inescapable failure experience before they will be responsive to help and/or advice.

2. They are much more likely to respond to criticism if they think that

it is coming from them, rather than from someone else. If the coach can get them to be the critic that may help.

3. Problems can be approached by providing a lot of positive feedback first, and then asking a rhetorical question that gently gets into a problem area. "You were great at. . . . What do you think about . . .?"

Low SES (below the 10 percentile):

1. These athletes will avoid a leadership role even when they are obviously the most qualified person to take charge.
2. Often it is very difficult for these individuals to use positive thinking in any general way, they do not believe in themselves enough. As a result, they need some actual success experiences.

Recommendations:

1. Avoid assuming too much responsibility for these athletes. They will need a lot of support and encouragement, but this should be contingent upon their assuming some independent responsibility, no matter how small that responsibility is.
2. Structure the environment so that these people receive support for any success they have. Get them to establish sub-goals that they can be assured of accomplishing.
3. Provide some relaxation and assertiveness training.

High OBS (above the 90 percentile):

1. These athletes have a tendency to worry and ruminate about problems without resolving them. As a result, they may have difficulty meeting deadlines.
2. Problems occur for these individuals because they fail to take advantage of opportunities that are presented. They over analyze and delay making decisions until it it too late.
3. Interpersonal problems can develop because the athlete tends to take home the difficulties they may be having in sport, and vice versa.

Recommendations:

1. Structure the sports environment so that there are external reminders (or distractors) that pull the athletes out of their head.
2. Help the athletes to develop a priority list or hierarchy that makes it easier for them to let go of a problem.
3. The coach or sport psychologist can often assume responsibility by making some of the athletes' non-performance related decisions. For example, making sure that rooms are booked, that they get to the competition on time, etc.
4. Get the athletes involved in a meditative training program that will

emphasize passively attending to some of their own internal distractions and worries.

5. Provide support and reinforcement for decisions that are made, and for any progress the athletes make in being able to drop issues.

Low OBS (below the 10 percentile):

1. These athletes tend to make decisions very quickly. If they score high on control and self-esteem they probably believe that their decisions are good ones. Others, however, may see some of their decisions as impulsive.

2. The feeling that other athletes and/or coaches may have, is that this person does not adequately consider all of the issues. When the athletes' control scores and self-esteem scores are low, this feeling is quite likely the case, especially if the athlete is overloaded attentionally.

Recommendations:

1. These individuals can learn to be more reflective. In critical situations (e.g., where they are attempting to get teammates to follow their instructions), it may be helpful to develop the patience to share more of the decision making proces that they go through. This will prevent others from seeing it as impulsive and will increase their confidence in the athlete's decisions.

2. Mental rehearsal procedures can be used by these athletes and coaches to teach them to increase their reflectiveness. They can learn to use a centering procedure to slow down their natural impulse to quickly respond. Following the centering, they consciously make an effort to be more reflective and/or to share thoughts with others.

High EXT with low INT:

1. These athletes need to be actively involved with others. They tend to use involvement with others as a means of reducing their own anxiety.

2. Problems can occur, especially if they score high on the BCON scale, because they get distracted by opportunities for social involvements. These distractions interfere with their dedication to practice. They may end up breaking training rules, etc.

3. These athletes and coaches may come on too strong in relationship to more introverted individuals. Pressure may increase because they don't allow others enough personal space. When their advances are rejected, they may become angry and/or hurt.

Recommendations:

1. Structure the competitive and practice environment so that the in-

volvement with others is contingent upon meeting training and practice goals.
2. Help the athletes learn to read nonverbal cues which let them know that others want to be left alone.
3. Relaxation and/or rehearsal training is likely to be more effective and the athlete will be more motivated, if training can be done in groups. Socialization will be an important part of the training process.

High INT with low EXT:

1. These athletes have difficulty dealing with unstructured social situations where they are not expected to occupy a specific role.
2. In a group situation, these athletes may lose out on opportunities for leadership, especially if they score low on self-esteem.
3. These athletes will have difficulty when practice, and travel, do not allow them personal space and privacy. They need some time alone.

Recommendations:

1. Attempt to make roommate assignments in a way which will allow the athlete some privacy.
2. In social situations, provide structure and a role which allows them to feel some involvement, but does not make them the focus of attention.
3. Because these individuals tend to be private, it will be important to provide them an opportunity to express their needs and feelings. This can be done on a one-to-one basis, not in a group or in front of the team. It should be done in a way which lets the athlete know you are interested, but does not appear to be a demand or an invasion of privacy. "Sarah, I haven't heard from you in a while and I just wanted to make sure that things are going well. Is there anything I should know?"

High IEX (above the 85 percentile):

1. These athletes may dominate a team discussion. This is especially true if they have a broad attentional focus (BET & BIT).
2. If IEX is higher than PAE and NAE, they may be seen by others as emotionally uninvolved. They tend to react in a logical analytical way and may not provide the emotional support that others need.
3. Often, these athletes are so turned on to ideas and techniques that they fail to see the feelings of others.

Recommendations:

1. Provide training to teach the athlete and/or coach to read nonverbal cues, to be sensitive to the emotional needs of others.

2. Teach the athlete to use a centering procedure to control their own impulse to dominate discussions and to overload others.

Low IEX (below the 10 percentile):

1. These athletes fail to share their ideas and often cheat themselves and others because of it. Many times they have excellent ideas and a tremendous sensitivity to issues. Their lack of confidence in verbal expression handicaps them.
2. If INT is also high, these athletes may continue to make mistakes because they fail to ask questions when they don't understand instructions.
3. Other people will tend to read silence as agreement. The result is that these individuals may feel used and manipulated because they didn't speak their mind. Resentment and anger build and this can interfere with interpersonal relationships.

Recommendations:

1. Assertiveness training.
2. Stress management training to help these people reduce anxiety in those situations that call for them to be intellectually expressive. This may involve centering, mental rehearsal, or discriminate cue analysis.

Low NAE (below the 10 percentile):

1. These athletes and coaches find themselves taken advantage of by others because of the difficulty they have in setting limits and in expressing their anger.
2. Often these people are out of touch with their anger, denying it. When anger is apparent to others through nonverbal cues, these athletes and coaches tend to be seen as dishonest. Trust then becomes an important and stressful interpersonal issue.
3. The inability to express anger reflects the athletes and coaches own need for positive support and acceptance. These individuals may be extremely sensitive to criticism and rejection.

Recommendations:

1. When anger is denied very strongly and yet it is behaviorally obvious to others, the only thing likely to modify the athlete's behavior is a therapy relationship.
2. Assertiveness training can often be helpful in getting these individuals to the point of setting limits.

High NAE (above 85 percentile):

1. These athletes and coaches tend to control others through their confrontation an threat. As a result, they may come on too strong

for individuals who need a lot of support. By the same token, they may find themselves driving other competent individuals away because they end up in too many confrontations. This will depend upon the technical expertise they have. If they are highly competent, others will stay with them (when they have high levels of self-esteem) because they know they can learn.

2. They may find that they are socially isolated and alone much of the time because others are afraid to approach them.

Recommendations:

1. These athletes and coaches need to learn to balance their affective expression. It will be important for them to learn to express more positive feelings. Often, team building can be a very helpful process for improving interpersonal relationships, and developing better communication skills.

References

1. DePalma, D. M., & Nideffer, R. M. Relationships between the test of attentional and interpersonal style and psychiatric subclassification *Journal of Personality Assessment*, 1977, *41*, 6, 622-631.
2. Jackson, D. The dynamics of structured personality tests. *Psychological Review*, 1971, *78*, 229-248.
3. McClelland, D. Testing for competence rather than for intelligence. *American Psychologist*, 1973, *28*, 1-14.
4. Nideffer, R. M. Test of attentional and interpersonal style. *Journal of Personality and Social Psychology*, 1976, *34*, 3, 394-404.
5. Nideffer, R. M. *An Interpreter's manual for the test of attentional and interpersonal style*. Behavioral Research Applications Group, Rochester, New York, 1976.
6. Nideffer, R. M. *Predicting human behavior: A theory and test of attentional and interpersonal style*. Enhanced Performance Assoc., San Diego, 1979.
7. Nideffer, R. M., Wolfe, R., & Wiens, A. N. The relationship between the test of attentional and interpersonal style and subjective measures of anxiety. Paper presented at the *Eastern Psychological Association* Meetings, 1975. Paper appears in: *Predicting human behavior: A theory and test of attentional and interpersonal style*, Enhanced Performance Associates, San Diego, 1979.
8. Nunnally, J. C. *Psychometric theory*. McGraw-Hill, New York, 1967.
9. Rotter, J. The future of clinical psychology. *Journal of Consulting and Clinical Psychology* 1973, *40*, 313-321.